The Key To Your Child's Heart

GARY SMALLEY

The Key To Your Child's Heart

THE KEY TO YOUR CHILD'S HEART, REVISED EDITION

Library of Congress Cataloging-in-Publication Data:

Smalley, Gary.
    The key to your child's heart / Gary Smalley. — Rev. ed.
      p. cm.
    Includes bibliographical references.
    ISBN 0–8499–0947–3
    1. Child rearing—Religious aspects—Christianity. 2. Parenting—Religious aspects—Christianity. I. Title.
HQ769.3.S63 1992
649'.1—dc20

                                92–12926
                                      CIP

Printed in the United States of America

In loving memory of our parents,
Uel Jefferson and Eleanor Deck
Frank and Emily Smalley.
And to our children,
Kari, Greg, and Michael,
we present to you our lifetime commitment.

Contents

Acknowledgments

It is with special appreciation that I acknowledge my debt to those without whose help this book could never have been published. To Judy Pitzmier for her dedication, talent, and warm understanding during the many hours of editing. To Al Janssen for his tremendous inspiration, encouragement, and editing skills when I couldn't "see the end." To Bill Yarger and B. John Trent, two of my outstanding and supportive pastors, who carefully evaluated the final draft. Last but certainly not least, to my wife, Norma, who walked with me every step of the way writing this book.

This book represents what Norma and I have learned through God's grace, trial, and error about parenting. It is with grateful appreciation that we express our love and indebtedness to our children—Kari, Greg, and Michael. They have been a tremendous inspiration and blessing to our lives. Each one is a special gift from God. Thank you for helping us to be parents!

Gary Smalley

The Key to Your Child's Heart

We were enduring our twelfth consecutive day of rain while traveling across the country one summer. Everything in our mini-motorhome was damp, and all five of us were tired of each other.

We had taken a drive up into Canada to see the beauty of Banff National Park. I had described the beautiful mountains and rivers we would see, but for three straight days, fog and rain had concealed the scenic beauty. Now, on the fourth morning, we were sitting in a restaurant trying to decide what to do. I urged us to return to our home in Phoenix where it was warm and dry. I'd fly alone from there to my next speaking engagement in Seattle. My wife, Norma, pleaded that we stay a fourth day in Canada and wait for the sun to break through. Kari, our fifteen-year-old daughter, wanted us to continue driving to Seattle. Our two younger boys "demanded" fishing in Washington.

As our volume increased in defense of each plan, Greg, our middle child, shouted, "Stop! I've got the solution!" He was so emphatic that even our neighbors in the next booth stopped to listen. "I think we ought to go out in the camper, get the gun, and shoot each other." All of us burst out laughing and that relaxed us enough to stay put another day during which the sun finally revealed the majesty of the Canadian Rockies.

Why is it that all five of us, and other families similar to ours, can go through very strained times like what we experienced in Canada and still witness a closeness and happiness together? Yet there are many other families that are so divided that even a minor crisis can permanently scatter the members in different directions.

There are many outstanding books on raising children, yet after reading some, I have often wondered "What's the use in trying? It's too difficult!" In my speaking and counseling all across the nation, I have found that many parents experience similar frustration and guilt.

In this book, you'll discover that we're an average family with very typical conflicts. But we have tried to find solutions to those conflicts that can be applied to almost every family. We will recount what has and has not worked in our home and will share with you the main factors that have drawn us into close relationship.

We'll also be summarizing what some of the parenting experts are saying today. For example, there are four basic types of parents. But only one of those four types produces the best results in children. We will examine why the children of these parents have much greater self-worth, are less rebellious, and are generally more successful in life.

You'll read about how we brought order and harmony to our family through the simple method of "contracts."

We will discuss several practical ways to help protect a child from becoming sexually involved before marriage.

If you're wondering how to get your children to clean their rooms, eat healthier foods, and avoid certain harmful activities, we have at least twenty-two ways to motivate your children. We will even share the secret of how you can actually increase your children's desire to listen carefully to you.

This book will give you several basic principles that I believe are *key* to raising children. In particular, the next chapter covers one principle that if diligently applied can virtually guarantee a closer relationship between parent and child. In my opinion, it is *The Key to Your Child's Heart*.

Violation of this principle has undoubtedly destroyed more families than any other single factor. It is the major reason why over one million children have run away from home and why millions more reject their parents' moral values and standards. Fewer teenagers would misuse alcohol and drugs if parents understood and practiced this principle.

Therefore, the concept presented in the next chapter provides the foundation for successful parenting. I suggest that you may want to reread it several times. Master this principle and I can assure that you will make significant progress toward experiencing the joys and rewards of a closer-knit family.

1

How to Overcome the Major Destroyer of Families

- A Closed Spirit
- Manifestations of a Closed Spirit
- Reopening a Child's Spirit
- Five Steps to Reopen a Child's Spirit
- Reasons Why One Might Refuse to Forgive
- Observing Voice Tone and Facial Expressions to Recognize a Closed Spirit
- How Children or Adults Can Reopen Their Own Spirits
- How Open Is Your Child's Spirit?
- Eighty-four Ways We Can Offend Our Children

ONE EVENING, WHILE I WAS in my bedroom on a long-distance phone call, my son Greg, five years old at the time, let out a bloodcurdling scream from the master bathroom. He came running to the door, screaming so loudly that I couldn't hear the other person's voice. I could feel my blood pressure rise as I signaled for him to be quiet. I dramatically patted my bottom to let him know what was coming if he didn't shut up immediately. But Greg continued to scream, so I quickly ended my phone conversation, telling the person I'd get back to him later.

When I hung up the phone, I grabbed Greg by the arm and shook him. "Why are you screaming?" I demanded. "Couldn't you see I was on the phone?"

Without waiting for an answer, I shoved him into the hall and said, "You get into your bedroom right now." He fell when I pushed him, but got back up, still crying, and hurried into his room. I grabbed the paddle we used for spanking—the entire family had helped decorate it—and told him to lie down on his bed. Then I gave him several hard swats. Satisfied with my discipline, I stood back and thought, *That's what you get for violating my rule.* You see, no one was supposed to scream while I was on the phone—I wouldn't want people to think my family was out of control.

It was our custom after a spanking to hold the child and reaffirm our love for him. But this time, something took place that scared me. Greg was still crying. He stood up and the look in his eyes said, "I hate you." He backed away from me to let me know that he didn't want me to touch him. I suddenly realized what I had done, and I knew that if I didn't take immediate action, there might be serious consequences in our relationship. Fortunately, someone had taught me what to do, and within a few moments, we were hugging each other on his bed, back in full fellowship and harmony.

What actually took place has saved our family time and time again from drifting into deep conflict. The principle I am about to share has, without a doubt, been the single most significant factor in establishing and maintaining harmony in our home.

In the United States, we are suffering from an overwhelming epidemic of broken relationships. We don't have to look hard to see the evidence. We see it to some degree in every relationship, both inside and outside of the home. I hope that I can explain in these next few pages what I know can have a very positive effect on all relationships, especially with our children.

I have taken what I've observed during my more than twenty years of counseling, with my own family, and what I've learned from experts in the field of building personal relationships. I've tried to develop a simple system of explaining the major factor that causes disharmony within the home, as well as outside of it. I would urge you again to reread this one chapter many times because I have found it to be *the key* to staying in harmony with *anyone*.

A Closed Spirit

The single most prevalent cause of disharmony within a home is what I have labeled a *closed spirit*.

What do I mean by a closed spirit? What causes it? Let's begin by saying that every person is born with a spirit, soul, and body, and all three are interrelated. I will define spirit as a person's innermost being, similar to one's conscience. It's the area in which people can have fellowship with one another and enjoy each other's presence without a word being spoken. Our deepest relationships are built on the spirit level. The *soul* would include our mind, will, and emotions. The *body* is, of course, our physical makeup. Together, we'll say the three comprise a total person. But the soul and the body are within the spirit.

Very Sensitive Tentacles

To help us understand how the spirit, soul, and body operate together, let's look at an example from nature. When I was a child, I enjoyed observing sea anemones on the California coast. They were often found in tidal pools among the rocks. About four or five inches in diameter, they look like colorful flowers with soft, wavy tentacles. But I noticed an interesting phenomenon. Sometimes I'd take a stick and poke one of them. Immediately the sea anemone would withdraw its sensitive tentacles and close up until it became a shell. It was similar to a beautiful flower closing. Now it was protected from further injury.

What happens with the sea anemone illustrates what happens to a person when he is offended. The tentacles of that sea anemone are similar to the spirit of a person. The sea anemone is completely open and vulnerable. But when the stick pokes him, he closes up. In a similar way, when a person is offended, he closes up. When his spirit closes, it in turn closes his soul and body. If the spirit is open, so are the soul and body. In other words, when the spirits of two people are open, they enjoy talking (soul) and touching (body). If the spirit closes, the soul and body close to the same degree. A person with a closed spirit will usually avoid communication.

Closing Tentacles

This is what I saw happening to Greg. When I pushed him in the hallway and screamed at him in harshness, *I had poked his spirit.* The greater the harshness, the greater the pain a person feels in his spirit. My harshness, pushing, and spanking without finding out the facts were three large poking sticks. Like the sea anemone, Greg closed his spirit to me with each jab. And when he closed his spirit, he closed everything else. He didn't like me. He didn't want to be near me. He didn't want to talk to me. And he resisted my attempts to touch him. These were the keys that told me that his spirit was closing. When a child resists affection—if you touch his hand and it's cold and limp, or if you put your arm around her and she turns her back, shrugs you off, and avoids conversation—that usually means the spirit is closing.

Manifestations of a Closed Spirit

When a child's spirit is closing there are many possible manifestations. He may argue and resist when you ask him to do something. He may be contrary, refusing to like anything you like! He may withdraw, and usually he is not very responsive to affection.

If his spirit is closed further, he may seek friends who are opposite from the kinds of friends you want him to have. He may swear or use disrespectful language. A closed spirit is a major cause for the misuse of drugs and alcohol, and a primary reason why children become sexually permissive.

At the very worst, a child whose spirit has been completely closed may run away from home or commit suicide.

All of these are symptoms of a closed spirit. If we can recognize them, and help to reopen the spirit, we will often take care of the symptoms in the process.

During my years of counseling, I've come to realize that this principle is the key to most relationships. When a man can't stand his boss, it's primarily because his spirit was "stepped on" or "poked." So the employee usually avoids his boss, silently disagreeing and resisting him. I see it all the time with professional athletes. They get offended by management or coaches and suddenly announce they want to be traded. Where once they were thrilled to be on the team, now they want to get away from it.

It happens in dating. When a girl meets a guy, usually her spirit is wide open to him. She likes him. She wants to talk with him. She enjoys doing things with him. When he touches her, she responds positively. Then something happens and suddenly she isn't as open. She guards her emotions more carefully and isn't as free with her affection. Somehow, her boyfriend has been closing her spirit, often without even knowing it.

It happens all the time in marriage. For years I did many little things to close Norma's spirit. I enjoyed telling little jokes about her to my friends or to my audiences when I spoke. I'd say things like "My wife treats me like a God. Every morning she serves me burnt offerings." Or this one: "Being married to Norma is like being married to an angel. Every day she's up in the air, harping about something, and she never has an earthly thing to wear." I'd laugh and others would laugh, but Norma wouldn't laugh. When she tried to express her hurt, I'd answer, "Come on! Can't you take a joke?"

What I didn't realize is that my jokes, kidding, sarcastic comments, and insensitive actions were closing her spirit a little more each time. After several years of marriage, Norma had closed much of her spirit to me. But I didn't know it. I only saw the outward results, like the times when I'd come home from work and she wouldn't greet me. I'd say, "Hi, Hon, I'm home," and there'd be no response. I'd ask, "Is there anything wrong?" and she'd say, "No." Gradually I began to learn that

"No" really meant "Yes." I needed to find out how I had closed her spirit, and take the steps necessary to reopen it.

During my seminars, to demonstrate how sensitive the spirit is, I often ask a man to come forward, close his eyes, and hold out his hand. First I put a large rock in his hand and ask him to identify the object. He usually correctly identifies it as a rock. Then I replace the rock with a pebble. Usually he can't identify it without feeling it for awhile. Most men, when they say something offensive to their wives, think they are only dropping a small pebble on her spirit. But she feels it like a large rock, which can close her spirit.

The same thing can happen in all relationships, especially between parents and their children. This is particularly dangerous with young children who need a lot of physical affection—touching and hugging. If a parent is harsh with a daughter so that she is offended, she will begin closing her spirit. But she still needs to be touched, and since she won't accept touching from Mom or Dad, she looks elsewhere.

Young men can easily pick up her need for affection and take advantage of her. She may resist at first, not wanting to compromise her standards, but her resistance breaks down with the boy's persistence. Because she has already closed her spirit to her parents and she can't take any more rejection, she has a tendency to give in to the boy. If, on the other hand, her relationship with Mom and Dad is solid, her spirit is open, and there has been a healthy degree of affection and touching between them, she is much more likely to have the energy and desire to maintain her moral standards.

Boys have a similar need for affection. However, some fathers won't hug their sons because they think it's not manly. And some have caused their son's spirit to be closed so that their sons reject any affection. It has been determined that this lack of affection may cause boys to find affection in ways that can even lead to a homosexual relationship. Dr. Ross Campbell, a psychiatrist who specializes in working with children, has discovered that in all his reading and experience, he has never known of one sexually disoriented person who had a warm, loving, and *affectionate* father. If, on the other hand, a parent is cold and offensive, a son can close his spirit, and many times adopt rebellious, antisocial behavior.

Fortunately, a child's spirit is somewhat pliable for the first several years. When children are offended, they are willing and ready to get back into harmony. But if we don't recognize when a child's spirit is closing, we can reap disastrous results.

A closed spirit can also occur between children. Once, Michael, our youngest child, exploded in anger at Greg to the point where he was ready to start slugging it out. When I intervened, I learned that Greg had been harsh with Mike, but Mike was responding far more vehemently than was normal. So I knew something else was wrong.

Alone with Michael, I started playing "twenty questions," trying to discover what had caused his spirit to close. I asked, "Did your sister hurt you?" "Was it me?" "Mom?" Finally, when I asked him if anything had happened to him at school, he put his head down and continued crying. Up to this point, Michael refused to tell me anything. Many times children will say they do not want to talk, but they really do. They will often open up when we gently probe to discover their problem.

Michael went on to tell me that his best friend at school had chosen a new friend, and the two of them had turned against him. My heart went out to him as he cried and I wanted to hold him, but he wasn't ready yet. That told me there was still another problem. Then Michael revealed that Greg and his friend across the street wouldn't play with him. The neighbor was taking his brother away from him. It was just like what had happened at school.

I told him that I felt terrible and asked if I could hold him. He scooted across the bed and held me, crying and feeling the full pain of rejection. Later on we got together with Greg, and Michael explained to him how he felt about the neighbor across the street. Together, the three of us were able to resolve the problem by taking the necessary steps to open Mike's spirit.

If I had not learned that Michael's spirit was closing toward Greg and his friend at school, I might have compounded the problem. I could have said, "Michael, shape up. You're getting to be a big boy now. I'm tired of the way you fight with Greg." That would have closed his spirit even more, especially toward me. Being harsh and demanding is like a big stick "poking" a person's spirit and causing it to close.

In the average home, it is impossible to keep from offending each other. Something seems to happen almost every day that will cause someone to be offended. *Yet, it is possible to stay in harmony as long as we resolve each offense.* One offense on top of another, on top of another, can build a wall cementing the spirit shut. It is much easier to reopen a child's spirit when it is closed slightly through one or only a few small offenses. But it is still possible to reopen a child's spirit even in the worst situations.

Reopening a Child's Spirit

There are undoubtedly many ways to help open a person's spirit that has closed toward us. I'll mention five ways that have been the most effective in our family and in my counseling. I'll show them in a particular order because this is how I've observed them to be most helpful. However, you may find it more effective to rearrange them or add other ways to the list.

Each of the five steps was used after I had spanked Greg for screaming while I was on the phone. After applying them, I witnessed his spirit reopen in a matter of minutes. Here is the sequence:

Once I had realized that Greg's spirit was closing toward me, I dropped to my knees and my attitude became *soft and tender*. Gently, I asked him, "Greg, *why* were you screaming in the bathroom?" With his voice trembling as he fought back the tears, he managed to say, "I fell and hit my ear on the bathtub." He showed me his ear which was swollen and bleeding. When I saw what had happened, I felt terrible. I gently said to him, "Greg, *I was so wrong* to have treated you this way. Daddy's the one who deserved the spanking." Greg wiped his tears and added, "Then when you pushed me in the hall, I hit my same ear on the toy box."

By this time, I felt like a child abuser. I was an irresponsible father and I recognized it. "Greg, Daddy was wrong." I handed him the spanking stick. "I'm the one who deserves to be spanked. I'm the one who needs it." He grabbed the stick and dropped it. He backed up again, still not wanting any part of me. I wanted to reach out and touch him, but his spirit was still closed toward me.

Finally, I said, again tenderly, "Greg, I was wrong. I know I don't deserve it, but I wonder if it would be possible for you to find it in your heart to *forgive me*." Immediately he threw his arms around me. We fell back against the bed and he laid on my chest for about a half hour as we held each other tightly. After some time, I looked at his ear again and asked, "Are you sure we're okay now?" "Yes, Daddy, I forgive you," he said, patting me on the back. "We all make mistakes." From the tone of his voice and the way he touched me, I knew his spirit was opening again.

It may take a little more time for some children to reopen their spirits, depending on the circumstances; but a child is certainly worth our time.

Let's go back now and examine more carefully each of the five ways to open a person's closed spirit.

Five Steps to Reopen a Child's Spirit

1. Become Tenderhearted

The first step that I needed to take to open Greg's spirit was *to reflect tenderness and softness*. Gentleness has a way of melting anger.

As we attempt to open one's spirit, our body language, our muscles, our facial expressions, and our tone of voice must become soft, gentle, tender, and caring. By doing this, we are communicating several things to the person whom we have offended:

We're saying:

(a) He is valuable and important. We express this importance in nonverbal ways. We are slow to move toward him. Our heads may be bowed down, and we are obviously grieved that we have hurt him.

(b) We do not want to see his spirit closed; we care about him.

(c) We know there is something wrong. We acknowledge by our softness that an offense has taken place and we are going to *slow down* long enough to correct whatever has happened.

(d) We are open to listen. It is safe for him to share what has happened and we are not going to get angry or hurt him again.

I was counseling a pro football player and his wife, and she was sharing with me how deeply offended she had been by some of the things her husband had said and done. He said he didn't understand why she got so mad and upset about the things he was doing. I could see she was hurting and that her spirit was closing toward him. So I asked him if he wanted to work on opening her spirit. He agreed to try.

"I want you to become really tender right now and put your arm around your wife," I said. "Pretend that your whole body is melting ice cream. Gently tell her that you know you have hurt her and you want to resolve it."

He started to do as I said, putting his arm around her, and she said, "Oh, you don't mean that!" Rather than understanding how hurt she was, he reacted: "I do too mean that. Don't tell me I don't mean this." The athlete was listening to his wife's words, rather than to the tone of her voice which was telling him how closed her spirit was. His anger and harshness were only further closing her spirit.

I suggested he let me demonstrate what I meant. Immediately, my voice softened and I became caring and gentle. I reached across the table and touched her hand and said, "You're really hurting, aren't you? And I know that the things I have done to you have deeply affected you." With my softness her facial muscles began to relax. Her head slightly bowed, her eyes started to fill with tears. Both of us were amazed how quickly her spirit was willing to open.

I find that the same thing happens with our children. Tenderness melts the anger and it begins to open their spirits.

2. Increase Understanding

The second step to open a person's spirit is to *increase our understanding of the pain he feels and how he has interpreted our offensive behavior.* When I asked Greg why he was crying and he said it was because he had fallen against the bathtub, my understanding of his pain immediately increased. I already was soft but my spirit became even softer because I had deeper understanding and could feel his hurt feelings. I probably would have screamed, too, no matter what the rule was, if I had fallen against the bathtub. Many times just these two factors—being *soft* and then *understanding* a person's pain—will open a person's spirit.

Children in various household arrangements often dream

that someday someone will understand what they are feeling and how they are hurting. Where there are single parents or blended families through a second marriage, a child can feel deeply offended by the partner who leaves or by new members of a family he's thrust into. Oftentimes a child will blame himself for a divorce. He may not say anything to either one of the parents, but he begins to express the symptoms of a closed spirit. He is argumentative and avoids his parents, even to the point of not allowing them to touch him. Either parent can begin to solve this problem by softening his or her heart toward that child and gaining more understanding of his pain.

One of the best ways to increase understanding of a child's hurt is through emotional word pictures. They help us feel the child's pain in such a vivid way that some conflicts are resolved in seconds.

One boy, whose father constantly criticized him, told his dad, "I sometimes feel like a bird in a nest. You fly in, and I should feel so encouraged to see you, because you are going to have some food or encouragement for me, but instead you jerk off one of the branches or little fibers that holds the nest together and fly away. I begin to think, 'Wait a minute. He's tearing this nest apart and I'm not ready to fly yet.' I have such an insecure feeling when I see you coming because you're always picking on me, tearing me down, and it's just like pulling those little pieces of string out of that nest." When the boy's father heard this word picture, he felt his son's hurt and insecurity. This one emotional word picture helped this father greatly reduce his criticism of his son.

As parents, we can ask our children to help us understand their feelings by asking them questions like, "If you were a rabbit, what would be happening to you right now because of what I just did?" or, "If you were a piece of cloth what would you look like?" or, "Give me a color to describe how you are feeling." Usually, if we give them time and encouragement, children can tell us exactly how they feel. If my daughter tells me she is feeling really blue, I might ask if it is a dark blue or a light blue, and if there are any cheerful spots in the color. One boy whose father traveled extensively said, "Dad, the way you've been avoiding me lately, I feel like a dishrag under the sink that's had a steady drip on it for the last two months. Nobody has noticed it so now it's rotten and mildewey." Most any parent could feel the pain of mildew.

We can also help our children express their feelings by relating to previous experiences. We can help them by saying, "Remember the time your friend across the street rejected you and wouldn't play with you? Am I sort of making you feel like that?" or, "Remember how you felt in school when you got that F, when you really studied hard for an A? Then your classmates made fun of you, and remember how you were embarrassed? Is that sort of how you felt today when I corrected you in front of your friends?"

Emotional word pictures are such an important tool in communication that we will talk more about using them in another chapter. It is very important that children know we really understand how they feel when they are offended. If a child refuses to talk, it may take a "cooling off" period for both child and parent. After a few minutes, a parent can continue gently probing to discover the level of hurt. Give a child time to understand his own emotional pain.

3. Recognize the Offense

The third step in opening a person's spirit is *admitting that we were wrong,* because what we did was offensive to him. It could even be that what we did was not wrong, but how we did it—our attitude was wrong. For example, I could spank my child for the right reason, but if I spank him in harsh anger, I need to admit my wrong attitude.

Even the world recognizes the importance of confession and admission of guilt. When Soviet fighter planes shot down a Korean 747 killing the more than 250 passengers, the world was shocked. Immediately, a number of the free-world countries demanded that Russia admit it was wrong and apologize. News commentators emphasized a previous example when Israel shot down a Libyan passenger airliner, and how it apologized to the world and paid restitution to all the passengers' families. But when the Soviets failed to admit they were wrong, and failed to make restitution, the free world became even angrier and more hardened toward them.

Children tend to be more aware of their own needs and wants and less concerned about the welfare of others. This self-awareness or self-centeredness increases the possibility of their being offended. As they grow in maturity, they find that people don't offend them as much, because they have become more understanding of people.

As parents, we must be wise enough to know what our child's level of maturity is so that we don't close his spirit unnecessarily. If we offend our child because he is immature, we can say, "I was wrong to treat you this way." We don't add, "You are only hurt because you are so immature." That would only offend him all the more.

One of the hardest things for many parents to do is to admit when they are wrong. It's especially hard for fathers. I do not necessarily like to find out when I am wrong and it's not always easy to admit when I am. But I must remember that a hardened, resistant attitude is extremely detrimental to children.

As a child hears his parents admit it when they are offensive and sees that they understand how he feels, he gains a feeling of importance. He realizes that he is a valuable person. Sometimes this is all it takes to open a child's spirit. But we should be careful because there are two more factors that are important to make sure that the spirit has reopened.

4. Attempt to Touch

The fourth factor is *attempting to touch the offended person.* There are several reasons why we want to touch a child when he has been offended. First of all, he needs to be touched. If he reaches out and responds to our touching, then we know his spirit is opening or has completely reopened. This is an extremely important time to take him tenderly in our arms and hold him for awhile. It lets him know that we care, that we love him, and that he is very important.

Second, touching allows us to find out if the child's spirit is not opening. Perhaps the offense was deeper than we realized. Or he may have been offended by someone outside the family, like Mike with his friend at school, and he has a general resentment toward everyone around him. If I have admitted I am wrong, am soft and understanding, and reach out to touch my child but he pulls back or moves away, it is an indication that he isn't ready to open his spirit. He may need more time or a greater understanding from the one who offended him.

When parents are not accustomed to touching their children, like my own parents who were reluctant to touch each other as well as their six kids, they may want to "warn" or explain to their children why they're starting to touch. A child who hasn't been touched may feel somewhat hesitant to allow touching even if his spirit is open. A gradual adjustment may be necessary.

Obviously, the lack of touching doesn't always mean that we have closed our child's spirit. Children go through stages where they may avoid touching, for example during puberty. However, if a parent is maintaining harmony with his child, he can usually detect if the child is offended or just passing through a stage.

There might be other reasons why our children resist our touch. One summer our family went fishing in the Colorado mountains. I offended Kari by being harsh. She had hurt her knee and I was trying to force her quickly up the bank so I could get back to my fishing. About halfway up the bank, I realized that I had hurt her spirit and that she was far more important than my fishing. So I stopped, took her in my arms, and told her I knew I had offended her and that I was wrong. She wiggled out of my grasp and asked, "Dad, did you use any deodorant today?"

5. Seek Forgiveness

The final step to open someone's spirit is to *seek forgiveness from the one offended*. When we have offended someone, we must give him a chance to respond. For me, the best way is to say something like, "Could you find it in your heart to forgive me?" This is when I knew I had reopened Greg's spirit, for when I asked for his forgiveness, he rushed into my arms. We can say at this point that *true restoration is confession of wrong plus forgiveness granted*.

Reasons Why One Might Refuse to Forgive

If we have followed these five steps and the child refuses to forgive us, there are several possible reasons.

Perhaps the offense was deeper than we realized. Or he may have been offended by someone outside the family and so he has a general resentment toward everyone around him. Maybe we rushed things and the child didn't have time to think through what happened. He may think that a parent can't possibly understand how he has been hurt and that simply asking forgiveness doesn't erase everything. Or perhaps the child might also want to see a real change in the parent's behavior first.

Whatever the reason, I have discovered that the best thing to do is start all over again. Be patient; don't rush. Begin at number one and continue to be soft and tender. Go to number two and increase your understanding. We can even say things like, "You know, I probably don't know how much you are hurting." Repeat that you are wrong. "I don't deserve to be forgiven for the way I have treated you lately, but I pray that you can. I want you to know that I love you and I was wrong. I really mean that." At this point, reach out and touch him on the arm to see if he has softened. If he hasn't, give him some time, but be persistent. And finally, ask for his forgiveness again.

One mistake many parents make is dropping the issue altogether. "Well, if he won't forgive me, that's his problem. I did my part." With that attitude, the problem may never be resolved. It's better to back off for awhile, allow a few minutes or even hours for things to cool down, then come back and repeat these five steps.

As parents, there is one additional effective way we can detect a closed spirit. I've found that if we carefully watch nonverbal expressions, we can add to our understanding of what's going on inside a child.

Observing Voice Tone and Facial Expressions to Recognize a Closed Spirit

One woman said to me after a seminar, "I hate my husband. I hate him so much that I can't even talk about him. I'll never go back to him." Yet four months later, that same woman was back with her husband and they were living together in harmony. I heard one husband say about his wife, "I hate that woman so much I can't even stand to look at her." Within hours that same man was loving his wife and regaining his feelings and desires for her.

Sometimes it takes several months, but I'm finding that regaining harmony is possible. My own hope for families and couples increases almost daily because I'm now aware that surface words like, "I hate you," "I'll never live with you again," "I'll always hate you," are reflections of a closed spirit.

A child may say to his parents, "I hate you. I can't handle any more of this. I'm through with this family. I've had it up to here and I don't want to talk about it. I don't even want to be around here." When people spew forth such words, I find they really are saying that they want to talk about it. They would love to resolve the problem but they want to resolve it in a certain way. We need to listen to how they say it, with what intensity. Learn to watch their facial expressions and listen to their tone of voice instead of limiting your understanding to the words they use.

Imagine for a moment a scale from zero to ten, with zero indicating the spirit is totally open and ten totally closed. If I reach for my daughter's hand after I have offended her and she turns her back to me and says, "Dad, you always do this to me and I just can't handle it anymore," chances are I have closed her spirit to about a three. It is not really major, yet it's still very important to reopen it. If I go to touch her and she jerks away from me and says, "Dad, just leave me alone. You're always doing this to me and I just feel like running away," her spirit is probably closed about halfway. But let's say that I knock on her bedroom door and she asks, "Who is it?" in a very hostile voice. I open the door and she says, "Just get out of here, Dad," and she takes a vase and throws it at me. I duck in time and say, "Hey, I know I was wrong . . ." but she yells, "I'm going to run away from this place. I just hate it around here." Those words and actions tell me that her spirit is closed to probably an eight or nine. Usually, the more violent and hostile the resistance, the tighter the spirit has been closed. Hostility may settle into apathy or indifference indicating "my spirit is cemented closed, don't try to reopen it." But when we realize that one's words don't necessarily reflect how one feels inside, we can continue to gently pry open someone's spirit.

The best way that I know to deal with such surface words is to become soft and understanding and admit we are wrong. Then persevere until we can touch and seek forgiveness. That is what they really want. But it may take time.

I have also found that offenses which happened many years ago can still be resolved in much the same way. A child may remember being hurt by a parent many years before. And if a parent really wants to make sure that a child's spirit is totally open toward him, it is appropriate to go back into the past and bring up these old offenses, *as long as the offenses are resolved once they are brought up.*

How Children or Adults Can Reopen Their Own Spirits

If parents are not willing to open their child's closed spirit, it would sound as though the child was destined to rebellion. But there are several things that a child or anyone can do to open his own spirit.

This simple but profound truth is taught in a prayer prayed millions of times each year—the Lord's Prayer. I had read this prayer for years, but continued to miss its true meaning. The prayer invites us to forgive those who trespass against us—who offend us—then God will forgive us of our trespasses. But if we refuse to forgive those who trespass against us, then God will not forgive us.

The word forgive comes from a Greek word meaning "to release" or "set free." It means to untie the chains that bind people. Therefore, when we set free those who offend us or trespass against us, God unties us, opening our spirit. He cannot reopen our spirit, however, if we refuse to help those who have hurt us.

Corrie ten Boom, who helped many Jews avoid the German torture camps in World War II, told me a story that illustrated what Jesus meant by His prayer. Sometime after she had been released from a concentration camp, she spoke at a church in Germany. As the crowd filed out after the service, she saw a man working his way forward. With horror, she recognized him. He had been a guard—one of the most cruel—in the concentration camp where she and her sister had been interned. He had actually been instrumental in causing the death of her sister, Betsie. She was almost nauseated by the sight of him. Her spirit had already been closed toward him years before. He reached out his hand and said, "Corrie ten Boom, I have become a Christian and I know God has forgiven me for the cruel things I did. But I've come to ask if you would forgive me." Corrie said her arms were frozen to her side. She couldn't move.

She told me it was the most difficult thing she'd ever done, but she did reach out and accept his hand and tell him that she did forgive him. At that moment, it was like the venom and hatred flowed out of her. "It was God's love flowing through me to him," she told me. "I really did release him from what he had done to me. And as I did, I was set free!"

As parents we can help teach our children that principle. First, a child can begin to recognize *that the person who has offended him has problems of his own.* Everyone who offends us has his own difficulties or unmet needs. He may have low self-worth. He may feel rejected, or guilty, or resentful toward someone. As soon as we start recognizing this, we start being free in our heart and our spirit can begin to open toward that person.

Second, *we can make a commitment to pray for someone who has offended us.* When our children were young, we lived in the Chicago area. When we went through the tollbooths on the expressway, our children would sometimes hand the attendants the money. They would reach over my shoulder to do so, but now and then the coins would drop and I would have to open the door to retrieve them. Some of the attendants became very irritated. As we would pull away, the children often commented about their anger. "You know why that person was mad at us?" I asked. "It's because he has an 'owwie' in his heart. That's his way of saying, 'Would someone please understand me?'" Sometimes we would pray for an attendant, which helped the children realize they shouldn't take someone else's anger personally.

The biggest problem is that people take offenses far too personally. Usually people are offensive because they have their own problems. Maybe they didn't get enough sleep, they've had a bad day, or someone at home or work has rejected them. There are any number of reasons why people can be offensive, and the sooner we recognize this, the less chance we have of being offended and having our spirit closed. However, even if it does close, we can begin to open it by recognizing that the offender has problems. Even if we never get a chance to help the offender with his problems, just wanting and intending to help many times is enough for God to open our spirit and clear our heart of resentment.

How Open Is Your Child's Spirit?

Test yourself with your children to see how open their spirits are. This is a simple, general evaluation that can help a parent detect whether or not a child's spirit is closing. Score each question from one to five. 1 = never; 2 = seldom; 3 = sometimes; 4 = usually; 5 = always.

1. Does my child (age two and above) enjoy touching me? ____

2. Does my child spontaneously touch me when I first see him after school or at home? ____

3. Does my child respect what I respect in life? ____

4. Does my child generally appreciate what I value in life—i.e., the Bible, my vocation, etc.? ____

5. Would my child's friends be my choice for him? ____

6. Does my child wear clothing and hairstyles that I approve of? ____

7. Does my child choose the activities I would choose for him? ____

8. Does my child's music reflect what I approve of? ____

9. Does my child enjoy having conversations with me? ____

10. Does my child agree in general with my opinions? ____

11. Does my child enjoy going places with me? ____

12. Does my child obey me regularly? ____

13. Does my child generally reflect a warm affection for me? ____

14. Does my child naturally enjoy looking into my eyes? ____

Total Score _____

These scores may indicate:

14–20—Danger, resolve immediately.

21–30—Warning, proceed with caution.

31–40—Watch out for falling rocks.

41–50—Things may be bumping along, but okay.

51–70—End of Construction. Drive carefully.

If you believe that one or more of your children are closing or have closed their spirits toward you, one effective way to start reopening their spirits is to take them out to dinner or get away for a weekend. During that time, let the child know you are trying to have the best relationship with him that you can. Then mention a particular incident that you think offended him and ask him if it did. If it didn't, you can ask, "If that wasn't it, what are some things you can think of that I have done in the past that have really hurt you?" Be prepared, however, to hear something that you do not expect. As offenses surface from the past, simply do the same things you would do with an immediate offense. Go through all five steps—being soft, understanding, admitting you were wrong, trying to touch, and seeking forgiveness.

Eighty-four Ways We Can Offend Our Children

As you seek to discover how you might have offended your child, you may need some help coming up with possibilities. In my counseling and work with children around the country, I have asked many of them how their parents have offended them. I took their answers and compiled them. Here are some of their actual responses:

1. Lacking interest in things that are special to me.
2. Breaking promises.
3. Criticizing unjustly.
4. Allowing my brother or sister to put me down.
5. Misunderstanding my motives.
6. Speaking carelessly.
7. Punishing me for something for which I already had been punished.

8. Telling me that my opinions don't really matter.

9. Giving me the feeling that they never make mistakes.

10. Not being gentle when pointing out my weaknesses or blind spots.

11. Lecturing me and not understanding when all I need is some support.

12. Never telling me "I love you." Never showing me physical affection.

13. Not spending time alone with me.

14. Being insensitive, rough, and breaking promises.

15. Being thoughtless.

16. Never telling me "thank you."

17. Not spending time together.

18. Being insensitive to my trials.

19. Speaking harsh words.

20. Being inconsistent.

21. Being taken for granted.

22. Being told how to do something that I was doing on my own.

23. Nagging me.

24. Bossing me.

25. Feeling unnoticed or unappreciated.

26. Being ignored.

27. Not being considered a thinking and feeling person.

28. Being too busy to care for me and listen to me.

29. Dismissing my needs as unimportant, especially when their work or hobby is more important.

30. Bringing up old mistakes from the past to deal with present problems.
31. Teasing excessively.
32. Not noticing my accomplishments.
33. Making tactlesss comments.
34. Liking me only for my physical looks or abilities, instead of what's inside me.
35. Not being praised and appreciated.
36. Being built up and then let down.
37. Getting my hopes up to do something as a family and then not following through.
38. Being corrected without being reminded that they love me.
39. Being disciplined in harshness and anger.
40. Not reasoning with me, and never giving me an explanation of why I'm being disciplined.
41. Misusing brute force.
42. Reacting to me in the opposite way I think a Christian should treat me.
43. Raising their voices to each other.
44. Not being interested in who I am.
45. Cutting down something I am doing or someone I am with as being dumb or stupid.
46. Using foul language when they are upset with me.
47. Being impatient, which often comes across as rudeness.
48. Saying "no" without giving a reason.
49. Not praising me.

50. Sensing a difference between what is said with the mouth and what is said through facial expressions.

51. Making sarcastic remarks about me.

52. Making fun of my hopes, dreams, and accomplishments.

53. Punishing me severely for something that I didn't do.

54. Being distracted when I really have something to say.

55. Insulting me in front of others.

56. Speaking before thinking through how it will affect me.

57. Pressuring me when I already feel low or offended.

58. Comparing me with other kids at school and telling me how wonderful they are and that they wish I could be better.

59. Forcing me to argue with them when I'm really hurt inside.

60. Being treated like a little child.

61. Not approving of what I do or how I do it. I keep trying to get their approval but they just won't give it.

62. Seeing them do the very things they tell me not to do.

63. Ignoring me when I ask for advice because they are too busy.

64. Ignoring me and not introducing me to people who come to the house or we see in public.

65. Showing favoritism toward my brother or sister.

66. Acting as if something I want is of little importance.

67. Not feeling like I am special to them. It's so important to me to have my parents let me know, even in small ways, that I'm special to them.

68. Seeing my father put my mother down, especially in front of company.

69. Seldom touching or holding me.

70. Hearing mom and dad bickering at each other to the point where one of them is really hurt.

71. Not trusting me.

72. Making fun of something physically different about me.

73. Seeing my mom and dad trying to get revenge against each other.

74. Sensing that my dad never approves of what I do or how I do it.

75. Not being able to control their anger.

76. Getting mad at me because I can't keep up with their schedule or abilities.

77. Making me feel like they wish they never had me in the first place.

78. Not having enough time for me.

79. Needing my parents but they are glued to the television.

80. Seeing my parents spend a lot of money on their pleasures, but when I want something, they don't seem to have the money.

81. Making me feel childish.

82. Not spending the time to understand what I am trying to say.

---

83. Yelling at me when I already know I'm wrong.
84. Making me feel like I hadn't tried to improve at something when I really had.

2

Parenting for Positive Results

- Four Basic Types of Parenting:
    The Dominant Parent
    The Neglectful Parent
    The Permissive Parent
    The Loving and Firm Parent
- The Two Most Important Factors in Raising
  Children

MY HEART SANK WHEN I saw the police car pull into our driveway. I knew why it was there. Too scared to move, I sat still, trying to look innocent while my mother opened the door.

The officer introduced himself, then turned to me. "Have you been with your friend Jimmy today?" he asked.

"Yes," I said, trying my best to hide my nervousness. "I see him all the time."

"Were you down at the river with him?"

"No. I wasn't anywhere near the river."

The officer looked at my mother and then back at me. "Jimmy told me you were down there with him. He also said that the two of you broke into one of the homes there."

I could feel the blood rushing to my face as I shook my head in denial. The officer kept talking: "You're going to have to appear at juvenile court next week. I'll have witnesses there."

I began to cry and then admitted everything. "I was down at the river. We did break into a house. But we only took a couple of small items."

This wasn't my first brush with trouble. A few of the town merchants had accused me of stealing money and items from their stores. I hadn't stolen anything from them, but my reputation was established, so they suspected me anyway. There were rumors going around town that I probably would be sent to reform school. Growing up, I basically did what I wanted to do when I wanted to. I'm sure that I deserved hundreds of spankings for my actions and irresponsible attitude as a child, but my parents never once disciplined me. As a result, there have been many areas where I have had difficulty adjusting as an adult. For one thing, rules never apply to me. If a sign says "no parking," I may park anyway because "I'm an exception." Because there were no rules in my home, I figured rules were for others, not me.

However, the attitude of my parents did have one very positive result in my life; it laid the foundation for a strong sense of self-worth. This fact could sound strange after reading about all of the trouble I was involved in. But as I look back to how I was raised, I can see that my parents were one of four types of parents we'll discuss in this chapter. I now understand how I was able to grow up with a positive self-image in a home void of discipline.

A few years ago, Dr. Dennis Guernsey described four basic categories of parents in an article for *Family Life Today*. His observations were based on a study by three Ph.D.'s at the University of Minnesota. Two types of parents tend to cause their children to resent authority. These children tend to dislike themselves. They may do poorly in school and are often convinced that they never will be successful. These same two types of parents also tend more frequently to close the spirit of their children, resulting in the various problems we mentioned in chapter 1.

The other two categories of parents—one of which characterized my mother and father—tend to produce more positive-acting children. These children are more secure and tend to like themselves. They do better in school and are more responsible as adults.

As we examine each type of parent, it is important not only to examine the kind of parents we would like to be, but also to evaluate our lives in light of how we were parented.

Four Basic Types of Parenting

1. The Dominant Parent. This type of parent tends to produce the most negative qualities in children. Dominant parents usually have very high standards and expectations. But they seldom offer warm, caring support and very few explanations are given for their rigid rules. They tend to be unbending and demand that their children stay away from certain activities because of their strong convictions. But because the children do not know the reasons why these activities are wrong, they may secretly participate in them.

A group of psychologists and psychiatrists studied 875 third graders in rural Columbia County, New York, from 1960 to 1981 and made several conclusions concerning dominant parents. They found that high aggression in younger children is caused by the actions of overly dominant parents. This high aggression usually lasts a lifetime and can lead to major violence. The study also showed that harsh punishment, like washing out children's mouths with soap, coupled with rejection can lead to aggressive behavior.

These are some typical statements and actions by dominant parents:

- "Rules are rules. You're late—to bed with no dinner."
- "I won't stand for your back talk. Apologize." (Or slap the child's face.)
- "You don't need reasons. Just do what I say."
- "I don't care how many of your friends will be there. You're not going and I don't want to hear another word about it, do you hear?"
- "No son of mine is going to goof off. You took the job; you get it done."
- "How many times have I told you to stop that? Get in there—you're going to get it!"

These are some possible reactions by children who have dominant parents:

- They rank lowest in self-respect. They have little ability to conform to rules or authority.
- The rigid harshness of the parent breaks the spirit of the child and results in resistance, "clamming up," or rebellion.
- The child usually does not want anything to do with his parents' rules or values. He tends to reject the ideals of his parents.
- The child may be attracted to other children who rebel against their parents and the general rules of society. They may use drugs and participate in other illegal activities.
- The child may be loud and demanding of his rights.
- In a classroom setting, he may cause disruption in order to gain attention from others.

2. The Neglectful Parent. Neglectful parents tend to lack both loving support and control over their children. They show an uncaring or immature attitude, lashing out at a child when pushed or irritated. These parents tend to isolate themselves from their children by excessive use of babysitters and to indulge in their own selfish activities. Children are viewed as a bother, "to be seen and not heard."

Dr. Armand Nicholi, psychiatric professor at Harvard Medical School, helped me understand that neglectful parents are not only absent when they are away from home. They rob their children of one of the most important factors in their lives—emotional accessibility. When they are home, they usually are not listening or paying attention to their children.

There are four main reasons why our children are being neglected today, according to Dr. Nicholi:

a. *The high divorce rate.* Statistics show that there are more than thirteen million children in single parent homes. The divorce rate has been upwardly spiraling since the early 1960s and has increased 700 percent since the beginning of this century. Most divorces require single parents to work outside the home, allowing less time for the emotional development of their children. It's very difficult for single parents to provide their children with the necessary time each day for listening and emotional accessibility. However, it's not impossible.

b. *The increase of mothers in the work force.* More than 50 percent of all mothers in the United States are working. This also greatly increased in the 1960s, with a strong emphasis being put forth that women were unfulfilled in their homes. The economic pressures of the times also forced many women to seek jobs. By joining the work force, mothers are often less accessible to their children.

The suicide rate among children ages ten to fourteen has tripled in the last ten years. Dr. Nicholi says this can be directly related to changes in the American home. One study he quoted shows that American parents spend less time with their children than parents in any other nation except England. The study quoted one Russian father who said he would not even think of spending less than two hours daily with his children. In contrast, a study at Boston University found that the average father in the United States spends about thirty-seven seconds a day with his children.

c. *Excessive television viewing.* This also increased greatly in the sixties and now more than 90 percent of American homes have at least one television. The problem with television is that even though people are physically together in a room, there is very little meaningful and emotional interaction. As parents neglect their children by watching television or through other activities, the children experience an emotional loss similar to that of losing a parent through death. They often feel guilty when their parents are not with them. Some even believe the reason is because they are bad, and if only they were better, their parents would spend more time with them. Obviously, this awareness lowers a child's sense of worth.

d. *An increasingly mobile society.* More than 50 percent of Americans change addresses every five years. This mobility robs children of their parents' time as well as the emotional strength and accessibility they have from friends and relatives in their former home. Yet even if we have to move our families, we can still provide emotional accessibility to our children. This can be done by setting aside time every day to spend with each of our children or together as a family. Dr. Nicholi stressed that this time should be used to counteract the effects of our mobile society.

To illustrate how prevalent the problem of emotional accessibility is, take a short break and try spending just five minutes concentrating on your family's welfare and how you can help meet each child's emotional needs. You may find it very difficult because we're not used to doing this in our culture.

Listed below are some typical actions and statements made by neglectful parents:

- "Work it out by yourself. Can't you see I'm busy?"
- "No! I'm expected somewhere else tonight. Get your mother to help you."
- "No, you can't stay up. Remember you wanted to stay up late last night. Stay out of my hair!"
- "That's your problem. I've got to get to work."
- "Good grief! Can't you kids be more careful?"
- "Late again, for heaven's sake. Would someone please pass the meat?"
- "So you think I'm stupid, huh? Well, that's your problem, buddy. Just get lost!"

Here are some possible effects on children of neglectful parents:

- The harshness and neglect tend to wound the spirit of a child, resulting in rebellion.
- The neglect teaches the child that he is not worth spending time with.
- The child develops insecurity because his parents are never predictable.
- The child may not develop a healthy self-respect because he is not respected and has not learned to control himself.
- Broken promises break the spirit of the child and lower his self-worth.
- The child tends to do poorly in school because he has little motivation.

3. The Permissive Parent. Permissive parents tend to be warm, supporting people, but weak in establishing and enforcing rules and limits for their children.

This was the type of parents that I had. My mother and father were very warm and loving and accepting of me. But as far as I can remember, there were no rigid rules in our home. They usually gave in to my demands. Even when I was in trouble, they would not spank or discipline me. My mother said she never spanked because her first child died of blood poisoning and she had spanked her two weeks before she died. She made my father promise to never spank any one of their five remaining children.

Although they meant well, that leniency affected me negatively. My parents left all decisions concerning how I would spend my spare time up to me. In fact I didn't start formally dating until . . . the third grade! This caused a number of problems in my life. Once my father caught me in a serious infraction as a young boy. From his firm voice I knew that I was in trouble. But later, he said he would let me off without punishing me if I promised not to do it again. I actually told him that I needed a spanking but he wouldn't do it. There was something in me that wanted to be corrected.

I found the same permissiveness in school. Once a teacher caught me passing notes in the third grade after warning me of the consequences if I didn't stop. She sent me to the principal. He talked to me for awhile, told me I needed to shape up, then said that he was going to spank me. I thought he really meant business, but about fifteen minutes later, he said he was going to give me another chance if I promised not to pass notes again. Of course, I promised the world, but inwardly I can remember being disappointed that he didn't follow through.

One of the major reasons why some parents are too permissive is an inner fear that they may damage their children if they are too strict. That fear of confronting their children may actually produce the very things they fear.

On the positive side, permissive parents are strong in the area of support. I am very grateful that my parents showed me warmth and love. They were very giving, very understanding, very comforting. Effective parents realize that a certain degree of permissiveness is healthy. That means accepting that kids will be kids, that a clean shirt will not stay clean for long, that children will run instead of walk, and that a tree is for climbing and a mirror for making faces. It means accepting that children have the right to childlike feelings and dreams. That kind of permissiveness gives a child confidence and an increasing capacity to express his thoughts and feelings.

Overpermissiveness, on the other hand, allows for undesirable acts such as beating up other children, marking on buildings, and breaking objects.

The following statements and actions are typical of permissive parents:

- "Well, okay. You can stay up late this time. I know how much you like this program."
- "You're tired, aren't you? A paper route is a tough job; sure, I'll take you around."
- "I hate to see you under all this pressure from school. Why not rest tomorrow? I'll say you're sick."
- "You didn't hear me call you for dinner. Well, that's all right. Sit down. I don't want you eating a cold dinner."
- "Please don't get angry with me. You're making a scene."
- "Jimmy, please try to hurry. Mommy will be late again if we don't start soon."

These are possible reactions by children who have permissive parents:

- A child senses that he is in the driver's seat and can play the parent accordingly.
- A child develops a feeling of insecurity, like leaning against a wall that appears to be firm, but falls over.
- A child may have little self-respect because he has not learned to control himself and master certain personal disciplines.
- A child learns that because standards are not firm, he can manipulate around the rules.

4. The Loving and Firm Parent. Loving and firm parents usually have clearly defined rules, limits, and standards for living. They take time to train their children to understand these limits—like why we don't carve love notes on the neighbor's tree—and give clear warnings when a child has transgressed an established limit. But they also give support by expressing physical affection and spending personal time listening to each child. They are flexible, willing to listen to all the facts if a limit has been violated.

The loving and firm parent is a healthy and balanced combination of the dominant and permissive parents. There is firmness with clearly defined rules like, "You cannot intentionally harm our furniture or anyone else's," but this firmness is combined with loving attitudes and actions.

Here are some typical statements and actions by loving and firm parents:

- "You're late again for dinner, Tiger. How can we work this out together?" (Parents spend time working out solutions with the child.)
- "Hey, I wish I could let you stay up later, but we agreed on this time. Remember what you're like the next day if you miss your sleep?"
- "When we both cool off, let's talk about what needs to be done."
- "You're really stuck, aren't you? I'll help you this time. Then let's figure out how you can get it done yourself next time."
- "You say all the other girls will be there. I'd like to have more information first."
- "Did you do your piano? I hate to do this, but we agreed—no dinner before it is finished. We'll keep it warm for you."
- "You may answer the phone, but before you answer, you must learn to answer it the right way."

Typical characteristics of children who have loving and firm parents:

- The warm support and clearly defined limits tend to build self-respect within the child.

- A child is more content when he has learned to control himself.

- His world is more secure when he realizes that there are limits which are unbending, and he understands why—the underlying principles.

- Because the spirit of a child is not closed, the lines of communication are open with parents. There is less chance of the "rebellious teen years."

- The children from loving and firm parents ranked highest in: (a) self-respect, (b) capacity to conform to authorities at school, church, etc., (c) greater interest in their parents' faith in God, and (d) greater tendency not to join a rebellious group.

The supportive and firm parent reflects the very specific biblical instruction for parenting. It stresses two important ways that parents must take care of their children. First, they must *discipline* their children, which partly means setting clearly defined limits in the home. Second, they must follow the greatest *instruction* in Scripture—to love one another.

The Two Most Important Factors in Raising Children

I have concluded that the two most important factors in raising children are:

1. Establishing clearly defined and understood rules in the home, limits that the children know they cannot violate without some consequence.

2. A commitment to love each child in a warm, affectionate, and supportive way.

In the chart below, each of these four types of parents is summarized. The dominant parents are lower in their ability to show loving, warm support and higher in the establishment of rigid rules and limitations. Neglectful parents have a tendency to be lacking in warm and loving support and also in establishing rules and limits around the house. Permissive parents have a greater tendency to be loving, warm, supportive, and approving, yet lack the ability to establish clearly defined limits and rules. The fourth type of parent, the loving and firm parent, has established clearly defined limits and is more diligent in communicating warmth and loving support.

Parents	Love and support for their children	Controlling children by limits or rules at home
Dominant	Low	High
Neglectful	Low	Low
Permissive	High	Low
Loving and Firm	High	High

3

Expressing Loving Support— The Most Important Aspect of Raising Children

- Unconditional Commitment
- Scheduled Times
- Availability to Children
- Tender Treatment
- Frequent Eye Contact
- Listening in an Understanding Way
- Meaningful Touching

THE TENSION WAS THICK in the front seat of our car. Greg stared silently out the window. "I know what you've been doing," I said. My thirteen-year-old son was involved in an activity he knew was wrong. But he couldn't admit it.

With tears streaming down his face, he said, "Dad I didn't want to tell you because I knew you'd be so ashamed of me." I held out my arms and he immediately grabbed me and began sobbing. I could feel his body relax as I told him, "No matter what you have done or ever do, remember I will always love you."

With those words, Greg was able to admit what he had been doing. As Greg sensed my love for him, he was able to relax and our communication was open. In this chapter we want to explore several ways of expressing supportive love to our children, the kind of love that builds stronger families and increases a child's sense of personal value.

Unconditional Commitment

One of the most important ways to express warmth and loving support to our children is *to make an unconditional commitment to them for life.* That's the kind of commitment that says, "You're important to me today and tomorrow, no matter what happens."

My family is reminded daily of my commitment to them. At the entryway of our home hangs a wall plaque that I made. It reads: "To Norma, Kari, Gregory and Michael, in assurance of my lifetime commitment to you."

Norma and I frequently tell our children that we love them. In many ways, we let them know that we are committed to them for their entire lives, no matter what they do. We are committed to help them be successful in whatever they want to do. We will be committed to them after they are married. We will be committed to them no matter who they marry. We will be committed no matter what happens during their marriage. We will be committed to their mates and to their children. We tell them we are always available to listen. Should they get into trouble, we will be there to help. That doesn't necessarily mean we will bail them out of a tight situation, for that may not be best for them. But they know how much we love them and that nothing can ever keep us from loving them.

Mark "Golden Boy" Frazie, a professional boxer, told me how his parents demonstrated their commitment to him. When I asked Mark who was the most encouraging person in his life, without hesitation he answered, "My dad." He told me that his father is his very best friend and always will be.

"When I was nineteen years old, I went through a real trial," Mark explained. "Some of my family resisted me and many of my relatives did not understand. But my dad told me that even though he was hurt by what I had done, I was his son. He would always love me and always be there to pick me up."

In contrast, lack of unconditional commitment can result in major conflict. A frightened eighteen-year-old boy standing in front of a stern judge listened as the judge, a close personal friend of the boy's father, told him that he was a disgrace to the community and his family: "You ought to be ashamed of yourself, disgracing your family's name, causing your parents a great deal of anguish and embarrassment. Your father is an upright citizen in this community. I have personally served on numerous committees with him and know of his commitment to this city. I count your father as a close personal friend and it is with deep grief that I have to sentence you this day for your crime."

With his head bowed in obvious embarrassment, the young man listened to the judge. Then, before sentence was passed, he asked if he could speak: "Sir, I do not mean to be disrespectful or to make excuses for my behavior. But I envy you a great deal. You see, there were many days and nights that I wanted to be my father's best friend. There were many times when I needed his help with school work, in some of my dating situations, and in some of the difficult times that I faced as a teenager. But my father was gone a great deal, probably on some of those committees with you, or playing golf. I've always felt like other things were more important to him than I was. I don't mean this disrespectfully, but I truly wish I knew my father like you do."

Stunned by the boy's words, the judge placed him on probation and ordered that the boy and his father were to spend time together every week, getting to know each other. The father obviously was humiliated by the sentence, realizing his lack of commitment to his son, but it caused him to get to know his son better and that was the turning point in his son's life.

Scheduled Times

A second way that we as parents can show our love is to *schedule special times with the family.* Communicating warm, loving approval to our children doesn't just happen naturally. I believe this time should be scheduled on a regular basis—preferably daily—because our children need us.

Schedule times that are meaningful for all persons involved. The activity itself is not so important, but it needs to be something that is enjoyable for both the child and the parent. Often the deepest relationships can be developed during the simplest activities.

As a family, we camp together frequently. It is during those times in the car, or lying in our sleeping bags, or waiting for a fish to bite when things are said that give us a deep understanding about our children. These special times help us understand where they are going in life and what concerns them. Just being with them communicates they are loved. A parent's willingness to wait for conversation to develop further amplifies his or her child's self-worth.

One summer night we were in our motor home driving from Portland, Oregon, to Chicago. It was about 10:00 P.M. and everyone was asleep. I had planned to stop at a campsite around 11:00, but Kari, who was about thirteen years old at the time, was awakened and wandered up front and sat next to me. She brought up the subject of dating and marriage and we got involved in a most meaningful discussion about the consequences of premarital sexual involvement. We had no place to go. There was no telephone to interrupt us. There is no way I could have planned a more meaningful time together. We didn't need to stop for food. And she was, of course, highly interested in the conversation. We stayed up until 2:00 A.M. while everyone else slept. These times seldom occur unless we plan time together. If our children see us neglect other things to spend time with them, they will realize how important they are to us.

I often wonder why we, as parents, are so reluctant to tell our children how valuable they are to us. We need to let them know regularly that they are tremendously important to us. On a scale from zero to ten, where do your children feel they rate in importance to you? My children know that they are about a nine to me. They are the most important things in my life other than my relationship with God and my wife. Sometimes I allow their value to drop to a four or seven, but I keep pushing it back up to nine with a conscious decision to value them. Gloria Gaither and Shirley Dobson have written a book called *Let's Make a Memory.* It is a super resource, filled with ideas for things to do during scheduled times for parents and children.

Availability to Children

Besides unconditional commitment and scheduling meaningful times together we need to *communicate that we are available* to our children both during scheduled and unscheduled times. Sometimes when I'm reading the paper, watching something special on television or heading out the door for a meeting, one of my children will walk up and say, "Dad, you got a minute? I've got this problem in geometry." Or Kari might say to Norma in the kitchen, "Mom, what am I going to do? I can't find anything to wear." We must be careful what we communicate at these times. If we say, "Not now, I'm busy," they'll observe what we are doing and compare their importance to it. Often we can say, "Now isn't a good time to talk, but I can give you my undivided attention in thirty minutes." Sometimes we can drop what we're doing, because our children are simply more important.

Children might go a whole day without asking for our help. But as Dr. Campbell explains in his book, *How to Really Love Your Teen-Ager,* teens have something like a "container" built within them and every once in a while they run out of "emotional gas." This is when they come up and need to be close to us. They need touching, listening, understanding, and our time. After we have filled their "emotional gas tank" they usually say, "Well, see you later." Maybe we haven't finished everything we wanted to say, but they're filled up. And that's okay. I want my children to know they are valuable and that I am available most of the time when they need me.

Being available does not mean that we wait around for our children. It does mean evaluating what is most important to us in life. Is it needlepoint? Golf? Television? Football? Work? How many parents would say that the newspaper is more important than their children? Probably none. Yet many parents appear to be unavailable or even become angry if their children approach them with some special need while they are reading.

It is natural for a father to become engrossed in his work, but a man must evaluate why he is working. Is he primarily working to meet the needs of his family or to meet his own needs? If he is working to meet the needs of his family, he should not rationalize that it is okay to spend many extra hours at work because he is feeding his children or preparing to send them to college. In reality, kids have a much greater need for *time with dad*, than knowing dad is away at work so they can eat or attend college.

Because I can easily get involved with my vocation and rationalize time away from my children, I reevaluate on a regular basis. I often ask my wife if she feels I am spending enough time with our children. I also ask our children the same question, carefully listening to what they say.

Children don't expect that parents give up all of their activities and fun times just so that they are always available for them. But they must see that these other activities are not as valuable as they are to their parents.

Tender Treatment

Another aspect of communicating love to children is how parents act while with them. *Children need to be treated tenderly.* Gentleness and tenderness are of prime importance in dealing with our children. Harshness and angry lecturing communicate to children that they are of little value and in some cases worthless. The phrase "If I meant anything to anyone, they wouldn't be so mean to me" is the frequent subconscious conclusion teens draw.

The calming effect of tenderness in a home has tremendously positive effects. Sometimes, while I'm reading in the evening, one of my kids will climb up on my lap. They may want to talk; other times they're content just to be with me. It's not unusual for Kari to come to me and say something like, "Dad, I'm having a problem with a friend at school. Do you think we could talk about it tonight?" She knows that I am usually open to that situation. And I have learned that when we do get together, she wants me to listen, remain calm, offer some suggestions, and especially try to understand her suggestions. She does not want or need a lecture. Above all, she wants me to be tender while I'm listening.

Recently I violated almost every principle I recommend in this book, but because Kari, now seventeen years old, knows I love her and our relationship is strong, it appeared that she was just barely affected by my insensitivity. Under the stress of finishing this book and several other major responsibilities I launched into a firm and serious lecture with her. "Don't you ever wait until the last day to finish a school report," I ranted. I threatened her social life and anything else that came to mind. I left the house with a close friend and halfway through dinner I excused myself and telephoned Kari. "Kari," I said, tenderly and apologetically, "Dad was wrong, wasn't he?" Often I think children are much more mature than their parents. She answered, "Dad, Mom explained the pressures you are under. The reason I never answered you was because I knew what you're going through. Thanks for calling though. I love you."

In the heat of a family argument I can forget all about being tender. I'm particularly vulnerable when I return home from a trip and am physically and emotionally exhausted. On one such day, Kari said she wanted to participate in some athletic activity but didn't know which one to choose. She had mentioned this on several occasions but never followed through on any of my suggestions. This time, I suggested she go out for track at school. She told me she had no interest in track. That angered me. "I want you to go out for track," I yelled. "If I tell you to go out for track, that means you're going out for track!" She was shocked by my response. Here she was, sixteen years old, a lovely girl with a great attitude, and I was upset because she wasn't going out for track. I knew I was wrong. I could see I was closing her spirit. But I was too upset to deal with it right then.

In situations such as this, it is often best to leave the conflict for awhile. Later that evening, when I'd calmed down, I gently approached Kari. (This was after I had made a deal with my family. Because they are all extremely valuable to me, I had told them I would give ten dollars to anyone if I ever took out my frustrations on him.) I felt so bad about what I'd said to my daughter, I made out a check to her for twenty dollars. I knocked on Kari's door and heard her say very hesitantly, "Who is it?" When I told her it was me, she said, "Oh, Dad, I can't take any more of this right now."

When I told her I needed to talk with her, she unlocked the door. I handed her the check, explaining, "Kari, I know this doesn't buy your love, and it doesn't get me off the hook. But what I did to you was very wrong, and you're too valuable to be treated that way. I want to give you this little gift."

A smile broke across her face and she was a little embarrassed. "Oh, Dad, you don't have to do this." I could tell that her spirit was opening as we spoke. Even if I hadn't given her anything, but had gently apologized, it would have helped begin the process of opening her spirit. When I gave her the money—twice the amount I agreed to give her—I was communicating in a small way how valuable she was to me.

It is easier for me to do this today, because I have been practicing for several years. However it wasn't easy at first. If you are not used to being tender and admitting wrong actions as a parent, it will be difficult for you to humble yourself. But it will pay valuable dividends in the lives of your children.

Frequent Eye Contact

Children need frequent eye contact with us. Frequent eye contact is a very effective way of communicating love to anyone. This can also help a parent evaluate whether or not a child's spirit is closing. A child whose spirit is closing tends to look down or away, or turn his entire body away from the parent. With younger children, it helps to get down on our knees and look them straight in the eye.

I've often heard Norma say, "Now, look me in the eyes," when questioning our children. She says that she can usually sense whether a child is telling the truth. It is difficult for a child to keep his eyes on his parents when he is guilty. He looks down, or away, or his eyes begin to blink. A child may confess something just because of our gentle insistence that we look each other in the eyes.

Listening in an Understanding Way

The sixth aspect of communicating love to our children is *listening in an understanding way.* Listening is one skill that many people take for granted. However, I believe listening is so important that I recommend parents purchase a book or enroll in a course on how to listen. Listening does not come naturally. Most adults are preoccupied with their own needs and problems and therefore have a tendency not to listen carefully to those around them. By not noticing the needs of others, we can communicate that we are not interested in them.

There are several important points to remember about being an effective listener with our children:

A good listener desires *eye contact* with the speaker. That means stopping our activities—putting the newspaper down, turning the television off—and giving our undivided attention.

A good listener *never assumes he knows what the other person is saying.* I have reacted to something one of my children said only to learn later that what I understood wasn't what he really meant. One of the fastest ways to close a person's spirit is to accuse him of something that he doesn't really mean.

I have found it helpful to ask questions to clarify what the other person has said. *I repeat in different words what I think they mean.* Then I ask them, "Is that what you are saying?" If they say, "Well, Dad, that's close, but that's not quite it," I say, "Well, we have plenty of time. Just what do you mean by that?" Then they will repeat what they are trying to tell me.

Greg is our resident comedian. But one time I thought he took it too far when I found Michael, at age three, lying on the bottom of a motel swimming pool. After rescuing Mike, I rushed him to our room so a local doctor could check him. Greg was chasing us when he yelled, "Dad wait, I can't keep up. He's okay, I'm sure!" and he started to laugh. I stopped, snapped my head around, and scolded him, pointing for him to stay with Mom. "What does he know about the seriousness of this situation?" I muttered as I continued running. Later, Greg tried to explain what he meant. Instead of reacting, I asked him to explain himself. He simply was trying to tell me that he wanted to help and in his nervousness he began to laugh without really knowing why.

Another key factor in being a good listener is to *not overreact or take immediate action.* One day I almost ran to Kari's school after hearing what one of her teachers had said about her in class. I was extremely upset that a professional teacher would say what he said to her. Kari immediately started crying and pleaded with me that I not confront the teacher. When I saw her fear I calmed down and reassured her that I would not go to the teacher without her permission. My assurance gave her the added freedom to share the rest of what he had said.

Later, after we'd both had time to think, I asked Kari for permission to see the teacher and she granted it. Norma and I confronted him, repeating what Kari had said he shared in class about her. The teacher confessed it, apologized to us, and asked if he could see Kari immediately. We took him to her and in tears he put his arms around her and sought her forgiveness. It was a special moment for all of us. Because I had not acted impulsively but instead asked for her permission first, Kari has continued to be open in sharing with us what happens in her life at school.

I have found that it is best to go through a whole conversation, then later on, after we have had time to think, take action with the agreement of the child involved. An immediate reaction causes children to fear bringing up things in the future, cutting the lines of communication.

Once I was locked in an argument with Greg concerning one of his grades. In my frustration, I said I was going to ground him from everything, forever. Kari calmly reminded me of my own commitment to wait a few days after a trip before changing or establishing a new rule that affected the kids. She was right. After a few days, I had forgotten all about the situation. Patience is crucial to building trust and openness between the parent and child.

In order to be a good listener, it is also important that we *not ridicule what our children say*. We may not understand what they are saying, but being critical or ridiculing a child lowers his sense of worth and can cut off meaningful communication.

In his book, *The Family That Listens*, Dr. H. Norman Wright outlines some additional ideas about listening:

1. Parents must be careful not to stereotype children. If you feel your child is a complainer, a whiner, a bully, or procrastinator, it may affect what you think he is saying. If we think, "Oh, he's

just a whiner, it's not important what he says," we may miss learning some vital information.

2. People tend to listen five times as fast as another person can speak. If your child talks at one hundred words per minute, and you can listen at five hundred words per minute, what do you do with the remainder of time? Often boredom sets in and we daydream. Or we try to help our children express their thoughts rather than taking the time to listen to what they really mean.

3. We need to listen with our entire body, not just our ears and eyes. We cannot listen effectively as we walk away, fix dinner, or flip through the paper. We listen most effectively with our body turned toward the speaker, leaning slightly forward.

Each of these areas—*unconditional commitment, scheduled time, availability, tender treatment, frequent eye contact,* and *listening in an understanding way*—increases our children's sense of worth and value. As they feel more valued, they feel loved.

Meaningful Touching

The last major way we express love for our children is through *meaningful touching*. There is a great deal of research emerging about the importance of touching and hugging our children.

According to some research, the skin is the largest organ of our body and has a built-in need to be touched. Physiologists contend that the nerve endings of the skin actually are associated with certain vital glands centered in the brain. These glands regulate growth and many other important functions of the body. Research suggests that some children, because of a lack of touching, actually have their growth stunted to some degree. At the University of Minnesota, they have what is called "hugging therapy sessions," where the nurses and attendants spend time hugging and touching neglected children in a mean-ingful way while telling them they are doing great. Research-ers found that these children actually caught up with their peers in physical growth.

In addition to stimulating their growth and aiding their physical health, touching also communicates to children that they are valuable. When I place my hand tenderly on my child's shoulder, I am actually communicating, "You are im-portant to me. I want to spend time with you." On the other hand, pushing our children away or hitting them with our hands communicates rejection. Refusing to touch our children communicates to them that they are "untouchable." Our touching must be meaningful from the child's point of view in order to be effective.

For a wife, a type of meaningful touching from her hus-band is when he holds her tenderly during a conversation. To find out whether his touch is meaningful to her, a husband can ask his wife. The same is true with children. We can actually ask them, especially as they grow older, if we are too rough, or if we touch too frequently or not enough.

It is important to remember that touching is a two-way street. Not only is it essential for parents to touch their children, but also for children to touch their parents. It is important for children to know that their parents need to be hugged. We don't depend on their hugs and touches like they do ours, but they may not realize that we have the same emotional and physical needs and we appreciate the spontaneity of their affection.

Once we were having our regular family meeting and the discussion turned to touching. During the conversation, we mentioned to Greg, who was fifteen years old, that we needed him to respond when we tried to hug him. He looked embar-rassed, so we talked further about it. He said that he didn't re-alize that by resisting some of our hugs we were feeling that he didn't like us. He changed immediately and became much more receptive to our hugs, even though at times we feel he is trying to rearrange our backbones.

There are several types of touching that are appropriate with children: holding them in our laps while reading to them, hugging them when they arrive home from school, or just holding hands. We have a family hold, where we interlock our little fingers. Every member of our family knows that this is our special, secret, family-tradition hold. Norma and I started holding hands like this when we were first engaged. It is a personal, physical sign of affection in our family. Obviously, as our children have grown older, we seldom hold hands with them. One of the problems in today's culture is that we have associated touching of any kind with sexual connotations. We need to realize that touching does not need to have such overtones.

A real sense of meaningfulness and security comes from touching. At times our children will stay in bed on a Saturday morning. I will go into their rooms and put my arm by their pillow and they will lay their heads on my arm. Other times I will touch them on the shoulder while we talk.

When Greg was about six, we were driving in the Chicago area, and he told me how terrible it would be if we had an accident and I was killed. I obviously agreed with him and told him I would miss him terribly. Greg looked up and melted me when he said, "You know what Dad? If you ever get killed, I want to die right with you. And I want them to put both of us in the same casket and I want to be lying on your arm." As dramatic as that was, it further illustrates how much touching our children means to them.

I haven't always been a touching person. I didn't come from a touching home. I don't recall my parents touching each other and I remember feeling uncomfortable when a relative, who liked to hug a lot, came to visit. Before we were married, I told Norma, "Now, don't expect me to be one of those 'huggy' husbands and fathers, because I'm just not like that." I had to learn over the years how to touch and enjoy it.

But touching has proven to be very meaningful because it builds a sense of value within our children. It helps meet their emotional, mental, and physical needs. To fully benefit from touching, I would say that parents should make a conscious effort to touch their children eight to twelve times a day in a way that is meaningful to them.

Expressing loving support is of paramount importance within the family structure. It is also important to remember that the *attitudes* of a parent in expressing his love are as important as *how* the love is demonstrated. We've discussed ways to express loving support to our children, and in the next chapter we will deal specifically with the second major factor in raising children—developing firm limits and understandable rules. Without the balance of love and limits, children are robbed of the wholeness God intended them to have.

4

Balancing Loving Support through Contracts

- Setting Limits through Contracts
- Enforcing the Contract—Our Experiments
- A Practical Way to Implement Family Contracts
- Don't Expect, Inspect
- Contract for Dating
- Contract for Driving
- Guidelines for Spanking

ONE OF THOSE RARE EVENTS took place when Greg was about seven years old. He awakened me at 6:15 one morning, pushing on me so as not to wake Norma. "Dad, could you get up and read the Bible with me?" he whispered. What could I say? This was a special opportunity few parents could pass up.

We tiptoed downstairs and Greg sat on my lap. We began to read, trying to memorize the short verses as we read. We discussed what it meant to rejoice, give thanks, and pray, and Greg seemed quite responsive. Then we prayed together and thanked God for Greg's messy room that he had to clean up and for all the hard work facing me at the office that day. By then the whole family was up. Amazed by what they saw, they gathered around for a quick time of prayer together. Then everyone scattered and I leaned back in my chair, bathing in the joy of my son's "spiritual maturity."

A sudden racket at the top of the staircase shattered my reverie. While returning to his room, Greg gave Kari a shove against the wall. She shoved back, and the fight was on. After breaking up the combatants I couldn't help but wonder how this could happen so quickly after such a meaningful experience.

Later that week, I related this experience while speaking in another part of the country. A woman in the audience graciously said in front of the group, "Don't worry. Your children are just in one of the stages they all go through. They'll be over it in about thirty to thirty-five years."

We have watched our children go through a number of stages, some of them good, some not so good. Looking back over more than twenty years of being a family, Norma and I have concluded that through all the stages, greatly valuing one another has been the most important ingredient that re-bonds us and "covers all our sins" toward each other. In other words, we have committed to love each other. Part of the meaning of love is "to attach high value or stand in awe of."

In the previous chapter we shared that we want our children to know how valuable they are to us. We try to communicate this value by spending time with them, resolving conflicts, motivating them, and keeping their spirits open. We carefully "listen" to them with our eyes. When they were younger, we got down to their level, on our knees. We take them in our arms, we touch them, we hug them, we talk with them—all to communicate the value we have placed upon them.

Shortly after we married, Norma and I made a very important decision that has affected every aspect of raising our children. We recognized that each of us was an individual, yet an equally important member of a union. Both of us had valuable skills and opinions. But we had also committed in our wedding vows to enter into oneness. Therefore, we determined to always strive to be in agreement.

Our decision to live in agreement does not mean that one of us has to compromise or give in. Rather it means *we will resolve our disagreements so that both of us are satisfied*. This commitment has given us tremendous strength in our marriage and with our children. Sometimes it takes a while to come to a decision, but because we value each other, we are willing to work for a negotiated resolution. We agreed together when we would start having children, the names of our children, and the type of training they would receive.

Before we could resolve how to discipline our children, we needed to do our own "homework." Norma began to read various books on raising children. We interviewed parents who had raised what we believed were successful families. Norma also took a course on raising children. We began to practice what we were learning. We observed which of these ideas seemed to work and which ones the children didn't respond to or caused disharmony in our home. We were constantly adjusting our techniques as we went along.

We studied the ideas of Dr. Robert Coles, one of the nation's most influential psychiatrists. He emphasized that parents seem to have forgotten that children need, perhaps more than anything else, rules of life that clearly establish what is right and what is wrong—practical rules that can govern our daily lives.

We read about a survey conducted several years ago with outstanding linguists, teachers, pastors, evangelists, and medical doctors. They were asked about the influences that led to their vocational choices and why they became so successful in their respective fields. Each said he came from a strict home where there were clearly defined limits. Studies like that encouraged us to establish our own rules and discipline.

We continued to read how children need a sense of discipline and authority in their lives to help them develop emotionally and physically. It gives children a sense of security to know what their boundaries are. Much of our security in life comes from order and regularity. We are relatively confident about entering an intersection when the light is green, knowing that the light for cross traffic is red. Limits are all around us. We know that if we purchase an apple from a grocery store, it has not been injected with a deadly chemical. We can be confident that the chair we sit on will not break, the walls in our home will not collapse, and that the tires on our car, when properly taken care of, will hold air because there are rules and limits regulating their quality. With inconsistency there is insecurity.

We read *Between Parent and Child* by Dr. Haim Ginott, who agrees that children need a definite sense of limits. They need to know what is right and wrong. Dr. Ginott states that one of the greatest philosophies undermining parents has been Freud's psychoanalysis. Freud perpetuated the idea that, "I'm the way I am today because of what my parents did to me." Today's parent is uncertain about how to raise a child. He is fearful that his mistakes will have costly consequences. Therefore a parent may experience paralysis when it comes to setting limits. Dr. Ginott forced us to examine the obvious—there are certain right and wrong limits for children's behavior. These can be as simple as, "You can hit your brother with a pillow, but you cannot hit him with a hammer." This may seem simple, but we read over and over again that *it is possible, right, and essential that parents establish what is clearly defined acceptable and unacceptable behavior for their children.*

Dr. Howard Hendricks, a professor at Dallas Theological Seminary and author of *Heaven Help the Home,* says that parents need to set some clear objectives and priorities for their children. "You can only achieve that for which you aim," Hendricks says. "If you aim at nothing, you will hit it every time." The same goes for setting limits. If we do not have clearly defined limits, and if we change our discipline from week to week, we will not know what we're aiming at or what we want to accomplish in our discipline.

Setting Limits through Contracts

If setting limits is so important, how do parents begin?

For us, it was important to have a *basis* for deciding what is right and wrong. In our family, much of that basis comes from what we believe the Bible says about living our lives. When our children were very young, we realized that it was extremely important that we nail down what we believed to be important family limits. We were even concerned about simple things, like courtesy and table manners.

As we began selecting family limits, we knew it was important not only to set clearly defined limits, but also to have very few limits. From our studies, we came up with two fundamental concepts. They are the same two concepts that Jesus Christ claimed are the greatest commandments in life.

First, we should establish a meaningful relationship with God. This includes an understanding of what He taught about Himself in the Bible as well as how to relate to Him. Norma and I agreed that our relationship with God was the most important element of our lives, and we hoped our children would also have a relationship with Him.

The second concept followed logically from the first. We should love and value people just as we value ourselves. God gave Moses ten very specific and clearly defined commandments, or limits. Each of the Ten Commandments is based upon the two established by Jesus in the New Testament—*valuing God and valuing people.* Jesus said that if a person lived those two commandments, he would naturally obey all the commandments in the Bible. The limits we set were based on these two principles.

When our children were around three years old, our very first and simple limits were:

1. We will obey God as we understand the Bible.
2. We will obey Mommy and Daddy.
3. We will be kind to people and things—God's creation.

With the first rule, we wanted to teach our children that we are not, as parents, the final authority. There is a higher authority. If we were to ask our children to do something that violated the Bible, we wouldn't want them to obey us. We explained to our children that we wanted to have these limits in our home because this would honor God. These were His commandments, not ours. By obeying us, they were obeying God.

The third limit naturally grew out of the first two—being kind to people and things. We didn't want to have the kids calling each other ugly names or doing anything that would make another child feel devalued. We also wanted them to learn that their brothers, sisters, and playmates were valuable because God created them.

As the children grew to six or seven, we began to revise and add to our limits. We included our children in this process and finally, years later, all five of us agree on six limits that are still in force in our home today.

Our entire contract is based on limits we have found in the Bible. We regularly remind our children that these are God's limits for our family. As they operate under the contract, they know that they are obeying God—it is God's learning process, not ours.

1. Learning to obey parents.
2. Learning to put things away after we have used them.
3. Learning to do our chores—responsibility.
4. Learning to have good manners and learning responsibility toward others.
5. Learning to take care of God's creation: people and things.
6. Learning appropriate inner character qualities.

These six limits represented our final draft of an actual written contract that each of us signed and dated. In a very real sense, this was just like any business contract. We discovered that having a written, objective contract greatly contributed to our family's harmony. It made disciplining the children so much easier because we simply pointed to the family contract, and they were much more willing to cooperate and adjust to it.

> Very simply then, discipline in our home consisted of clearly defined limits with our children. These limits became our written family contract.

Most of us live by contracts, but the majority are not written out or signed. Marriage vows and driver's licenses are contracts. Agreeing to do a certain job for an employer is a contract. There are even contracts that no one mentions. For example, you keep your yard in a certain condition or else the neighbors will complain to city officials. Drive your car eighty miles an hour and you will discover that you have a contract with the city or state and it's going to cost you a stiff fine.

The basis of a contract is that all parties participate in the negotiations. All must agree on each point and on the consequences when a point is violated. Then everyone signs the contract, putting himself under its authority.

Our children were very involved in defining the limits. For example, in our first limit, "Learning to obey parents," we asked them what it means to obey. They said it meant two things. First, it meant not complaining. Examples of complaining included, "Why do I have to do it? Why can't Kari do it? I'm always the one chosen. Why is it always me? Why can't you do it?"

The second part of obeying was not nagging. "Please Dad, can I do it? Can I? Please, everybody is doing it. I mean, couldn't I just do it one time?" Constant nagging was interpreted as disobedience and a violation of the command for children to obey their parents. They finally helped us define the word *obey* to mean, "Yes, I will do it and I won't complain."

The second limit that all of us were concerned about was cleaning the house. The house was messy a great deal of the time because the kids would leave their belongings strewn about the floor. At night there was usually a stream of clothing and toys from the bathroom to their bedrooms. Together we agreed it was too much for Dad, and especially Mom, to follow them around and pick up after them. They decided that each person would learn to be responsible for his own property.

The third limitation was responsibility. We talked about the importance of each member in the family and the need to work as a unit. Everyone had responsibilities. There was homework and cleaning the bedroom and feeding the animals. Someone had to take out the trash. Piano practice was part of each child's responsibilities. Once we established all the chores that helped make our home run smoothly we felt it was important for each of us as members of the family to take an active part. This was all part of learning responsibility and sharing our part of the load.

The fourth limit was learning good manners. We defined what that meant. At meals, it meant holding silverware properly, placing a napkin on the lap, and chewing food with the mouth closed, unless of course one had wiry braces or retainers. There were also certain responsibilities for being in public. You didn't run in a grocery store or in church. You didn't crawl under a church pew and bite a sweet old lady on the ankle. *We understood that our behavior in the presence of other people was a reflection of how we valued them.*

The fifth limit dealt with taking care of God's creation—people and things. Part of taking care of God's creation is taking care of our own body. On school nights, for example, that meant the children were in bed between 8:00 and 9:00, depending on their ages. Brushing their teeth after meals was part of taking care of God's creation, as was bathing, washing hair, and wearing clean and neat clothing.

This limit also included taking care of others, such as asking questions instead of arguing. It meant trying to really understand others because what they say is important. It also included playing carefully, not hitting someone with intent to hurt, getting revenge, or calling someone a degrading name.

After writing down these first five limits into a contract (we will discuss the sixth later), we made a place for everyone to sign. If they were not old enough to sign, they scribbled in the appropriate place and I put the date next to it. This showed that we all agreed to the direction we were going to go as a family. Because we involved the children, from the earliest ages, in helping write these limits, they considered them *their* limits, rather than standards their parents were imposing on them.

We never considered any of these limits lightly. We wanted to see these five, simple limits as a part of our children's lives. That meant we had to figure out how to motivate them and what the best means of correction was when they got off course. That's when the fun began. We tried many things that didn't work before choosing a method that accomplished our goal.

Enforcing the Contract—Our Experiments

We tried spanking when one of the limits was violated. But even though spanking is very useful in discipline, it was not effective for us to regulate our family contract daily by spanking.

We tried memory exercises where Norma, the children, and I all memorized the limits. I expected that after they memorized the limits, they would naturally want to follow them. It wasn't that simple.

We tried things like washing their mouths with soap if they called someone a degrading name. We only tried that a couple of times because we found it was actually degrading to the children. It was violating the very thing we were punishing them for.

We tried cutting their allowances and fining them. I had some violation tickets printed, just like a policeman would give. When they violated one of the five rules, I would write out a ticket. Fines ranged from ten to twenty-five cents, depending on the violation. It was cute for a couple of days, but it soon turned into a burden for us as parents.

The list of our punishment experiments is a long one. We tried having them write the limit they violated and how they were going to change fifty times. That was effective to a degree, but again, it only lasted a few weeks. We tried push-ups and running around the block, but both of those only accomplished the loss of weight.

We tried punishing the kids by not giving them dinner. The children thought this would be a good form of punishment because it would make them aware of how important the limits were. The first time we tried it was also the last. Greg sat about fifteen feet away from the dinner table, his tongue hanging out as we ate. Halfway through the meal, Norma said, "This is harder on me than it is on Greg." To Greg's delight, we asked him to join us.

We tried punishing by prohibiting talking, playing with toys, and staying in their bedrooms. We tried turning off the air conditioner in their rooms, no camping trips, no snacks, extra piano practice, and many others. I chuckle now as I write this. But I didn't come from a disciplined home, and there was little written about this area, so we had to experiment.

Unfortunately, nothing seemed to help our children consistently live within these five limits. Plus the methods of correction were difficult on us as parents. Sometimes it seemed like a full-time job trying to keep up with all these little rules and regulations.

In our search to discover how to implement these rules in our home, we met an outstanding pediatrician and his wife, Dr. Charles and Dorothy Shellenberger. They explained how they had implemented their limits in a practical way. It was not only effective, but provided the missing element in training our children.

A Practical Way to Implement Family Contracts

Using the contract method in a home is a very effective way to balance love and limits. Drs. Charles P. Barnard and Ramon G. Corrales found that a family is forced to clarify limits by writing them out on paper. Before anyone is willing to sign his name, he usually desires to understand what he's putting his name to. The question then, is how to implement the contract on a daily basis.

Here's where Dr. Shellenberger greatly helped us. He taught us that there are three parts to the process:

1. Set clearly defined limits by writing a contract.
2. Supervise the living of these limits regularly.
3. Consistently handle resistance through lost privileges.

Number three was the missing ingredient for us. We had set limits and written the contracts, but we hadn't incorporated the violation consequences in the contract in a practical, workable way. So we gathered again as a family and reworked the contract. Since 1977, though our contract has been amended several times, the format has remained basically the same.

First, we negotiated our family contract into something like Chart #1 on the following page:

Chart #1

Family Limits

1. *Learning to Obey Parents*
Answer by saying "Yes, Dad/Mom" immediately and accomplish the request right away.

   • Do not complain: "I don't want to do that." "Do I have to?" "Can't someone else do it?" "This is not fair."

   • Do not nag: "Oh, please, please can't we do it?" "Can't I go, Mom? Can't I go, Mom? Can't I go, Mom?"

2. *Learning to Put Our Things Away After Use*

   • Toys in our closet or garage

   • Clothes in the "dirty" box or hung up in closet

   • Towels on the towel rack

   • Have a place for everything and everything in its place

3. *Learning to Do Our Chores*

   • Clean bedroom before school

   • Place used dishes in the sink after meals

   • After school: homework and piano before play; take out trash Tuesdays and Fridays; feed cats; bring paper to Mom

   • Special chores when Mom or Dad need help

4. *Learning to Have Good Manners*

   • Meals: Walk to the table, fold hands in lap, no talking before we pray. Chew food with mouth closed. Say, "Kari, please pass the _____."

- When others are talking, wait for a pause in the conversation and say, "Excuse me Dad, could I _____?"
- When we disagree with someone, do not say so, but rather, be a learner and ask, "What did you say again?" or "I always thought it was _____."

5. *Learning to Take Care of God's Creation: People and Things*
People (Self):

- 8:30 P.M.: Bath, if needed; brush teeth; put school bags by front door; read, listen to record or story

(Others):

- Asking questions—not arguing
- Playing gently—not roughhousing
- Praying for our "enemies"—not hitting
- Being kind and sensitive—not calling names (love and kindness are gifts from God; He changes our heart)

Things:

- Protecting house and furniture: Not jumping and playing on chairs, beds, etc.; not throwing balls in the house or against the house; not climbing the small trees

Second, we decided as a family what lost privileges each member would have when one of the limits was violated. The children had dozens of ideas—no toys, no television, no movies, no eating out, no snacks, no dating, no telephone, no dinners for a month, being grounded. Some of their lost privileges were much harsher than we as parents would have ever put down. After we made a list of thirty or forty possible lost privileges, we went back over the list and agreed on twenty-four hours of lost privileges for each of the five limits. We revised each limit to start with the letter C; the limits came to be known as the "Five C's." See Chart #2.

Chart #2

Our Family Limits

Responsibilities	Lost Privileges for 24 Hours
1. *Conforming:* Obeying Mom and Dad—not complaining, arguing, or nagging	All toys
2. *Cleaning:* Clean room every morning; clean up after using toys or other items	Television
3. *Chores:* Lawn once a week; trash every evening; piano by 5:30 P.M.	After-school snack
4. *Courteous:* At meals; at church and outings	Joining the family the next time they eat out
5. *Caring:* To bed on time; brush teeth; kind to people and things (God's creation); not teasing, hitting, or arguing	Seeing friends

Signed: _____   Date: _____

You can see from Chart #2 that when any of our children violated one or more of the limits they might lose toys or the opportunity to watch television for twenty-four hours.

We met for ten to fifteen minutes each night after dinner to evaluate how everyone was doing in each of the five areas. We kept the chart on the next page by the kitchen table. It was covered in plastic so we could mark on it with a grease pencil and erase it the next evening. We also used this time to correct our children rather than reprimand them throughout the day, unless of course they had committed a serious offense, then we would take care of it immediately.

Chart #3

Responsibilities

	Kari	Greg	Mike	Lost Privilege
1. Conforming	❑	❑	❑	toys
2. Cleaning	❑	❑	❑	television
3. Chores	❑	❑	❑	snack
4. Courteous	❑	❑	❑	eat out
5. Caring	❑	❑	❑	friends

Responsibility is a daily decision.

This chart made keeping up with our contract simple. Each evening as we met after dinner, we would go through this chart with our children. For instance, if Greg had not been responsible with his chores that day, we would place an "X" in that square, and he would not be able to have an after-school snack the next day. He could use that time to catch up on his chores.

Don't Expect, Inspect

For three years, we met every night after dinner, applying the old Henry Brandt proverb, "People do what you inspect not what you expect." We inspected and evaluated their behavior every day. After three years we no longer met daily, because the limits had become a regular part of our children's behavior. However, the contract still serves as our family constitution. It is open for amendments, but we can revise it only if all five of us agree with the recommended change.

As our children entered their teen years we wrote separate contracts to include more specific areas, particularly dating and driving.

This brings us to our sixth and final limit—developing character. We added this as our children became more aware of the opposite sex. We agreed that rather than set a specific age when they could start dating, we wanted instead to see a certain level of maturity in their character. In order to define this, we again looked to the Bible. Our standards of maturity became the nine qualities found in Galatians 5:22–23, the eight beatitudes (Matthew 5:3–10), and the attitude of Christ displayed in Philippians 2:5–8. We'll list a few of the main areas that we discussed with our children.

The first area of importance was that they be able to withstand peer pressure and not compromise the standards they believed were important. Norma punctuated this by relating a story about one of her first dates in high school. She was double-dating with a girlfriend, and they had both agreed not to allow any physical contact on their first date. Norma said that all of a sudden, she looked up and noticed her friend in the arms of this new-found boyfriend. That put pressure on her. Her date began to pursue her, but Norma said "No!" When her date became angry, Norma told him to either take her home or she would walk. It took all the strength Norma could muster.

It takes a great deal of courage for a teenager to be assertive in such situations. But that is the type of character quality we wanted to see in our children before we felt they were mature enough to date.

Another inner quality we felt was important is what the Bible calls being "pure in heart." That means having a single focus on what is most important in life. We wanted our children to understand that having a solid relationship with God is essential to establishing good relationships with people.

The Bible has a certain standard for living that leads to an enjoyable life. Its limits are not designed to restrict us from happiness, but rather to keep us from certain activities that can rob us of joy and peace. For example, the Bible gives us several consequences of premarital sex. We have taught our children that sexual actions from petting on up to intercourse prior to marriage, or after marriage with someone other than our mate, have several negative results. As a family, we discovered in both religious and secular studies at least twenty negative consequences of premarital sex. Here's a sample:

- It immediately reinforces our desires for greater and more frequent sensual fulfillment.

- It reinforces our self-centered nature. As the Scriptures say, it causes us to have a hardened or calloused heart. We become less sensitive to the needs of those around us, because we spend more time looking for ways to have our own sensual needs met. We tend to observe life as a means to stimulate our own senses instead of loving those around us.

- Immorality also reduces our faith in God, because the more we violate God's limits, the more we must rationalize that "God doesn't exist" or His rules are invalid. This can lead to questioning the very creator of those limits. Thus I've observed those who practice an immoral lifestyle have more and greater doubts about the existence of God.

- Sexual "freedom" and promiscuity can actually lead to slavery—slavery to our physical senses and impotency. A certain cigarette company has a slogan that says, "Smoke this cigarette. It *satisfies*." That's a clever twist of the word satisfy. Have you ever known a smoker who could smoke just one cigarette and be satisfied? He has to have another and then another. The same can be true with sexual immorality.

There are so many lies circulating in our world. We're told that we live in a day of sexual "freedom." Implied by the word *freedom* is the opportunity to experience sexual contact before and after marriage with a variety of partners. Just look at the inconsistency of this statement, "We're free to make love." Making love means sexual involvement and the more involved we are the more we lose our freedom to restrain our desires and the more our senses enslave us. It is important for children to understand these consequences of immorality. Even though they have strong and normal sensual drives, they must gain the ability to say "no" for their own long-term benefit and the fulfillment of lasting, loving relationships.

Contract for Dating

The first part of our dating contract deals with a child's character. The second part deals with the actual dating practice. Here are some additional elements in the dating contracts:

With the first few years of dating, we evaluated each dating situation on its own merit, but we especially favored well-organized, school-sponsored activities that were adequately chaperoned. Next, every member of the family must approve of the potential dating partner. This has been a very effective safeguard designed to protect against a potentially harmful relationship. It is a reflection of a close-knit family, each concerned about the well-being of the other.

We also discuss and set a curfew for dates. The greater a child's trustworthiness, self-control, and purity of heart, the greater freedom in dating privileges. Likewise, if any of the character qualities is tarnished or violated, then the dating privilege may be lost for an agreed-upon period of time. For example, if one of the children lies about some activity, even if it has nothing to do with dating, he may lose the privilege of dating for a week or two, depending on the severity of the offense.

We all agreed to this simple dating contract and as the children get older, we will continue to evaluate the contract. We probably will revise it a few times, which is what we encourage families to do. Stay current and up to date with children in the areas of training and correction.

Contract for Driving

Driving a car is another privilege that comes with age and character development. Even before our children were old enough to drive, we agreed as a family on the following contract:

1. Upon receiving my driver's permit, I will be allowed to drive on local errands when accompanied by either parent. I will assist in driving for extended periods of time on long family vacations under all types of driving conditions.

2. Before using the car, I will ask either Mom or Dad if I can use it and explain the purpose.

3. If I want to go somewhere for myself, both my homework and piano practicing or other chores must be completed first.

4. During the first month after receiving my driver's license, the radio will not be used while driving.

5. During the school year, I will be allowed to drive to activities at night but cannot take anyone home without permission.

6. I will not allow anyone else to use the car under any circumstances without permission from my parents.

7. I will not carry more than five passengers at a time.

8. I will not give rides to hitchhikers under any circumstances, and I will use extreme caution in accepting assistance if I should have difficulty with the car.

9. I will pay half of the increase of insurance costs whenever my grades fall below a B average. In case of an accident, I will assume half of the deductible costs.

10. If I receive any moving violations, I will lose my license for up to one month. On the second violation, I will lose it for up to three months.

It took us several weeks to negotiate this simple contract and our children signed it only after several revisions. We are certainly open to future revisions, but again any changes must be understood and agreed upon by each of us.

Guidelines for Spanking

Our final contract deals with the important area of spanking. Most violations of our limits are punished by a loss of privileges. But it is part of our written contract that we will use spanking if anyone is obviously resistant or rebellious, especially showing strong defiance against a parent.

Spanking can be very effective to guard against rebellion, but as Dr. Armand Nicholi says, the main problem with spanking is that it can be a release for the parent's frustration, guilt, or anger. It may therefore benefit the parent more than the child. He advises parents to ask themselves who will benefit most from the spanking. Spanking certainly can be used when a limit is violated, but it must be used cautiously.

I have also come to see the effectiveness of spanking on a decreasing scale. It's most effective with preschoolers, but it should rarely be used after age thirteen. If a spanking is necessary, it should be taken very seriously, so as not to close the child's spirit. Usually a loss of privileges is more effective for older children.

Before we developed our contracts, we discovered that the majority of spankings in our home took place before meals. This is often the hardest time because everyone is hungry and tired. Our blood sugar levels are low. The children are restless and impatient, and the aroma of food heightens tension. A number of things can happen at this time to flare up disobedience within children. We found I could reduce some of the tension by simply spending more time with the children when I came home from work.

We also allow our children to call for "court" if they believe that they are being disciplined unjustly by spanking. We started this after I saw Greg push a plate of chips and sandwich across the kitchen table. The plate hit Kari in the chest and the sandwich and chips went all over her and onto the floor. I immediately grabbed Greg's arm and told him, "You're going to be spanked." He was trying to tell me it wasn't his fault and Kari was trying to intervene, but I didn't pay any attention.

Only after I had spanked Greg did I gather the facts—after all, I saw it happen. But I didn't know that Norma had asked Kari to make Greg a sandwich, but Greg said he wasn't hungry. Kari retorted, "Mother told me to make you this sandwich, so you're going to get it whether you like it or not." He shoved it back. The sandwich passed between the two of them at least three more times. I walked into the kitchen just as Greg was shoving it the final time out of complete frustration.

Had I taken the time to get the facts, I would not have spanked him. We initiated the court alternative to avoid similar mistakes. The defendant can call the whole family together, even call in a witness or bring in a friend to act as lawyer if he wants to present his case concerning why he believes he does not deserve this spanking. After all the facts are gathered, we go around the table asking each member of the family for his verdict. If everyone votes "guilty," we ask the person accused what he thinks. Every time we have done that, the guilty party has agreed with the others, admitting his guilt.

Here are ten factors to consider when spanking is used as a method of correction:

1. *Give clear warning before the spanking.* Children need to understand why they are being spanked. We have told our children that they must show obvious signs of rebellion against clearly established rules to get a spanking. Examples might be if they physically harm each other or if a parent tells them not to do something and they say they don't care and do it anyway.

2. *Establish a child's responsibility for his or her disobedience.* When a child disobeys after instructions and warning, the child must assume responsibility for his disobedience. We ask our children *what they have done* so they can see for themselves that they violated our family limits. Sometimes it takes a while for one to admit his wrong. He will want to blame someone else and rationalize his behavior. We must be persistent with our question until he admits what he has done wrong.

3. *Avoid embarrassment and outside interference.* When spanking or correcting a child, make sure you are alone with him, especially when the child's offense occurs in public. If the parent brings up a problem in front of a child's friends and attempts to correct him, the child will be more concerned about his reputation than the offense he has committed. Such a correction demoralizes the child and can produce a closed spirit. It also might motivate a child to figure out ways to justify his action to those who saw him being punished so that they will side with him.

4. *Communicate parental grief over the offense*. This is important because it causes the child and parent to reflect on what has taken place. It also gives them both a chance to calm down. The ultimate goal of this time is to bring the child to a sincere repentance, where he wants to be corrected.

5. *Associate love with spanking*. *It is important to explain the age-old adage,* "This hurts me more than it does you," to children. My children have questioned that many times, but it is true.

Once when I was going to spank Kari, she tried to talk her way out of it. She promised never to do the offense again. She begged me not to spank her. I decided to take that opportunity to illustrate an example of real love and sacrifice.

I told her how when Christ died on the cross, He paid the penalty for our sin. Then I told her that I wanted to show her a small example of what Jesus did. I was going to let her spank me.

"Someone's going to be spanked today," I told her. "But I'm going to take your punishment for you because I love you and want you to know that I'm not spanking you to hurt you. I'm doing it because I think what you did was wrong and we are correcting it."

Kari stopped crying, her eyes lighted up and she looked at me as if to say, "Are you serious?" I told her I was, gave her the paddle, and lay down on the bed just as I had asked her to do. But when she tried, she couldn't do it. I told her it was okay, but if she didn't want to spank me, I would spank her. She quickly said that she thought she could bring herself to do it. After a long struggle, she gave me a good one. And it stung. I stood up and she gave me a big hug, like we always did with her after a spanking. This only happened once, but it gave Kari some understanding of what her parents go through.

6. *Use a neutral object for spanking*. It is important that a neutral object be used for spanking because a child has a tendency

to associate the pain with the object used to spank him. If a parent uses his hand, the child may feel uncomfortable when that same hand is used to touch, hold and hug, especially if the child is spanked in harsh anger. We have found that it is very effective to use a thin stick that we decorated as a family. We call it the "teacher." Using the "teacher" also helps calm everyone because usually it takes a few minutes to find it.

The first time I used "teacher" was when Kari was about three years old. She jumped on the bed and started screaming. When I reached for her, she jumped behind the bed, then under the bed. I calmly told Kari I was going to follow through with the spanking if it took all day.

Finally, she lay down on the bed and I gave her a swat. As soon as I did, she was jumping on the bed and screaming again. I told her to lie still until I finished. So she lay down again and I gave her another swat. Again, she jumped up and started screaming. I stayed calm, but firm, and the process was repeated three more times. Finally she realized that I was serious and stayed still. Kari never jumped around like that again because she knew I meant business.

From that episode, we both learned that correction can reveal the level of a child's resistance. Persistent correction can break stubbornness, which brings us to the seventh point about spanking.

7. *Discipline or spank until the will is broken.* It is very important that we do not spank our children in harshness or severe anger, even if this means getting away for a few minutes to cool off. We must take the time to communicate love to them, but we must also communicate that we are going to spank them until they understand we mean business. If we spank children in harsh anger, it has a tendency to break their spirit, which can be worse than if we didn't spank them at all.

When Greg was in the seventh grade, he went through a period of blaming a poor grade in school on his teacher, his mother, even the time of day. Everyone and everything was at fault but him. I tried talking to Greg about the importance of assuming responsibility and not blaming those around him. The showdown came when Greg deliberately and willfully told me, "Dad, it's not my fault. It's their fault." He became very disrespectful to me as his father. Then I spanked him. About five minutes later, after I had spanked and hugged him, Greg sat on my lap and said, "Dad, thanks for spanking me. You know, I can see that it really is my fault." Then he sat down, got his books out and started studying. I could see the cleansing in his life because he had been corrected firmly and his stubborn will was broken.

8. Comfort a child after the spanking. Kari and Mike almost always crawled into my arms for a hug after a spanking. But with Greg, sometimes it took an hour or two for him to warm up and want to be touched. Once Kari and Greg chose to be spanked in the same room at the same time. They wanted to be together so they could comfort each other. They hugged each other prior to the spanking and asked who wanted to be first. They both took their spanking, they both cried, and we all hugged each other afterward. Hugging reinforces our love for the child.

9. *Discuss any restitution that might be necessary.* If a child is spanked because he hit a neighbor willfully and deliberately, it may be important for you to discuss how he should go and seek forgiveness from that neighbor. Or if he stole money from someone, you may discuss with the child how much and in what manner to repay it.

10. *Evaluate your correction and your child's response to it.* If you have wronged your child in any way, through false accusation, anger, attacking him as a person rather than his wrong behavior, embarrassing him, lacking love, or overpunishing, it is important to go to him and follow the steps of opening his

spirit. This should be done when both parent and child have calmed down emotionally and can evaluate what took place more objectively. A child has a keen sense of fairness and will be highly sensitive to his parents' offenses. One of the most common accusations children have against their parents is that they rarely admit when they are wrong. This pride makes future correction very difficult because it can cause a child to close his spirit.

My worst spanking experience took place when Greg was about two years old and I tried to break what appeared to be his "strong resistant will." I wasn't swatting him hard enough to really harm him physically, but I did persist many times, trying to "break his will." As I continued I could sense his fear, frustration, and inability to explain himself. I finally stopped in grief and held him, seeking his forgiveness because I could see his resentment growing toward me. We waited until he was almost three before he received any more spankings. I felt he wasn't old enough before that to really benefit. It was, and still is, more important for us as parents to have a warm, loving relationship with our children than to have a strict "military" type atmosphere at home. The strictness is important, but I would say in training children, the emphasis should be about 45 percent strictness with limits and 55 percent a loving relationship.

Along with unconditional love and support for our children, successful parents must balance this love by establishing clearly defined rules and limits. This is the area where we had a lot to learn. And we're still learning. What I have shared in this chapter has evolved over years of trial and error.

Parenting is not something we do once and get an "A" and it's over. It would be nice if it were that easy. We must continue to learn and relearn. An NFL quarterback, Jim Zorn, told me that every year for two weeks, the quarterbacks on his team take a class where they review the fundamentals of quarterbacking. Then during preseason training camp, they practice the same techniques over and over again. The same should be true with parents. We need to continually learn, review, practice, and relearn the basics of parenting. Norma and I are still learning. Our children were ten, fifteen, and seventeen years old when this book was first written, and we were committed to continue learning until all of them were raised. Now that they're nineteen, twenty-three, and twenty-five, we look forward to reading, studying, and learning about how grandparents can enrich their grandchildren's lives. We hope we never stop learning.

5

Giving Yourself the Freedom to Fail

- Discipline in the Home
- Communicating Emotionally with Children
- Building Friendships in the Family
- The Value of Being Together without Spending Much Money
- What They Didn't Like
- The Long-Term Effect of Words
- Gaining a New Perspective
- The Principle of Empowerment

You REALLY FIND OUT what it means to be vulnerable when you ask your grown children to rate your successes and failures as a parent. That's exactly what Norma and I did last Thanksgiving. We were having a family meeting with just the five of us in the living room, and I said to our children, "I'm thinking about revising our parenting book, *The Key to Your Child's Heart*, and I was wondering if the three of you would like to help?" Kari, Greg, and Michael responded virtually in unison, "Yeah, we'd love to help."

I wasn't sure they would want to help me or have anything to do with the revision, so their sudden, unanimous response surprised me. Getting down to business, I said, "Can I ask each of you a couple of difficult questions? Can you really be honest and share what you appreciated about the way we disciplined you as children and what you appreciated about us as parents? And then can you describe what you wish we had *not* done as parents? What would you have done differently? How would you have done it differently? Tell me what you don't plan to do as parents yourselves because of what your mother and I did when you were growing up. I remember several times when all of you said, 'Boy, I'll never do that with my kids!'"

I said that I thought this was the kind of information a lot of parents would like to know. So in this chapter I would like to share some of the positive and negative aspects of our own parenting.

As parents, Norma and I did what I suspect you are doing as readers. We looked around and saw the large number of families around us who were hurting and falling apart. Like you, we started a search to find reliable training methods for raising our three children. Because our own parents were dead and since every day counted when it came to parenting, we talked to anyone who seemed to know something about parenting or who seemed to be good role models.

One of our best sources turned out to be our own godly pediatrician, Dr. Charles Schellenberger, and his wife, Dorothy. We sought out Charles' advice almost every time we visited his office—which seemed to be practically every week with our kids' runny noses and whatever.

Now that all three of our children are grown and out on their own, our questioning of what they appreciated about our home was a chance to evaluate some of the methods that we had discovered and applied. It was interesting to hear their varied and precise remarks. Before I summarize that, however, it might be helpful to know how the three of them turned out as adults and what they're doing these days. You can see from their "before" and "after" pictures how they changed over the years.

Kari is our oldest. She's twenty-five years old as of this writing and just married to Roger Gibson of Phoenix, Arizona. Basically, she is a practicing missionary school teacher in an inner-city public elementary school in Phoenix. Each year Kari takes a large group of kids from this school to a summer sports program called Kids Across America at Kamp Kanakuk, a Christian camp in Branson, Missouri. During the year she and Roger disciple this group by taking them to church and meeting with them weekly. Norma and I are extremely pleased with the way Kari's life has worked out. Her warm heart, her genuine love for children, and her deep desire to see that they know the Lord and grow up in Him are evidence of the kind of person she is.

Greg, our second oldest, is now twenty-three years old and finishing his first year at Denver Seminary. He's planning to be a clinical psychologist. Greg's gone through some tough times during his university experience. Later in this chapter he'll explain some of the struggles he went through as a young man and how he was able to climb out of a deep hole he had dug for himself. We are very proud of Greg and the commitment he has made to help troubled children and their parents. Greg is also getting married this year, to Erin Murphy.

Mike, our youngest, is nineteen years old now and finishing his first year at Baylor University in Waco, Texas. Michael is our "all-everything" child, and he utilized almost every opportunity to his best advantage during his high school years and especially his summer camp experiences. Mike has often said that he really developed the personal skills and attitudes of confidence, leadership, and dependence upon the Lord that have been his greatest assets when he was at Kamp Kanakuk in Missouri.

Discipline in the Home

Our discussion of discipline focused on the training times and the spanking times. As a parent, it was interesting for me to see that these were what Kari, Greg, and Michael remembered most about discipline in the family. As they looked back, these emotional experiences came to mind immediately; these are the experiences that stick in their minds.

According to our family contract, the only time we ever spanked any of our children was when they deliberately or grossly dishonored something of God's creation. If they used some degrading word against us or against their brother, sister, or even a friend, we said that they were really devaluing God's creation. It was a lack of proper respect, and Norma or I punished them for that.

We never spanked any of our children for something the children didn't know they would be punished for ahead of time. That would have been unfair. If it wasn't in the contract, we stopped and talked about it and pointed out how they were supposed to behave in those situations. The contract was our rule book, and we all had to agree to live by it.

The family contract is a great system. I don't think we can overstress how valuable it was to us in raising our children. If I were raising children again, I would start the contract process when each child reaches five years of age. By then kids are fully capable of understanding how rules work, and they will come to appreciate the fact that there are clear, written guidelines for good behavior in the family.

Our children all agreed that this was an important principle, and when Norma or I talked to them about what they had done, they generally agreed it was wrong, and they understood they would be spanked. It was understood that breaking the contract was grounds for punishment. However, if they didn't think the punishment or the accusation was fair, then we would have a family meeting (a kind of family court) to clarify the situation. Everybody would vote, and if the child was guilty and everybody agreed on that, then the child would usually see it too. If the facts showed that the child was innocent, then we would settle things as quickly and fairly as possible.

There were times when Norma and I *were* wrong, when we made a mistake in assuming what had happened when it wasn't really the case at all. Whenever that happened, we would listen to the child's explanation, hear the other side of the story, and when it was appropriate we would say, "We're wrong. You don't deserve a spanking."

Kari told us that she could not remember any time when we spanked her in anger. "I'm sure there were times when they got angry with us for something we said or did," she said, "but they always took time to cool down before disciplining us. Any time I got a spanking my parents would sit me down and talk to me, remind me of the rules we had agreed to, and also remind me of the consequences. Those certainly weren't happy memories, but I don't remember ever thinking that my parents were bad or unfair. In fact, I felt they were more than fair."

I believe Kari's memory of these occasions is correct. Rarely did we ever spank in anger, as an emotional response, or as a sort of knee-jerk reaction. The children appreciated that. Whenever we had to discipline them, either Norma or I would take them to their room and talk there. We always took the time for them to admit what they had done, and we would always hug them before a spanking and say, "We feel as bad about this as you do," and "I know you agreed with this rule." We'd hug them after the spanking, but we'd never spank any of our children publicly and never in front of the other children.

Physical discipline is a very private, honoring experience, and it was not administered all that often in our house. Over all those years, Greg got the most spankings, and he seems to remember them as daily experiences because it was such an emotional experience for him. Today those spankings are what he remembers most vividly about his growing-up years. On the other hand, Michael got the least. He was our most even-tempered, happy-go-lucky child. Michael always wanted to do what was right.

When we did spank, we were always careful to assure the children that we loved them and that we wanted them to be our friends before, during, and after any disciplining. That was really more important to us than the spanking. Proper training was preeminent in our thinking. We wanted each child to know that honor—which is valuing all of God's creation, people, and things—was the greatest value they could have. And we taught the concept of honor on every occasion.

Now that we look back on those experiences, we realize that honor was truly the most important thing that we taught our children. It was the fifth point in our family contract. If we were just now establishing the contract I think we would make it the first point, because now we see that it covered and over-shadowed everything else we did.

I think it is important to note that we never slapped the children and we never used our hands to spank them. The children's spirit was so important to us, and even when we felt that a spanking was necessary, we were always careful to do it in an honoring way. It's not a very happy time when you have to spank your children, but we spent as much time as we had to with them to ensure that they truly understood the lessons we were trying to teach them. We both felt that it was impor-tant that we discipline them in an honoring way.

Whenever Norma would discipline them, she would take them to their own room and sit down with them. She would look into their eyes and ask, "What did you do?" Their differ-ent reactions were interesting. Kari and Michael would admit immediately what they had done.

It always took longer with Greg. There were times when he was very young that a spanking time might take up to two hours. We knew it was important for him to admit what he had done, but he did not want to do that. After the spank-ing, we wanted to hug him and we wanted him to hug us—this was to affirm him and to assure him that even though he had been given a spanking we still loved him—but he didn't like that at all.

We knew Greg had a strong will, and this was another in-dication of that, but we also knew how important it was to see that he understood and agreed with what we were trying to teach him. On some of those early occasions, Norma would stay in the room as long as it took. It was about a year before Greg was able to bring himself to accept our discipline and to hug us, but that was an important part of the learning experience too.

We did not spank our children after they became teenagers. If parents are consistent in their discipline, by the time the kids are ten or eleven years old they are really obeying you. After that age, as we used our contracts (and when they were allowed to help us set up the rules for the home), the most effective punishment would be the loss of privileges or missing something they would have enjoyed if they hadn't broken the rules. We have counseled with many parents who say they wish they could have used this system with their own teenagers; it is such a fair and logical way of doing things.

Even Greg, our strong-willed child, accepted the rules more easily after he was ten years old. It's sort of like putting a bridle on a young colt: When he knows the restraint and the guidance are going to be there, he actually begins to relax. That's how it worked for us. Greg was constantly probing and testing us when he was small, but he was an easy, fun teenager, and he came to understand the importance of playing by the rules.

After the children became teenagers, our family contract became the family constitution. Decisions of this kind involved the whole family and we had to vote on it. When a serious breach of the rules occurred, it was like having the Supreme Court in session. And since the family constitution provided the guidelines and the law for the family, that meant that spankings, yelling, shouting, and all those kinds of things didn't have to take place.

It was really a wonderful experience then, and I become more and more positive about the idea of a family contract or constitution every year. So I urge every family to write their own constitution. I truly believe that the information on contracts and constitutions in chapter 4 may be some of the most practical and helpful advice we ever received on maintaining discipline in the home.

Most of the time when Greg broke those rules, he would lose certain privileges for twenty-four hours. Spanking was the least-administered punishment, but Greg's spankings are the things that stand out in his mind today because they were the more painful experiences, the physical reminders. With Michael it was different: He received few spankings. Kari received very few because she simply did not like to be out of harmony with the family. If you have read *The Two Sides of Love*, which I wrote with John Trent, you know something about personality types, and you will recall that two of those personalities simply do not like spankings. Children in these categories will go to almost any length not to get themselves in a situation where punishment is necessary. Kari and Michael are like that, and throughout their growing-up years they hated to disappoint their parents.

Now I know that, as a parent, you are praying that if you have any more children they will have personalities like that! These are wonderful children. They are so easy to raise. But in God's providence—or maybe His sense of humor—there often seems to be a mixture of personalities within a family. Kari and Michael were the agreeable ones, and pleasing their parents was very important to them. But we also had Greg. In our house Greg was what John and I called the lion personality. Greg was—and still is in some ways—a strong personality.

To put things in perspective I should add that we didn't have all that many stormy incidents, although it probably seemed like more because of the tensions involved. You know, I wasn't surprised when both Michael and Kari told me that they plan to write a family constitution with their own children. They were both very comfortable with the terms of our agreement. But, believe it or not, Greg also plans to do the same thing. So apparently that was one of the best things we ever did.

As I said earlier, the number one article in your constitution ought to be, "Honor God and His Creation." That was the central principle and central truth we wanted our children to learn. When young people honor God and His creation, they will naturally honor people and things.

Communicating Emotionally with Children

The second outstanding memory our kids had of their childhood was that I told them a lot of stories. I told them all kinds of stories, the typical children's stories, of course, but almost all of them were emotional stories. These were the ones they remembered best. The more drama to a story and the more it involved their own feelings, the stronger their memories are today of that story.

Sometimes I would make up stories, but often I would tell them about my own growing-up adventures. When we discussed these in our family meeting, I found it especially interesting to discover that the stories they remembered most vividly were the stories about my childhood, especially those in which I was in danger. Some of these stories were about my parents, my brothers, my sisters, or just the various dangerous situations that I got myself into while growing up in Washington state. But those stories had a great impact on them.

There were times when I would gather all three kids around and say, "You want to hear a story about what happened to me when I was a little kid?" And to arouse their curiosity, I'd say, "I bet you are going to wonder how I ever got out of that mess!" And I would tell about the time when I stepped into a sawdust pile and discovered it was on fire, or the time when I fell through a bunch of logs. Maybe it was the idea that these were true-life adventures, or that they involved Daddy; whatever it was, my children were fascinated and listened to these stories with real enthusiasm.

Growing up in the Northwest where the lumber industry is so important, there always seemed to be an adventure around every corner. What is really interesting to me today is that my children's memories of these stories are confused and out of sequence! They each remember the facts somewhat differently, and all of them are slightly wrong. What they remember distinctly, however, was that Dad was in danger. They remember the story about the time I ran into a rattlesnake pit during a time when the snakes were all going underground for winter hibernation. They remember the drama, the suspense, and hearing me tell how I narrowly got out of that. Not only do they remember the story, but they still like for me to tell it. And I guess they will probably want me to tell it to our grandkids someday!

I also told a lot of Bible stories during those years, and, again, the ones the kids liked best were the really emotional stories. They liked the one about the time the disciples brought a demon-possessed man to Jesus, and Jesus drove the demon out. You remember, this demon was so powerful it scared the disciples, and they weren't able to cast it out without Jesus' help. So I said to my children, "Do you want to make sure that you never get any demons inside of you?" And, wide-eyed, they said, "No, we don't want any demons in us!" And I said, "Well, make sure that your conscience is clear before God and man." Boy, they confessed every sin they ever had . . . so did I!

In fact, telling the story to the children affected me as much as it affected the children, and I remember that night vividly. I remember lying there in the dark and having a little revival of my own in bed.

Some of the other highlights our children remembered about their growing-up years were the stories I read to them, like C. S. Lewis' Chronicles of Narnia. Whenever the adventure would build up to a peak in those wonderful tales, I'd look at my kids and I could see their little hearts start to pound with anticipation. When something exciting would happen in the story, they would jump under the covers next to Daddy and snuggle up. Isn't it amazing that the casual, comfortable little stories I read or told them during those times have all but faded from their memories, but the stories that gripped their hearts and their emotions remain in vivid detail?

Now as a parent I had a pretty good repertoire of stories. At least I knew some basic endings, and I would just invent the stories to go with them. I'd make them up on the spot, and I would make them as wild and complicated as I could, adding all sorts of crazy things. If I saw that I was losing their attention, I'd say, "Uh, oh. I can't go on. I don't know if I should even tell the rest of this story, it's so scary."

Of course, when I was saying that, I was thinking, *What can I tell them that would be so scary?* I didn't want to scare them into being fearful, but I would say, "Oh, I'm not sure you're old enough for this." And they would always say, "Daddy, we're old enough! Come on, come on. Pleeeeze."

I would always try to give the story a biblical meaning and a good practical point. It might be something about forgiveness, about honoring people, or something about how Jesus loves us, that He'll never forsake us, and that no matter what happens, God always turns the bad things that happen to us into something good if we let Him.

I would use verses like Romans 8:28, 1 Thessalonians 5:16–18, and 1 John 2:9–11. Those verses would give me a certain direction, and I would make up the stories and the plots to try to come to some sort of biblical truth. I think I enjoyed them as much as the kids. Those were wonderful times.

Building Friendships in the Family

Camping was another highlight of our kids' growing-up years. Without a doubt, they said, some of their greatest memories, some of the times they loved best, and some of the times they appreciated most were the family's camping trips. We camped a lot when they were small. As they got older we couldn't go as often because they were all involved in sports—football, basketball, track, everything you can imagine. It was too hard to get away then, but when they were younger, we camped all the time.

In the early years we frequently camped in tents, sometimes in those little pop-up trailers. Later we bought a used motor home, so it was always ready to go. We would just jump in it and take off on a Friday night, drive to a local campground, and camp overnight. We would find a place where we could do a little exploring, tell stories, and have hot dogs around a campfire. They were wonderful, wonderful experiences. Sometimes we would take a week or two, sometimes as much as three weeks, and we would go camping in Canada, Colorado, Texas, or the California mountains.

I remember some disastrous experiences, but those were really the times that bonded us together, as you will see in the last chapter on the secret of a close-knit family. Sometimes the disappointments, the surprises, the battles, even the accidents were the most important parts of the overall experience. But however great or terrible things may have seemed at the time, we all knew that we were in it together. We were a family, and somehow that was enough to hold us together.

In our meeting last Thanksgiving, the kids said that one of the things they appreciated most was the fact that they were all so close in age. There are eighteen months between Kari and Greg and five years between Greg and Mike. That has been a nice age span. Whenever we did do things together, whether it was camping or anything else, they were not just siblings but best friends to boot. That was a big help for Norma and me, and it helped make our outings more fun for everybody.

The real and lasting importance of our camping trips was that it allowed Norma and me to be involved with our children on a personal basis, developing personal friendships with them, and forming memories and bonds with them that would be there the rest of our lives. I cannot overstress how important that has been.

In our family, Kari was usually the one who could come up with the great ideas for fun things to do. Whether it was a family cookout, a talent show, or a night out together, she could always think of fun and original ways to enjoy ourselves. During our family meeting, Norma asked Kari if she would come up with a list of creative ideas for family fun. So, at this point, I would like to give you Kari's list.

Fun Things to Do with Your Family

Home Activities

1. *Lunch Bunch:* Pack a lunch together and "Do Lunch"!

2. *Saturday Blast:* One Saturday a month, do something special, such as visit the zoo or go horseback riding. Whatever you choose, vote on it as a family. If one member votes no, that vote wins the next week.

3. *Lazy Day Saturday:* Before getting up and starting the day, everyone stays in bed and reads a book. (This has been known to be done even when the children are grown and come home to visit!)

4. *Let's Cook:* Get matching aprons and once a week (or more) all cook together. You can make dinner, bake cookies, cakes, or even Play-Doh! Get the kids involved.

5. *Sun (Cozy-Bed) Day:* Everyone snuggles up in bed and reads a story, sings a song, or reads Bible verses before getting ready for church.

6. *Kids' Friday Night Bash:* This is an excellent way to start off the weekend. Play a game, cook out, picnic with an early dinner, go hiking (don't forget a snack!), paint rocks that you have collected, watch home movies or a fun video.

7. *Family Talent Show:* (Home or camping) Plan all day what each person will do for a talent. This activity is even better with a whole bunch of "family relations"! That night, "Let the show begin!" Be prepared for lots of laughs.

8. *Dad's (or Mom's) Night:* This night honors Dad or Mom in a very special way. Kids cook their parent's favorite meal! Bring out the candles and set the mood. The honoree even gets to choose the activity for the night.

9. *Dear Dad (Dear Mom):* If one of the parents travels or is out of town, put special notes in his or her luggage, handbag, suit pocket, and other places. Mailing them is even more fun!

10. *Let's Go to the Store:* Give the kids a food list and the fun begins. Remember to get hamburger buns, all the sandwich trimmings, chocolate milk, and dessert. You can even plan ahead to load the food and family in the car and go to a friend's house for "food, fun, and games."

11. *Fancy Sandwiches:* Let your kids cut out their bread, cheese, and meats with different shape cookie cutters. What a fun way to gobble down something healthy!

12. *Warm, Rainy Day Fun:* Load up a few warm blankets and make a tent. Cuddle up and watch it rain. This is especially fun if you have a big porch, but if it's too cold to go outdoors, you can have your tent adventure inside the house. Don't forget a good book.

13. *Time to Wash:* If your little girls love dolls or Barbies, then this activity is for you. Outside, set up a mini laundry line including tiny clothespins. Show them the "old-fashioned" way of washing and drying.

14. *Paper Dolls:* Buy them or make them yourself. I bet you forgot how much fun they are!

15. *Jacks Anyone?:* Another fun game for all ages—all too often neglected these days.

Outings and Outdoors

16. *Let's Go to the Show:* It is so important to give your child a taste of culture: symphonies, museums, science exhibits, community events, the zoo, etc. They may dislike some of these things at first, but they will come to appreciate them if you show your own interest.

17. *Friday Fun:* It's a perfect time to bowl, play miniature golf, or even skate.

18. *A-Z Search:* Hike and look for things that start with each letter. You can write down your list on mini notepads or make it a contest.

19. *Hunting:* Boys love to hunt with their dads, but girls can enjoy it too. Be sure to check local and state regulations; some require certificates of training. As an option, target shooting can be a lot of fun.

20. *Feed the Ducks:* Take leftovers and feed the ducks at the park. A bag of bread crumbs can provide loads of fun.

21. *Fish for It:* On a long drive, make a small fishing pole and tie a clothespin to the end. The children can fish over the car seat and catch all sorts of things, from crayons and coloring books to snacks and treats.

22. *Bait for Bears:* On your next camping trip to a wilderness area, put out some "food bait" for wild animals. National and state parks have regulations about feeding the animals, so be sure to check on the rules, but it can be fun to watch the critters come for the bait.

23. *Backyard Camping:* Can't get away to go camping? Pitch a tent in the backyard and camp for the night. Try having a cookout of hot dogs. Music around the campfire, and s'mores—what could be better?

24. *Fire Tower:* Whenever you go camping or to a wilderness area, visit the local fire tower. Rangers and parks department employees can arrange tours; most are glad to see visitors. The experience is exciting and helps kids realize how important forest rangers and firefighters really are.

I hope these suggestions will help you to think of many other creative ways to have fun with your family. The dividends of this kind of investment in your family relationships are greater than you can ever imagine. Stocks and bonds don't come close.

The Value of Being Together
without Spending Much Money

Recently, Greg told me that knowing that his father and mother considered him to be not just a son but a friend was one of the most important things in his life. He reminded me that way back when, I told him, "You know, Greg, one of the neat things about having kids is that you get a chance to raise your own best friend. And Greg, you *are* one of my very best friends."

Norma and I were very involved with our kids as friends through all the years of their schooling—junior high, high school, and college. We went to all their sporting events, and Norma even went to watch them practice. We planned it into our week. We made it clear that basketball games were more important than board meetings. It was just something that we did automatically. Greg and Michael told me that even though they didn't always acknowledge the fact that we were at those activities, they really appreciated knowing that we were there.

Greg remembers that in high school he didn't want to relate or hug or care, but we kept up a steady pressure on him to do those very things. We never got discouraged. He often resented or resisted the talks we had about the importance of touching and hugging, and the importance of caring between us, to our parents, and to each other as brothers and sisters. But more important than the fact that he resisted it, he would also have *hated* it if we hadn't wanted to talk to him.

He always knew that Mom and Dad wanted to be friends with him and that they accepted him no matter what. Today Greg believes that our desire to be not only parents but friends with our children was a key part of his maturing experience. We always tried our best to treat our children like people, not just kids, but like very valuable people. There had to be a balance. We definitely knew that we were the parents, but we also knew that we were best friends, and our kids later acknowledged that we were able to be not only parents but, at the same time, their best friends.

An important part of our relationship with our children was what we called Family Night. Before they started high school, we would have Family Night every Friday, and these were very important times for us. All our kids agreed. We would play games, have a conversation or a debate, go out for the evening, or maybe we would just have a special dinner.

During most of our kids' growing-up years we didn't have a lot of money, but we still managed to do a lot of things because there was so much we could do that was absolutely free. Camping is about as close as you can get to free entertainment. At one time we could rent a space for about four dollars a weekend. I think campsites run about ten dollars a night these days, but there are still a lot of free campsites around.

Our kids said they never realized we didn't have a lot of money. We could always do the things that mattered. We had food and clothes, and there was plenty of fun. There seems to be a tendency in modern society to believe that money is the only thing that matters. When people don't have very much money they drag around, complaining, feeling underprivileged and depressed because they don't have the things they see on television.

The fact is, we were able to do very simple things that didn't require a lot of money. We might not have money, but we were doing just fine. We made that a point. There were times when we had to buy our kids' clothes at second-hand stores. We would find good quality, name-brand things, and our children didn't know the things we brought home weren't brand new. They were *great* clothes.

It was difficult for Norma and me to go to some of those places at first because we didn't want anyone to see us there. We were struggling with our pride. But after a while we got used to it and it was fine. We felt that it was important not to say that we didn't have a lot of money, or even to make money an issue, because we felt that all of life should be honorable. Money was a convenience: We were glad to have it, but we didn't have to be rich to be happy.

I recently received a testimony from our secretary who was in South America. She said that most of the people she met had no money at all, yet they were happy, loving, hospitable, and gracious. These people know what Norma and I learned many years ago: Money is not the thing that gives honor to a family. Real honor is a decision that we make as parents, and it transfers to our children. It is the attitude that life is worth living, and people have value that doesn't depend on their possessions.

What They Didn't Like

Well, I said I wanted to share some things that our kids didn't like, things they don't plan to do with their own children. I want to preface this, however, by saying that the last item in this discussion concerns what I believe now was about the biggest thing I did wrong as a dad and as a parent. At the time I really didn't realize what was happening under the surface, but I wish I hadn't done it.

This particular problem turned out to be a major obstacle in my relationship with Greg. Even though some great things eventually came about in Greg's life because he responded in the right way, it was nevertheless something I would not do— something I would not say—if I had it to do over again. I would encourage you to consider seriously whether or not you may be saying something like it to your own children.

But the first thing I want to talk about is the matter of discipline: in this case, physical punishment. When it comes to discipline, it is easy for parents to forget what it is like being a child and how fragile children really are. Whenever Greg got into trouble as a child, I would sometimes tell him to go find the spanking stick and bring it to me. The spanking stick was just a little stick that the kids had made and decorated, and we used it to paddle the children, but it stung when they were paddled, and I thought that going to find it would make the kids think about the consequences of what they had done wrong. I thought it would just be beneficial for them to think long and hard about what they had done. I think now that I was wrong, especially in Greg's case.

The problem was that Greg became so fearful inside while he looked for the stick, his little heart would just be pounding. I didn't realize how strongly my plan really affected him. Even though Norma never used this method, I reasoned that he had disobeyed, and if he spent fifteen or twenty minutes looking for the stick then that was fifteen minutes he would have to consider what this was all about. But it was not worth the fear, the hurt, the resentment that this lesson cost. Yes, he was antici-pating the spanking, but in Greg's mind I was a big mean per-son who was about to hurt him. That was a very negative and unproductive message. It did not produce the behavior change I truly hoped for, and I was not even aware of it at the time.

On a couple of occasions Greg has told me that this was the part of his childhood discipline that hurt the most. It was not the physical hurt but the emotional hurt. In fact, in our re-cent conversation about this, Greg said that he remembered a couple of times when he brought the stick to me and I asked, "What's this for?" He'd be standing there, holding the stick, al-ready in tears, and he could tell that I had completely forgotten that I had sent him to get it.

When Greg told me this as a twenty-three-year-old, I just blushed in my heart. I had to ask myself, How could I have been so insensitive? I learned an important lesson. But I think that the point here is that parents need to realize that a child's heart is very fragile. We need to be honoring and careful, especially in the area of discipline and spankings, so that we don't do things in the process of training that are actually dishonoring to them. I know that if I had that to do over again, I surely wouldn't do it the same way.

Another thing that our kids all agreed was a major problem actually developed as a result of our lifestyle and relationships as a family. When the kids were small, we were very active in our church because I was the assistant pastor. We were very involved in the various activities at our church, and Kari, Greg, and Mike were each involved in Sunday school, Bible school, and all the regular church activities. But then I changed jobs.

When I started my full-time ministry in family life, our church in Texas sent me out as a missionary to families, and that meant I was gone a lot of weekends, speaking at conferences, in churches, and at a lot of seminars. Whenever Norma had to stay home with the kids, they were involved in church, but it wasn't the same as before. They went every week, but the sense of family unity had changed. Even when we would take the kids with us when I had to travel on weekends, we ended up visiting a lot of different churches in a lot of different towns. Consequently, we didn't feel that we really had much of a church life.

Sometimes we would wind up traveling on weekends and we couldn't go to church at all. Today the kids feel that, in the long run, this probably hurt them. They weren't involved in our church on a regular weekly basis. They didn't have regular contact with youth groups or youth leaders or church activities, and now they realize they didn't get discipled by our church in the way they wish they could have. That was a serious problem.

In some ways I felt that our family life substituted for church: We had quiet times and devotions and prayer together. But for all the good things that came out of those experiences, I now believe that every family needs a strong local church. Our kids say they really missed the local church experience.

Later the children attended a Christian school and the school became a sort of church for a while, but it wasn't what they really needed. Even very good schools aren't designed for discipleship: That's a job for the local church—the schools will tell you that. So my kids now look back and say they wish they could have had more direct discipleship from older, committed Christian kids. They wish they could have been "plugged-in" to their local youth group.

Looking back now, I totally agree with them, and I wish that we could have done it that way. Even though they are all growing in their relationships with the Lord today, and even though they have strong commitments to God and to other people, I think they missed an important stepping stone in their spiritual walk. In fact, that was probably the area that hurt Greg the most, and that's the area that we will go into with Greg because he was really the one who struggled in this area.

The Long-Term Effect of Words

I made a statement to my kids when they were young. I thought it was a good statement, not really thinking it through carefully, and I thought it was important to say. I said that because of my work and my various responsibilities, we were probably more vulnerable than a lot of families. I said, for example, that if they ever got involved sexually with someone before they were married, then I wasn't sure I would be able to stay in the ministry. In fact, on a couple of occasions I even said that I wasn't sure I would want to.

Now there are a hundred things in life that I could do—and would probably love to try some of them—but they *knew* that I loved what I did. They knew that I was having a definite effect on families all over the world, and they did not want to keep me from doing that. They did not want to be responsible for harming my work in any way. So even though I said that they could always say whatever they wanted to say to their mother and me, the fact that I had said that their behavior could force me to leave the ministry actually became an obstacle to open communication when they were teenagers.

Greg told me, "Dad, you told us we could tell you anything, but we knew that if it was something really bad, it might possibly cause you to leave the ministry. Maybe you would; maybe you wouldn't. We didn't know. But it was an obstacle. When I was in college, I saw a lot of really worldly stuff. There were constant temptations. Sex was all around me: in our dorm, in our room at times. Girls were always talking about it; girls propositioned me; there were magazines. I simply couldn't avoid it."

He went on, "The world is a very different place than when you were a kid, Dad. In our world sex is so prevalent and so talked about that sometimes it is more than a person can ignore. I was away from home, away from my family, and I was struggling with all these problems but I never felt I could talk to you openly about it. I felt that the potential consequences were just too great.

"Sure," Greg told me, "I 'surface' talked to you about it, but not really, not directly. When I went off to the university, I got into serious problems with sex, and before I knew it I was living in two worlds. In one world I was a 'bad person.' In the other world, with my family, everyone viewed me as this 'good kid.' You all loved me and told me how valuable I was, how good I was. But then I would leave your world and go back to my 'bad' world."

When all this first started to come up, I talked to Greg about it to clear the air, to encourage him to just talk things out. This was at Christmas time and we were both relaxing in the Jacuzzi, so it was an honest heart-to-heart talk. Greg said, "You know, Dad, you and Mom saved my life in some ways. I was trapped in sin. I felt guilty and ashamed. There were even times when the thought of taking my own life crossed my mind, but in the end I always knew I had a safe place to come back to. I knew that no matter how bad I felt, I could still get love and support here at home. I suppose I could have gone off the deep end and just gone deeper and deeper, but your support gave me the strength to accept God's love and grace and forgiveness. I am really grateful now that I was able to return to Him and to be able to pull myself out of the ice water I had fallen into."

I could see that Greg had really gotten in over his head. He started to feel like a total "scuzz ball." He said, "I felt like a totally rotten person, and I was so ashamed. But what pulled me out was when I realized that you could screw up and God would still love you and that He could still use you. That didn't mean I didn't feel horrible: I did. But, you know, I made a decision to be better, not bitter. It had to be my own decision. There was nothing my parents could have done."

He continued, telling me, "It always boiled down to my own choice. One reason I decided for a while I wanted to be a lawyer was because I figured that God could never use me in any sort of ministry. But then I remembered the story of Saul of Tarsus. He had killed people, persecuted Christians, and did so many awful things that, by comparison, his sins were so much worse than mine. Yet, God still used him, turned his life around and made him into the Apostle Paul. That seemed to prove that you could never do anything so bad that God couldn't turn you around and use you."

"So, Dad," Greg said, "that's what happened to me. I eventually got my act back together and became best friends with my Savior. I needed to let Him heal me. It was a long process and it has been very painful . . . over two years. But through the pain and the healing I have become what I am today."

I can't tell you how my son's honest confession and his beautiful understanding of what he had been through touched my heart. The shame and the guilt he had felt were so strong that it held him down. He said he felt like he had stepped through the ice into freezing cold water and he couldn't get out. The cold water was immobilizing his muscles, and he was not strong enough to pull himself out of the water.

"The guilt and the shame," he explained, "were the ice, and I couldn't get back through to the good world. I needed some kind of tool to break through it and get out. The Bible became my tool, and I started learning more and more about my personal relationship with Christ and how He could work in my life. I made a deeper commitment to Him at that point, even before I knew all the right things to say. But once I finally made this very real, sincere, personal choice to become a personal friend of Jesus Christ, He gave me the tools to break through the ice."

Our pastor said recently, "When we are in God's will, following His way, then and only then does He empower us." That was the principle Greg discovered. As Greg began to feel the power of God's grace and love, he was able to get his head back above the ice water and start to breath again. He was still freezing and cold and paralyzed, but he was on the way back.

"Months passed," Greg told me, "and I realized that the guilt and the shame were only in my mind. I had to understand that it was okay for me to have done those bad things. I mean, now that they are in the past and I've confessed them, they're not going to hold me down any more. God can truly forgive. He has mercy on us every day, and He can ritualize those old habits and pull us into new patterns. We can actually look back on those old things, and God can turn them into something good."

Greg was so right. Isaiah 61:2–3 says that Christ came to "comfort those who mourn," "to give them beauty for ashes, the oil of joy for mourning, the garment of praise for the spirit of heaviness; that they may be called trees of righteousness, the planting of the Lord, that He may be glorified." God turns ashes to beauty and sorrow to joy if and only if we are dependent on Him. Now Greg was learning all of this on his own.

He said, "I think I have a much greater sensitivity today than I ever did before, a greater love for people. I have a level of understanding that I never had before. I realize now that messing up your life doesn't have to be fatal. I'll soon be married and into my second year of seminary, training for a career in counseling, and I believe that my own past really is a sort of a foundation for my understanding of how to help other people in the future."

Gaining a New Perspective

Now I am not telling these things about our struggles as a family or about Greg's experience to point out how much pain we had to overcome as a family. My purpose is to show how an attitude I had expressed to our children, a verbal caution that they were not allowed to get into any sort of serious trouble, may have been partly responsible for Greg's decision to lead a double life. One of the things we both acknowledged was that my saying that I might have to leave the ministry if he ever told me about those things actually caused him to stay out in the cold.

Greg didn't have access to me and Mom during those lonely nights when he was struggling in the ice water of immorality. That really hurts. But the good news is that because he didn't have me to turn to, he turned to the Lord. It's not exactly the way I would have wanted it to happen, but what a great opportunity my mistake actually became! God turned it into something good: joy for ashes.

Greg and I went to see Dr. Bill Retts, a terrific Christian counselor, and Bill said something wonderful to Greg. He said, "Greg, all of Scripture is the story of how God uses people's lives and their personal stories to tell God's truths. You now have your own story. It's not your dad's story that you are living on, it's your own story. Here's where I was before; here's what happened to me; and here's how God took me out of the ice water. So Greg, I hope you will see this experience as a chance to help other people understand how God changes lives."

Dr. Retts also encouraged me as a parent, just as I now encourage you as parents, to let your kids know that they can tell you the whole truth. You may want to tell your teenagers about your own rocky times, what you were like, and how God pulled you out of the icy waters and put your feet back on the solid rock of Jesus Christ. Tell them the whole story and humble yourself, which I didn't always do. Now I wish I had done more of it. God's walk in our life is a process. It is the story of how God is taking us from victory to victory despite the mistakes and the stumbling we may experience along the way.

Greg's decision to be a youth leader is a real challenge for him. Teaching and leading young people has helped him to grow and it has also helped him to help other kids. It didn't really teach him anything new, but it kept him on that continual upward path. It helped him hold his head above water.

Greg has told me that, looking back, he could say that it was what God did in him through his failure that really turned him around. You can learn those things in many other ways, but he had to go through it because he needed to experience God's grace. Maybe there would have been no other way for him to discover what God wanted to teach him.

Greg knew he was a strong person, very insensitive and very judgmental. I think God knew that and realized that he needed to go through something really humbling in order to soften him up. Now he has a much greater empathy for other people's problems. He can cry with and for people now. Before, he didn't have a clue.

Sometimes when he's talking with kids, either in a counseling situation or just one-on-one, he can feel their pain, their enslavement, their grief. He can see the icy water they've fallen into and know that they are trying to swim out of it. And then, having a new understanding of God's great compassion, he can say, "Here's how I crawled out." He couldn't do that before, and he used to think it was a little wimpy. His reaction would have been to say, "Hey, man, what are you doing? Come on, crawl out! What are you doing in that water anyway!" He had a very hard-hearted attitude toward people he thought were weak. In his own mind he was on a pedestal, and he needed something or someone to take a sledge hammer and bounce him off that block. And that's exactly what happened!

Later I asked Greg, "Did you know that we would accept you even after you told us all this stuff that you'd been going through?" And he said, "Dad, you told me that you'd always accept me no matter what I did, but I never wanted to tell you because I was so proud of what you were doing and who you were. I could see all the people that you were helping, and there was no way on earth that I was going to let my actions make you give up something that I knew was so dear to you. That would have messed me up more than anything else. Home was so good. Whenever I came home I could disassociate myself from what I was doing in my other world. If you hadn't given us that warning about how our mistakes might affect you and your ministry, I would probably have been able to talk to you about it. But despite everything else, I am really thankful now that things worked out the way they did."

Kari's, Greg's, and Michael's comments really confirmed for Norma and me the importance of the concept of honor in the family. We told them that we felt this was the most important concept we had learned as parents.

The truth is, we all go through the experience of parenting as beginners, and we're going to make mistakes. Mistakes are inevitable. God allows us to learn how things are supposed to be done as we go along. As long as we are honest with ourselves and our children, as long as we honor them and are totally honest with them, we have the freedom to make mistakes and still develop character and responsibility in our children.

I sometimes think that the freedom to fail may be the most important lesson we learn as parents, and it is one of the most important things we can teach our kids. We all do it.

The Principle of Empowerment

As I reflect on the lessons my children have taught me and how they have responded to our discipline and our family life, I am truly gratified by the evidence of God's love and protection in our home. I am also humbled to know that the efforts Norma and I made to empower our children with God's love and our own has returned back to us tenfold over the years.

As I spoke with Michael about his thoughts on what we had done positively and negatively as parents, I was struck by his observations.

"Dad, just encourage the parents who read this book to instill godly values in their children *when they are young.* Don't be afraid to take stands on movies or friends, what is right and what is wrong. They need parents *to be parents* while they are in the formative years . . . and then a mom or dad can loosen up and give them the opportunity to adopt these standards as their own as they get older."

There is so much wisdom in what Mike shared. It was King Solomon who wrote the words, "Remember also your Creator *in the days of your youth. . . .*"

When our children are young, we need to be their guides, their encouragers, their teachers and coaches. We need to empower them with the unshakable knowledge of how incredibly valuable they are to us. We need to make stands on right behavior and attitudes and be strong enough to discipline them. But we also have to let them go and grow . . . grounded in our values . . . and secure in our love.

For eighteen years we sought to empower Michael with our efforts and actions. And as Mike talked to me, I realized that he had turned the tables. Now he was empowering *me* to go out and encourage other families by his love and support.

"Dad, I've chosen to follow the guidelines you and Mom set for me. I think you did a great job with us. And I would encourage parents not to spend all their time worrying about what their child 'might' do wrong when they're older, and concentrate on giving them—*when they're young*—the values they'll need to make the right choices on their own."

Norma and I have always taken comfort in the fact that while we haven't done it all right, we've done our best to follow God's will. And you can know that feeling as well. In God's love, you can find the power to be whole and complete yourself and to overflow that love onto your children. This lesson has come back so often and so forcefully in our family, I'm convinced it can be a guiding principle in your home as well.

As we turn now to some practical examples for parents, I would like to offer some useful guidelines and principles for motivating children.

6

Three Powerful Ways to Motivate Children

- Use a Child's Natural Bent
- Use the Salt Principle
- Use Emotional Word Pictures

*I*T WAS 1957, IN SAN FRANCISCO. A tall, skinny ten-year-old boy was waiting to sneak inside Kaiser Stadium. He had waited all year for this game between the San Francisco 49ers and the Cleveland Browns and the chance to see his idol, Jim Brown, the All-Pro running back who held almost every rushing record in the NFL. He knew that at the end of the third quarter the gate guard left and he could slip in. Even that wasn't easy for him because he had trouble walking. Raised in the ghetto, malnutrition had taken its toll and his legs were weak and bowed. He had to walk with the aid of steel splints.

After he made his way into the stadium, he stood right in the middle of the entrance to the players' tunnel, where he patiently waited for the game to end. As the final gun went off, the wiry lad struggled to stand tall so he wouldn't miss this moment. Finally, he saw Jimmy Brown turn the corner and walk toward him. As he passed by, the boy held out a piece of paper, asking politely for an autograph. Brown graciously signed it, then turned for the locker room.

But before he could get away, the boy tugged on Brown's jersey. The great running back turned and was met with this proud confession, "Mr. Brown, I have your picture on my wall. My family can't afford a television set but I watch you on the neighbor's set every chance I get. I know what your records are and I think you're the greatest. You're my idol."

Brown put his hand on the boy's shoulder and thanked him before heading on to the locker room. But the boy reached up and tugged Brown's jersey again. Brown turned and looked into the boy's big brown eyes and asked impatiently, "Yes?"

The boy cleared his throat, held his shoulders back and head high and matter-of-factly said, "Mr. Brown, one day I'm going to break every one of your records."

Brown was so taken aback by the statement that he asked, "What's your name, son?"

The boy answered, "Orenthal James, sir. But my friends just call me O.J."

In 1973, O. J. Simpson broke Brown's long-standing single-season rushing record and became the first player to gain more than two thousand yards rushing in one year. He was second behind Brown in career rushing yardage when injuries forced him to retire. Why was O. J. Simpson so motivated? Why did he have such great success?

There are many, many reasons why people are motivated—it might be the applause, the cheering of a crowd, awards—but as with O. J. Simpson, real and lasting motivation must come from within. If Simpson had viewed Jimmy Brown's records as something he never could achieve, he might have ended up in a wheelchair. But he didn't. He set a goal and believed in himself enough to accomplish that goal.

When a child uses his own energy and drive to achieve a goal he has set, he is truly motivated. That goal may be inspired by parents or friends, but it is important that the child actually set the goal and see that it is attainable and that he will benefit by reaching that goal.

Notice we stress the child setting his own goal. There is a fine line between motivation and manipulation. Dads and moms alike need to be so careful not to use their children as pawns for their own needs. Have you ever witnessed a Dad forcing football on his son because Dad needs it—not his son?

True motivation comes from one or a combination of two factors:

1. Desire for gain.
2. Fear of loss.

Imagine waking a child on Christmas morning. He doesn't need to be motivated to get up. Eagerly he jumps out of bed because he knows there is something waiting for him. That same child will not stick his hand into a fire because he fears pain and loss, and this motivates him to avoid the flames.

Working with young children, teenagers, and college-age young people for more than thirty years has made me aware of over twenty ways to motivate children. At the heart of each of these methods is the desire for gain and the fear of loss. In this chapter, we will focus on motivating through a child's natural personality and the use of two communication tools. In the next chapter we'll cover nineteen other ways to motivate children.

1. Use a child's natural bent.

I could tell that Norma was down in the dumps by her voice on the telephone. It was Mother's Day and I was away from home teaching a seminar. She was lonely and I wished I were home. While we were talking, Greg walked into the house and presented her with a bouquet of flowers. I was pleased with his thoughtfulness, especially since he was only thirteen.

The next day I called Norma again to see how she was doing. "Oh, I'm just sitting here looking at these beautiful flowers Greg gave me," she said. I asked where Greg had gotten the flowers, hoping that he had picked them from our garden and not from the neighbor's.

"Oh, no," Norma said. "He ordered them from a florist."

"He ordered them? Where did he get the money for that?"

"Oh, he just used your charge card."

Greg is very sensitive and helpful whenever his mother is feeling down. He will vacuum the house, wash the dishes, sweep the floor—anything to make his mom happy. But our other children respond differently, and this reflects their different personality types. Kari and Michael tend to empathize with Norma if she's feeling low; they sometimes even get discouraged along with her. But neither one tends to "kick in" like Greg does.

A person's personality type, as I'll be describing, is a result of his total physical make-up, especially his gene structures. I like to call it his "natural bent." Often there is a *combination* of personality types in a child, but usually one is predominant.

Certainly his upbringing and environment affect his "bent," but I have observed that at least five different temperaments can be found in children and it is important to understand each of them. I've arrived at these five through my observation of children through reviewing a number of studies. Each child is motivated differently, according to his or her "natural bent."

Within each of the five personality types, the behavior of children will vary because of birth order. For example, firstborn children tend to be more pushy and prone to give orders. Secondborn children tend to be more sociable. Other factors account for variances within temperaments: being an only child, living with only one parent, being the only boy in a family of girls, and so on. Yet despite these variances, children tend to fall within one of the five general personality types. (For a more complete treatment of a child's and a parent's personality make-up, refer to *The Two Sides of Love,* which I coauthored with John Trent.

The summaries on the following pages illustrate the predominant personality types and general characteristics of each.

Also explained is how to motivate each type of child so that he or she will want to respond in a positive manner.

The Strong-Willed

General Characteristics

- They believe they're usually right
- Often critical, pointing out the mistakes of others
- Perfectionist tendency
- Believe there is a right and wrong way to act
- Prone to "foot-in-mouth" disease
- When doing a task, they want to do it right or not at all
- Negative thinker
- Persistent
- Very loyal
- Good memory of others' actions toward them
- Can be warmly touched by sad stories

Dos and Don'ts in Motivation

- Spend time fully explaining things, because once they see that certain actions are right, they usually comply.
- Be careful not to interpret their ability to be blunt with others as a sign that they can receive blunt, terse words in return. They are much more motivated by sincere grief, even tears, but they are experts in detecting insincere or manipulative motivation.
- They like to know where they are wrong if adequate time is taken, and they know if we are sincere and willing to wait until they really understand.

- Avoid prolonged arguments because the "strong-willed" often feel slightly hypocritical in discussing what they "know" is right—their own opinion.

The Peacemaker

General Characteristics

- Conforms to others
- Pliable
- Dependent
- Supportive
- Tenderhearted
- Agreeable
- Avoids persistent arguments
- Somewhat introverted
- Careful in what they say or do so as not to cause conflict
- Not the flamboyant type

Dos and Don'ts in Motivation

- They need to know that we sincerely like them as a unique individual.
- They react to being stereotyped or placed in a box.
- They respond better to someone they consider a friend.
- Patiently discover their personal goals and motivate them by helping them meet those goals.
- If the peacemaker disagrees, encourage discussion on personal feelings and opinions rather than objective facts.

- Avoid harshness or demanding attitudes because they are very stubborn when offended.
- When disagreement occurs it is better to have a soft, tender conversation as you gently touch them: "You're feeling hurt, aren't you? I sure don't want you to feel badly. Let's resume this later when we can both be calmer."

The Cheerleader

General Characteristics

- Manipulative
- Excitable
- Undisciplined
- Reactive
- Promotional
- Expressive
- Desires to be helpful
- Creative
- Approachable
- Warm
- Communicative
- Competitive
- Impulsive

Dos and Don'ts in Motivation

- Discover their opinions and ideas. Help them figure out how to reach their goals in a realistic way. Many times their goals are not realistic.

- "Cheerleaders" have opinions on almost everything. When motivating them, find out what they are most interested in and develop a friendship on this level of interest.

- They are most responsive to a good friend who likes their ideas.

- When faced with a problem, discuss possible solutions and let them come up with their own solutions, with your help as a parent.

- If you disagree, avoid prolonged arguments because "cheerleaders" have a strong need to win. Look for alternative solutions that you both can live with.

- "Cheerleaders" tend to do what you inspect, not what you expect.

The Pusher

General Characteristics

- Objective
- Uncommunicative
- Cool
- Independent
- Competitive
- Initiates action
- Pushy
- Tough-minded
- Dominating
- Harsh
- Determined
- Decisive

Dos and Don'ts in Motivation

- Help them see the results of their behavior. Be objective.
- They are interested in knowing what will happen, not so much why it will happen.
- When an argument starts, use facts and ideas, not feeling statements. "Pushers" are motivated by cold, objective facts.

The Helper

General Characteristics

- Somewhat like the peacemaker in temperament, but more concerned about assisting people in need rather than empathizing with them
- Tends to be exacting; their way is the only way to do it.
- Undependable
- Impulsive
- Avoids long-range planning
- Conforming because they avoid conflict
- Would rather do a job right than delegate it
- Usually overcommitted

Dos and Don'ts in Motivation

- They run on genuine, sincere praise.
- If you expect them to do a certain job, they'll probably avoid it and do something unexpected for someone else.
- They are stubborn if harsh demands are made.

- They usually try to accomplish more in one day than they can finish so they become frustrated. Help them organize their day, but don't demand that they follow the plan.

- If you want their help with a particular project, it is best to start it in their presence and wait for them to help. They may prefer to finish it by themselves, without your help.

When motivating a child by using his or her "natural bent" it is important to learn the child's basic interests and talents. You can use this knowledge to motivate that child to be a better student, eat healthier foods, read books, and do many other things.

Kari is a lot like the peacemaker and her strong interest is in teaching. We used this goal to motivate her to eat healthier foods, play on the high school basketball team, and study more diligently in school by showing her that she would be better prepared physically and mentally to be a good teacher.

When Michael was ten years old he wanted to be a pro football player. We used this goal to motivate him to eat more nutritional foods and take care of his body. "Have you ever met an unhealthy football player?" I'd ask him. Then he decided that he wanted to be a zookeeper. We visited different zoos and talked about what it takes to be a good zookeeper. Because a zoo must be neat and orderly, we motivated Michael to keep his room more neatly arranged. We gave him books about animals to encourage him to be a better reader which has motivated him to do well in school. And that strong interest in animals helped him to develop his research skills, which helped him throughout his school work and especially now in his college studies.

Our other son, Greg, started taking pilot lessons when he was twelve. He is a good pilot and because of this, his sense of self-worth has increased. Because he wanted to learn more about the history of flying and the various geographical areas over which he flew, his interest in school and reading also increased.

Greg said one of the reasons he wanted to be a pilot was so that we could travel together as a team, speaking together across the country. He took public speaking classes to help him meet this goal. He also became more interested in spiritual matters and living a consistent Christian life, because he realized that if he were going to speak about these matters, he needed to start learning them now.

When parents use their children's interests to motivate them, the resulting progress is often amazing. Motivating a child through his interests is effective because it comes from within him. It reflects his bent.

Parents must be careful, however, not to "force" a child into a particular "bent," especially when considering the child's temperament. People can take on characteristics of other temperaments, so the five general temperaments should only be used as a guide and not as a rigid mold. They can be very useful in communicating with and motivating children, but it can be very harmful to make statements like, "You're the strong-willed type, and this is the way you'll always be." Realize that they can adjust or even change their personality type in time.

2. Use the Salt Principle.

Using a child's interest can motivate very effectively, but what are we as parents to do if we can't even get their attention? What if they avoid our attempts to enter into a serious discussion with them? I have found a simple tool that can grab and keep their attention. It's called the *Salt Principle.*

We were driving back to Phoenix from Los Angeles a few years ago. Norma and the boys were in the back of our motor home, and Kari was sitting up front next to me. "Kari, would you like to date during the upcoming school year?" I asked. Shyly, she answered, "Yes."

"What type of boy would you like to date?"

"Well, he needs to be nice—polite. I want him to be sensitive. He should be interested in a lot of different kinds of things, especially sports."

"Sounds like a hunk," I said. Kari smiled, blushing a little at the name I'd used. "Kari, would you like to be sure that your dream date will come true?"

She looked at me with surprise. "Sure!"

"Well, I've been reading lately about two or three things you can do that will be attractive to a boy like the one you mentioned. Let's talk about them when we get back to Phoenix, okay?"

"Why wait?" Kari asked. "Let's talk about it now."

We spent the rest of our drive talking about several inner attitudes that make a person an outstanding dating partner. We discussed patience in understanding men and how they are different from women. We discussed what it means to have genuine love, and how she will gravitate toward a certain type of boy because of her temperament. It was a very profitable time, and it all happened because I used the Salt Principle.

> Simply stated, the Salt Principle involves using a child's *interests* to teach specific things that a parent believes are important.

We are all familiar with the saying, "You can lead a horse to water but you can't make him drink." But that's not necessarily true. If you dump salt in the horse's oats, he will become thirsty and want to drink. The more salt you dump on his oats, the thirstier he becomes and the more he wants to drink.

When I use the Salt Principle, I'm creating curiosity. That's what I did with Kari. I knew she was highly interested in dating, and I used that interest to share some things that would help her be successful in that area. I was able to hold her interest for hours because she was motivated.

The Salt Principle motivates children to listen carefully and thereby learn some important truths about life. I used it with Kari another time when I said to her: "Do you realize that there is something that could occur in your life this next year that could cause you to doubt God? Just this one thing could cause you to become extremely self-centered and have a difficult time in your relationship with God. You'll have a hard time reading the Bible and praying and you'll find you're less interested in school. You'll also find several other negative things happening to you."

After dumping on all this salt, I asked if she would like to discuss what it is that could cause such a devastation in her life.

"Yes! What's that?" she asked with excitement. "Let's talk about it, because whatever it is, I don't want to do it." At that point, I again shared some of the dangers of premarital sex. It was another very meaningful discussion.

The Salt Principle can be used to teach children many important lessons. Here are some guidelines for using salt effectively:

1. Clearly identify what you wish to communicate.

2. Identify your listener's most important interests.

3. Using their areas of high interest, share just enough of your idea to stimulate curiosity to hear more.

4. Use questions to increase curiosity.

5. Communicate your important information or idea only *after* you see you have your child's full interest and attention.

Not long ago, I wanted to teach Mike an important lesson. If I had said, "Hey, how about a Bible lesson together, just the two of us?" you can imagine the response: "Yeah Dad, maybe later, okay?" or perhaps, "Oh no, not one of those again." We are an ordinary family and I realize that my children often are not interested in what I consider to be important for their lives. But I can salt their interest by relating to things they are interested in. Here's how I used it with Mike:

"Hey, Mike? Want me to tell you a story?" I asked.

"No, Dad. I'm playing right now. Maybe later."

"Well, okay, then I won't tell you about a crazy, wild man who lived in the mountains, and he was so strong he could break chains and no one could hold him down and he made these horrible screams so no one would get near him."

I paused and Mike immediately piped up, "That's in the Bible?"

"Yes. And you won't believe what happened to him. Maybe sometime I'll tell you the story."

"No, tell me now, please!" So I proceeded to tell Mike the story about how Jesus healed the demoniac in Gerasenes.

The Salt Principle is a highly motivating tool when used with a child's natural bent. For example, I could take Greg's interest in being a pilot and use it to motivate him in a number of areas if I combine it with the Salt Principle.

Once I was talking to a commercial pilot, and I learned that you cannot fly commercially if you take certain types of drugs. You must swear to have never taken drugs and pass a lie detector test. I knew this would impress Greg deeply, so I arranged a meeting between the pilot and Greg.

Before the meeting, I salted Greg: "You know, there's one thing you could do which would prevent you from ever being a commercial pilot." Greg naturally was curious about what that could be, but I told him I wanted him to hear it directly from a pilot. When the three of us got together, the pilot asked Greg if he had ever taken drugs.

"Why no, I've never done any of that," Greg replied.

"That's good, Greg, because I want to warn you that if you ever do, you won't become a professional pilot. You can't even experiment with drugs or you can forget about being a pilot."

Talk about motivation. What took place in that discussion was far more effective than anything I could have said. And it was the Salt Principle that motivated Greg to listen to that pilot.

I had a high school English teacher who used salt to motivate us to read books. He would read to the class from a book. Then just when he got to the most exciting part, he'd stop reading and close the book. Naturally, we'd all say, "What happened?"

"It's in the book," would be his reply.

"What page?" we'd beg.

"You'll find it."

And so we'd dash to the library to check out the book, and many times we'd read the entire book to find out what happened. Norma used that same method to motivate our children to read fifty books one summer.

Look around and see how many people use salt. Television shows you twenty- or thirty-second previews of upcoming programs. They show you the most exciting scenes, but don't let you know how they are resolved. They'll show a car flying over a barrier in a chase scene, but in order to find out if it lands or crashes, you have to watch the show.

Gossip is the Salt Principle used in a negative way. You can walk up to someone and say, "You'll never guess what I heard about so and so." The immediate response is "What's that?" If you say, "Well, I promised not to say anything about it to anyone," you have just increased the salt level even more. This negative use of the Salt Principle demonstrates just how effective it really is. It can be used for manipulation, which is very negative, or it can be used in a very positive manner.

It's important to remember that the Salt Principle stems from a desire to serve a child's real or felt needs and interests. It guides that child toward fulfillment of his goals, while helping him gain important information that is vital to becoming a mature adult.

The next area is as equally effective in motivation as using a child's natural bent and using the Salt Principle. However, using it not only motivates a child, but I have never used anything more effective to communicate with children. This is the best method I've found for causing positive adjustments between parents and children.

3. Use emotional word pictures.

During most ordinary days, family members can offend each other and experience hurtful and difficult times. They often wish that another family member could understand how they are feeling. Using emotional word pictures is one of the best ways to have others enter into our feelings and it can motivate them to stop hurting us.

> An emotional word picture is associating our feelings with either a real or imaginary experience.

Using word pictures to motivate others is identifying with them emotionally. It's motivating on an emotional level.

A teenage girl once told me how she motivated her father to listen and understand her. She used an emotional word picture relating to her father's job as an auto mechanic to tell him about something that was troubling her.

"Daddy, you know how sometimes you will tune up a car and it runs okay, but not exactly the way it ought to? Then the owner will bring it back and say it's not running exactly right. Frustrated, you take out all your tools and check everything again and sure enough, you'll make a minor adjustment that makes the engine purr. Well, you're a super dad and our relationship is running along fine, but there's a little part of it that's out of adjustment. I wish we could spend some time so that I could explain from my point of view what we could do together to fine-tune our relationship."

The girl's father understood immediately because he could imagine someone returning a car for an adjustment. Because he understood how his daughter felt, a positive change occurred in their relationship.

I've used word pictures in counseling to help couples open up their lines of communication. Once, the wife of an NFL player used this graphic illustration to describe how she felt about their marriage: "I feel the way you have been treating me lately is like the way a little baby rabbit would feel out in the back yard. It's cold and raining. You've come out of the house and wandered out to the trash can and stepped right on my back and broken both my hind legs. I'm terribly frightened and I'm trying to get away." Tears welled up in her husband's eyes and he said, "I had no idea you were feeling this way. I didn't know I was hurting you like that." Once a person starts to *feel* the pain another is feeling, he increases his understanding and becomes softer in his spirit.

The use of emotional word pictures is useful for children as well as adults. Children can be affected by them at almost any age, as long as they can talk. Here are two steps for successfully using emotional word pictures. First, we need to clearly identify what we are feeling—what's going wrong or how do we *feel* about what's happening around us? Second, once these feelings are identified, we must make up a story that illustrates these feelings. If one is feeling discouraged he can say, "I feel like the color blue," or "I feel like a damp, smelly dishrag," or "I'm in cold water up to my neck in a deep well." Word pictures can be created by using things that are common to our experience: animals, water, mountains, desert, furniture, the seasons.

An example from the Bible demonstrates how powerfully motivating word pictures are. In the story of David and Bathsheba, David became sexually attracted to Bathsheba, lusted after her, and eventually caused her pregnancy. Feeling guilty about his actions, David arranged for her husband, Uriah, to be brought home from the battlefield to be with his wife. David thought this would get him off the hook, but Uriah refused to return home, saying he didn't want to offend his fellow comrades. David was angered, so he arranged for Uriah to be sent to the front lines of the battlefield where he was killed.

David wasn't motivated to repent or change until the Lord sent Nathan, who painted a powerful emotional word picture. Nathan related a story of two men, one very rich with many sheep, the other poor, with nothing but one lamb. The poor man raised the lamb with his children, and the animal became like a member of the family. One day a traveler came to town, but the rich man was unwilling to take one sheep from his flock to prepare for the visitor. So he took the poor man's one lamb and prepared this for his guest.

The story angered David, who said the rich man should make fourfold restitution for the poor man's lamb. David demanded that such a man deserved to die. Boldly Nathan said, "David, you are that man." The emotional word picture was so powerful that David cried out to God in grief and repented of his sin.

Jesus Christ was a master at using emotional word pictures. He used natural things and experiences to teach truth. He said things like, "The kingdom of God is like finding a valuable pearl." Or "Unless we fall to the ground like a seed and die, we will never produce the true fruit of life." "I am the Good Shepherd." "Faith is like a mustard seed." "I am the light of the world." These word pictures illustrate truths that are understandable to man because they are put in the context of human experience and emotions.

I've witnessed the power and effectiveness of emotional word pictures in my own home. It took five minutes to help my son change an irritating habit. I travel frequently throughout the country and am often gone for several days at a time. When I arrive home, the whole family usually greets me. It is an encouragement when they rush out to hug me and yell, "Welcome home, Dad!" When our son Greg was twelve, he would usually join in the welcome, but there was a time when, after the initial greeting, he would avoid me for an hour or two. I would try to touch him or ask him what he'd done while I was gone, but he'd say, "Just leave me alone. I don't want to talk."

That bothered me. He was acting like his spirit was closed toward me, but I hadn't done anything to him. I asked Norma what she thought was wrong and she explained that Greg was probably angry because I had been gone, and this was his way of punishing me.

I wanted Greg to understand how his rejection hurt me, so one evening a couple of days after I'd returned from a trip, I took him out for dinner, just the two of us. After dinner, I made up a story relating to his participation on the school basketball team.

"Greg, suppose you made first string on the basketball team and you were playing well, and suddenly you got an injury. We took you to the doctor and he said you couldn't play for two weeks so the injury would heal. So you don't play, but you show up at practices. Then after two weeks, you're ready to play again, but the rest of the players and the coach just ignore you. They act like you aren't even there. How would that make you feel?"

"Dad, that would really hurt. I wouldn't want to go through that."

"That's somewhat how Dad feels when I come home from a trip and you welcome me home, but then reject me for an hour or two. I want to get back on the family team, but I feel you are ignoring me."

"I didn't know that," he said. "That really makes sense. I won't do it anymore."

About two weeks later, I left for a trip. As I was getting into the car after saying goodbye to my family, Greg yelled, "Have a great trip, Dad. And get ready to be rejected when you get home." We all laughed, but he remembered, and never again did he reject me when I returned home.

Emotional word pictures can be used with anyone. Try using emotional word pictures with your mate or a good friend before trying it on your children. The more you practice, the better you will become, and you will see that this simple motivating force is very powerful.

In the next chapter we'll continue sharing an additional nineteen ways to motivate children.

7

Nineteen Additional Ways to Motivate Children

- Help Children Choose Their Own Goals
- Expect Children to Do Things Right
- Expose Your Children to People You Admire

I REMEMBER LYING DOWN next to our youngest son, Mike, just as he was falling off to sleep. Somehow we began talking about how special he is to me. I asked him the same question I've asked many times, "Why does Dad love you so much?" Unhesitantly he responded, "Because I'm a boy and have blue eyes, right?" "Yes," I answered, "but remember there's one more big reason." He thought and smiled, "I brought you back to the family, huh?" "Yes, but there's an even more important reason" I answered. He had been a major reason I changed vocations in order to spend more time with my family. Mike thought a moment more and said, "Because I'm me." "That's it!" I said. This special time with Mike reminded me of a major problem with motivating children.

Motivating children is a powerful way to change their behavior. However, performance to gain acceptance can cause an emotional drain on children as well as on adults. Parents should be very careful not to withhold acceptance if a child does not perform to their expectations. A healthy parent-child relationship is to accept children for who they are, not what they do. Acceptance adds to their strength and desire to change.

Again, true motivation is from within a child, not from external pressure from parents.

These nineteen remaining ways to motivate are suggested not for manipulation or for performance, but so each child can attain his full potential and experience his own goals.

---

1. Help Children Choose Their Own Goals

The football coach at Texas A&M asked each of his players to write down a number between one and ten, with ten being the best, representing how good he wanted to be. Jeff, a walk-on, wrote down "10" because he wanted to be good enough to play pro football. The coach then asked each player to write down specific goals for the season. Jeff set goals for weight lifting, including a bench press of four hundred pounds, running the one-hundred-yard dash in eleven seconds, and so on. The coach told the players to post their goals in several places, in their lockers and at home so they would be reminded of them at all times. Every week he had them read their goals out loud to each other and evaluate their progress. Jeff said the goal-setting procedure was probably the most motivating force he had ever experienced because the goals he was striving to attain were *his*.

We practice the same type of goal-setting technique with our children, whether it involves sports, school work, or any of their other interests. We say, "From zero to ten, how good do you want to be? We're committed to help you, but we want to understand your goals first."

In the past our children did not set their goals as high as we felt they should, and this led to some conflict. However, once we understood what their goals were, we also understood why they weren't as motivated in some areas. For example, we pushed and shoved Kari for years to be above average in her piano playing. We wanted her to be good enough to play in front of a group. We finally asked her to rate how good she wanted to be from zero to ten. She picked five—average. We had picked eight for her but that was not her goal. Consequently we practically had to sit with her to get her to practice. She finally stopped practicing when she was sixteen years old because she had reached her goal.

Part of loving children is helping them reach *their goals*—not superimposing our goals upon them. If we press our goals, their motivation won't last because it will be from an external pressure rather than true motivation from within themselves. When helping your children choose their goals, try to expose them to people who have succeeded in areas in which your children are interested. If they're interested in both animals and medicine, set up an appointment for them to spend several hours visiting and watching a veterinarian. Something might be said during the experience to help motivate them. (If they don't faint as the vet patches a broken leg!) The motivational force is often more powerful when it comes from someone outside the family.

2. Help Children Visualize the Positive Results of Achieving Their Own Goals and the Negative Results of Not Reaching Their Goals

It was early in the basketball season and the team was doing quite well. But they were about to face a team which had humiliated them last year by thirty points. The coach knew he had to motivate his players, so he pulled out the film of last year's game. The game looked as bad on film as it had that night. It even captured the fans' shameful expressions, disgusted with their team.

At first that may not sound like the best motivational tool, but then the coach pulled out a film of his team winning a big game. This time the fans were screaming and cheering. "Look how well you played against that other team," the coach said. "This year you can play just as well against the team that embarrassed you last year. What do you say? Let's go get 'em!"

The coach's purpose was to help his players visualize beating the opposing team. He wanted them to see and hear the fans cheering for them, to see themselves out on the court, to recall the joy of beating a tough foe and the pain they would suffer if they failed.

A very popular high school football coach in Southern California motivates his players by finding out what each boy wants out of football. One boy might want to please his father, another wants to impress his girlfriend, while a third hopes to win a football scholarship at a major university. During practice, he might take the boy who wanted to please his father off to one side and say, "You know that play you've been working on? You're not quite getting it right. Now if you use this technique, can you imagine how proud your dad would be when you shoot through the line and make that tackle? Can't you just picture your dad cheering, jumping up and down in the stands?"

To the player who wants a scholarship the coach might say, "College scouts will be impressed if you use this technique. They spend hours trying to teach it to their players. Can you imagine them smiling as they see you make that play? They'll put a special note in their reports about that."

We've watched our son Michael's eyes and facial expressions as he admiringly follows in his older brother's footsteps. We know he wants to be as good as Greg in everything, especially in sports. The main reason we encourage our children in sporting events is because it can help build inner character such as patience, humility, and learning to lose and win graciously.

I witnessed the force of this motivational tool while Mike was telling me how much he wanted to be a tight end on the football team, like Greg. But he was in gymnastics and several years away from being in high school. I said to him, "Mike, can you just imagine how much fun it will be to go out for a long pass in football, catch it, and do a flip completely over the defender because of your gymnastic skills? I can see it now. I'll jab the person in the stands next to me, 'Did you see my son! He jumped completely over that guy—great move!'" Michael was laughing and I could see he was right with me; he was getting motivated.

3. Remember the Power of Praise

If, as a father, you had less than one minute each day to talk to your children, what would you tell them? Studies show that fathers, on the average, spend less than sixty seconds a day talking to their children, and most of that time is spent pointing out negative behavior.

However, the opposite of criticism is one of the most powerful motivating forces available to parents—praise. It can be used in a variety of ways. You might give your children ribbons for good behavior. You could take a picture of your child doing something that you really appreciate and put it in an album or hang it on the wall for everyone to see.

Michael was extremely dejected after his first wrestling match. He had lost and as I walked over to him, I could see tears trickling down his face. "Michael, that was great," I told him, ignoring his tears. "Your opponent has wrestled for two years and just think, the score was only two to one after two rounds. Mike, how did you keep up with such an experienced wrestler?"

Mike looked up and said, "They cheated me. They should let me wrestle someone my own age and with the same experience." He paused and then added, "But I did put him down twice. Did you see that, Dad?" His face began to shine with excitement.

A year later, Mike had decided not to go out for the wrestling team again. But the coach told him, "That's too bad, Mike. You have very good moves and great potential in wrestling." The conversation between Mike and the coach lasted no longer than one minute, but Mike's outlook on wrestling changed completely in those few seconds. That night Mike told me his coach said he was good in wrestling and asked if he could go out for the team.

As parents, we can motivate our children through praise. Instead of mentioning to them the two things they did wrong today, let's talk to them about the ten things they did right. You'll be amazed at the results.

4. Expose Children to a Variety of Activities

Some of the motivational methods that we have discussed so far come from top university students and athletes who serve as staff members at Camp Kanakuk, a nationally renowned sports camp in Branson, Missouri. A top collegiate gymnast at the camp told me that her parents exposed her to a variety of sporting activities when she was young. They introduced her to different people, including a girl who was one of the top baton twirlers in the nation. This personal contact greatly influenced her. Her parents noticed her tremendous interest, paid for her to take lessons, and later she became one of the top twirlers in the nation.

The key is letting the child choose what he wants to do. Expose children to a variety of activities, then carefully watch their response and interest. Wait until they ask to become involved, then support them the best you can.

5. Expect Children to Do Things Right

When I was a youth director for three hundred junior high students in Southern California, I *expected* those kids to show up for activities on time, to leave activities at a certain time, to produce various programs, and to do them well. I demanded the best by my attitude, and I was always fascinated by the outstanding, creative jobs the students did with any assignment I gave them.

I have learned that children can sense whether or not you expect the best from them. If they sense that they can get away with doing less than their best, often they will do just that. If they sense that you expect that they cannot do any better, they may drop to your level of expectation. I also have seen children who were highly motivated when great things were expected of them. I still hear from some of those junior high students I worked with. They tell me that they remember many of the things they were taught because they were *expected* to learn and perform at a high level.

6. Believe Your Children Can Achieve Great Things

Imagine how little you could do if you were only able to use 8 percent of your brain. What things would you have to give up with a 92 percent loss?

Most of us would give up little or nothing at all. Most humans only use about 8 percent of their mental capacity. That helps me realize how much more we are capable of doing. So many of us limit ourselves because we don't believe we can accomplish great things. Doctors say that even if we lose large portions of our brain in an accident, it's amazing what we can relearn through rehabilitation—like learning to walk and talk all over again.

Many of us have watched the television specials where three-year-old children in Japan are trained to be concert violinists. The school attributed the seemingly remarkable feat to the fact that the tots *didn't know* that they weren't supposed to be capable of such a feat.

Our mental capacity is so powerful, but unfortunately we often talk ourselves out of achieving things that are possible. And we can talk our children out of doing what they could accomplish. "Well, I wouldn't try that," we say. "You could never be like that."

Given the right opportunity and encouragement, children can accomplish incredible things. What a miracle when Kari was willing to try basketball in her junior year of high school. She had never played any competitive sports. She didn't even understand the difference between defense and offense. But she tried out for the team and made it. In her first game a teammate threw her the ball and Kari ducked, thinking it was meant for someone else. *Why would anyone want to throw her the ball?* she thought. She was amazed at how much she learned and improved over the year. How thrilled we were when she made her first basket, and when she started for the first time. She was so motivated, she majored in basketball at her summer camp in order to be better prepared for her senior year.

If only we wouldn't limit ourselves. God has created each of us with tremendous potential no matter what level we're starting at. As parents, we must communicate to our children that if they want to give something a try, they should do it. Even strain for it. That is one reason why I ran my first marathon at the age of forty-two. I wanted to show my children that even an "old man" can do things that appear almost impossible.

7. Help Children Develop a More Positive Self-Image

A young boy who looked on the bright side of everything was given a ball and bat by his father. The father told the boy that when he got home from work, he would play a whole inning of baseball with his son. Sure enough, when the father arrived home, he took the son out in the back yard to see what he could do.

The little boy threw the ball up, swung the bat, and missed. "Strike one," the father said. The boy tossed the ball up again, swung, and missed. His father said, "Strike two." With more determination than ever, the boy threw the ball up a third time, swung a mighty swing, missed, and spun around, falling to the grass. His father said, "Strike three. You're out. What do you think?"

To this, the optimistic little boy answered, "Man, am I a good pitcher!"

A little positive thinking can go a long way in motivation. However, the lower a person's sense of self-worth, the less that person tends to accomplish both physically and mentally. A low self-image affects a child in virtually every aspect of life—dress, conversation, facial expression, future employment possibilities, even the future of his or her marriage.

In my counseling of young children, teenagers, and even adults, I have found that certain individuals seem to be programmed to fail. But I also have found there is something we can do to enhance a person's level of self-worth.

It's essential that we get our children involved in at least one activity where they can be successful. The more successful they become in various activities, the more it raises their self-worth. We should literally help them through at least one accomplishment, whether it is playing the trumpet, swimming, painting—anything. A child may say, "I can't do that." But we must find an activity that interests the child and then let the child know that we believe in him and that he is capable of accomplishing the task.

I can still recall when my high school basketball coach yelled at me one day, telling me I was too slow. It took me years to get rid of the memory of those words ringing in my ears, "Smalley, you're too slow." When I went out for track, it was difficult for me to run because I kept reminding myself I was too slow. My low self-image actually inhibited my ability to run.

8. Reward Your Children

Parents who were trying to get their daughter to stop sucking her thumb decided that they would give her a little surprise every time she went seven days without sucking her thumb. When she went thirty days without reverting to the habit, they gave her a bigger surprise. Rewards have a way of motivating and changing behavior and they can be particularly effective with young children.

Of course, we must be careful that children do not learn to expect a reward every time they accomplish something, such as routine chores around the home. Children need to learn that they are part of the family, and that everyone must work together to do things around the home without expecting any reward.

When Greg was fifteen, we discovered a very effective way to motivate him with major chores around the house. We simply placed a list of jobs to be done on the refrigerator with the wage amount written next to each job. These were jobs that were not part of our household chores, such as cleaning the garage, weeding the backyard and garden, and trimming the trees.

These jobs were open to any of our kids, but Greg would rush through as many as he could. It seldom seemed to bother our other two children that Greg earned the most money. But sometimes they would write their name next to a job signifying "Hands off! It's my job."

9. Use the Ol' You-Can't-Do-It-Can-You? Principle

What happens when someone tells you, "You probably don't have time for this," or "You can't do that, so I'll get someone in here who can"? If you're like me, such statements bother you, so you usually jump right in and tackle whatever has to be done. I've seen the same type of motivation work with my children. I'll say, "You probably can't handle this" or "I need someone *strong* to do this. Who can I call?" The result is that the children often get right in there and do the work.

The head of my college math department called me into her office one day and suggested I reconsider my decision to minor in math. "Gary, I know you're having a difficult time in calculus," she said, "I'm not sure you can handle the more advanced courses."

I boiled inside. "Hey, wait a minute," I thought. "Are you telling me that I can't handle math? I'll show you." I politely asked for a chance to prove I could do it. She gave me that chance and, motivated to study harder, I went on to graduate with a minor in math.

While this technique can be very successful, it must be used carefully. If used on a person with a low self-image or someone who has trouble believing in himself, you may only succeed in discouraging him further, or causing him to give up completely.

10. Expose Your Children to People You Admire

My children's inner motivation has greatly increased by exposing them to some very successful people. I've taught at several pro athletes' conferences and my children have come to know Bob Breunig, then an all-pro linebacker for the Dallas Cowboys. Bob and Mary Breunig can talk to our daughter Kari at any time about any subject and she absorbs every word they say. The same thing occurs with Steve Largent, the all-pro receiver for the Seattle Seahawks. Our children already know of his personal faith in Jesus Christ, and when Steve takes time to sit down with our kids and chat, they remember what he says and are motivated by his encouraging words. They never forget these special encounters.

Chuck Snyder, a very successful businessman from Seattle, visits with us a few times each year. When he does, he usually takes Kari out for lunch. Each time he brings her home, it is obvious that Chuck has influenced her life. He carefully listens to her, he praises her, and he really encourages her.

Not long ago, I asked Chuck to help Kari clarify her goals in life. When she came home from their luncheon, she enthusiastically announced that she now knew exactly what her goals were. The impact was tremendous. Not only did she set her own goals, but she began helping us all with our goals. Her motivation level tripled after this one meeting with Chuck. An evening spent dining and conversing with these quality people is such an inspirational experience for my children. I'm not sure I can have the same type of *instant* impact on them. There is no amount of money I could pay Bob Breunig, Steve Largent, and Chuck Snyder or any of the other leaders for what they have taught our kids.

You may be saying, "Well, that's fine for you who know some of these pro athletes and business leaders, but what about me? I don't know people like that."

You might be amazed how easy it is to rub shoulders with some of these outstanding people. Many of them want to share their lives with others, particularly young people. There are many influential people who would love to meet with your children, if only for a few minutes, so that some of the qualities that have made them successful could rub off on your children.

For example, consider inviting your pastor to dinner. Prepare for the time by asking him to share how he started in the ministry and let the discussion after dinner stimulate and inspire your children. Try the same experience with a businessman you admire or an outstanding leader in your community. Let these leaders know what your purpose is. Invite a retired missionary or statesman to your home. Take your children to visit a prison facility. Have them ask some of the administration officials why people generally get into trouble. Try to spend time with someone of influence at least two or three times each year.

11. Be Persistent

As a parent, I never realized how motivational persistence can be. But knowing this, we must be careful to not confuse persistence with nagging. Nagging is basically negative, a criticism of someone who is not acting in the manner in which we would like him to. Nagging usually reflects selfishness: "You haven't started to clean your room yet? You didn't do it yesterday. When are you ever going to get that room cleaned up?" The same topic and the same tone of voice, repeated over and over again, can cause resistance in children and can eventually lower their self-image. They begin to believe what they continually hear—"I can't do anything right."

Persistence, however, is when we creatively and enthusiastically bring up something that we believe to be important. We mention it in different ways and at different times and in different tones of voice.

Many years ago, I came to the conclusion that everyone in our family, myself included, was watching too much television. We were hooked. I was watching too much sports, the kids were watching too many cartoon programs, Norma was hooked on "soaps." I felt uneasy about the control television seemed to be having over our lives. Yet every time I mentioned the subject I was met with a howling reaction. I soon realized it was my fault. I was nagging with statements like, "Let's stop watching television," or, "This television set ought to go." These types of statements did nothing but create negative feelings and reactions to me. No one was motivated to change.

Once I realized what was happening, I decided to become persistent in a calm, loving way. I said things like, "I would really be grateful if we would cut back on the amount of time we spend in front of the television." Then for weeks I would say no more, because I didn't want to pressure anyone. A few weeks later, I made a statement about how much television we were watching, but again, I dropped the matter immediately.

To set an example, I began to spend less time in front of the "tube" myself. Often I'd read in another room. However, I was careful not to appear like I was superior, "Mr. Good Guy." I watched certain programs from time to time, but they were carefully selected. The most powerful statement I made, but didn't realize it until later, was after dinner one evening. I casually mentioned that it would really make me happy if someday we could live in a home where we didn't need a television because we enjoyed life so much without it. But I added, "That's probably not possible."

About a year later, Norma called me at work and mentioned that she and the kids had a surprise for me. When I opened the front door, the kids were all giggling and Norma was smiling. I took a glance around the house, but I couldn't figure out the surprise.

"Don't you see it, Dad?" the kids yelled. "You mean you really can't see it?" I couldn't see "it." Finally, they pointed toward the table where our television used to sit. The table was empty.

"What do you think, Dad?" they asked. I was speechless. They had put the television in the attic. They wanted to go "cold turkey" and forget about television, at least until they had gained control over their habit.

I was overwhelmed and immediately wanted to do something for them since they had changed their life pattern for me. I reached for my wallet and said, "Hey, let's all go out for dinner."

Their reaction astounded me again. They didn't want me to repay them. They didn't put the television away thinking they would get some reward. They told me they did it out of appreciation for my feelings. They did it out of love. I truly felt the love in what they had done. I never sensed that they were pressured into putting the set away. After a year or so we brought the television back, and we watch occasional programs together. But now television doesn't control our lives. We control the television.

---

12. Be Enthusiastic

Waking up in the morning has never been one of the highlights of my day. I'm one of those people who has to drag himself into the shower to wake up. Norma, on the other hand, is one of those people who wakes up every morning with a smile on her face. She starts singing as soon as her feet hit the floor. She even makes up her own songs. She is excited about seeing the new day, and her enthusiasm fills the whole house. Because of her attitude, everyone feels a lot better about getting up and going to school, to work, or doing whatever has to be done that day.

Being around an enthusiastic person is like being around someone who is laughing. It's contagious. Even when you don't know what someone is laughing about, you start grinning, then chuckling, and before long, you're laughing too.

I have found that, as a parent, if I am really excited about something, my family tends to get excited too.

One year I spent several months trying to convince my family to spend four weeks at an outstanding summer camp. But no one was even interested in hearing about it. Whenever I brought up the camp, I was met with disinterest. Later I met with a musical recording artist who had spent some time at the camp and he gave me all the enthusiasm I needed. That evening, I telephoned home and asked everyone to pick up an extension.

"Are you ready for this?" I asked enthusiastically. "Listen to this great place I just heard about." I went on to describe the camp in full. I told them in detail about all the fantastic activities available, the food, the lakes, slides, and giant water balloons. When I finished, I asked, "Have you ever heard of a place like this?" Their response was "No." They wanted to hear more. Then I told them it was the same place I had been talking about. We all signed up to go that night. Enthusiasm is contagious!

---

13. Develop Strong Inner Convictions

I believe it is very important that parents periodically evaluate their convictions. What do we believe is right for the family, and what do we believe is wrong? What is right for our children and what is wrong for them? What does the Bible say is proper behavior, and what is behavior that contradicts God's standards?

The average woman probably has no idea how tremendously influential and motivating she can be if she has deep convictions. The Old Testament speaks of a "virtuous" woman. It says that when you find a woman like that, you have found a woman more precious than jewels. In the Hebrew language, a "virtuous" woman was one who had strong convictions and who had influence because of her convictions.

If a woman believes it is very important for children to learn communication skills, for example, she will tend to spend time gathering information on how to teach such skills to her children. She will be *alert* to anything that will help her attain her goal. Her conviction that it's important for her children to know these skills greatly increases the likelihood that they will learn them.

This is a major reason why children learn from their parents nonverbally. When parents approve of what their children are doing, they get excited, and it shows in their eyes, their facial expressions, their nonverbal actions. Our children understand this nonverbal communication, and they tend to get excited, too. When we are displeased, we display negative facial reactions such as frowning and tightening our lip muscles.

Nonverbal communication can be a very motivating factor for children because they are alert to facial expressions and body language. The stronger our convictions, the more our nonverbal language will communicate those convictions.

How many people have had a lasting influence on your life? Think about it. They probably were people with strong convictions. The same is true for us. The stronger our convictions, the greater our influence on the people around us.

When talking with some of the Dallas Cowboys football players, I have learned that former Coach Tom Landry had very strong convictions about how to play football. He had his ideas about how to prepare the offense and defense. The players say they could feel his convictions. Even the television audience could sense his seriousness as the camera scanned the sidelines on Sunday afternoons.

14. Use Contracts

Chapter 4 covered how we involved our children in drawing up our contracts. We have found it very motivating for a child to conform to a contract that he helped prepare. We have watched our children make adjustments in their lives because they have agreed to terms of the contract. For example, Greg decided on his own to change schools, with our blessing, after we had written out a contract that outlined the major reasons children attend school. After he saw the finished contract, he suggested a change. The school he was attending didn't include some of the important areas we had written into the contract. Here's a sample of that contract.

A school should include:

- activities that involve the whole family
- students that I can develop close friendships with because we have many things in common
- an atmosphere where students can pray and interact about their faith in God

There were also several other factors involved. More items were added to this list by our other children. Then together we all chose the school we felt came the closest to our contract on schooling.

15. Encouragement from Peers

When Greg started attending a new high school, he wanted to try out for the basketball team. But he held himself back because he didn't think he was good enough. During the year, he ate lunch with some of the players and shot some baskets with them after school. When the players told Greg he should try out for the team, their encouragement was just the motivation he needed. He did try out the following year and made the team.

Then there was a thirty-second, life-changing experience for Kari. Kari almost dropped out of basketball after practice one evening. I went into the gym to pick her up, and as we walked off the court she announced, "That's it, I've had it. I just can't play basketball!" The front gates were locked so we had to walk around the school and in front of the boys' locker area. When the boys' team saw Kari, they were so excited about her trying basketball that they were patting her on the back and saying things like, "Hey, Kari, go for it!" Thirty seconds later as we were driving home she said, "Dad, I really like basketball. In fact, I can't remember now why I wanted to quit."

16. Create a Positive Successful Experience

Many times we fear that if our children get involved in a certain activity they will fail because they lack some basic skills or knowledge. We have this inner sense that tells us, "I don't think they can handle this," or, "I don't think they're ready for this."

In such cases, I believe it is appropriate for us, as parents, to intervene to help our children gain the *knowledge* or *skills* that they need before attempting an activity that appears to be certain failure.

17. Wait for the Children to Act on Their Own

From time to time, parents must "light a fire" under their children. But there are also times that we need to wait for them to see what we see. We have found, for example, that it occasionally is very motivating to allow our children to let their rooms become extremely messy. Eventually, they get upset with the contrast between their messy rooms and the other orderly rooms in the house. Before long, they become tired of the mess and the room gets cleaned. If a child has never lived with the mess and disorder, it's harder to appreciate order.

It is true, of course, that some children will never clean their rooms without direction from a parent. But the idea is to give a child time to initiate the desired behavior himself.

18. Accountability and Support

When we share our goals with others, whether with family members or friends, we become increasingly motivated to attain these goals because we know we will be held accountable. There is a great deal of discomfort associated with knowing that we have not attained our goals, and that others we care about know this, too. This feeling of accountability, when coupled with support, is a tremendous motivating factor.

When we get discouraged or disappointed that we haven't progressed as far as we would like, the support of our family and friends can generate energy within us. This energy drives us to go forward, even when many times it seems easier to give up. Just having someone say, "How are you doing?" or "You can do it," is tremendously energizing.

19. Tender Touching and Listening

Children can become discouraged for a number of reasons—an injury, lack of progress, knowing there is always someone who is just a little bit better. Any of these reasons can make a child lose his energy. The easiest way for children to regain that energy is for someone who cares to put his arm around them, touch their hand, or pat them on the back. When someone really listens to how they are feeling, it pumps energy into them and motivates them to pick up at the point where they otherwise would have quit in discouragement.

While training for my first marathon, I was running on the shoulder of a major freeway in Portland, Oregon. Lost in my thoughts, I was startled by a motorist shouting at me with his fist clenched in what appeared to be a hostility toward runners. Then I noticed his smile and heard him shout, "Go for it! It's great to see you out here! You can do it!" Tears came to my eyes as he drove off and a burst of energy surged through my body. I literally bounced down the highway. Support like that is highly motivating.

When a child is discouraged, try the touching and listening approach: "Tell me about it," you say as you put your arm around the child. "You're really hurting today, aren't you? Do you want to talk about it?" or "I know it's hard, but you can do it."

As you touch your child, you are not only sharing with him, you are energizing him. You are not pitying him, as that can bring you both down. What you are doing is touching to listen, to understand.

After trying this, let some time go by before you start telling your child how to get back on course. Sometimes we try to get everything corrected too quickly and we drain the child's energy. Give him time. You'll be surprised at just how energizing touching and listening alone can be.

With any motivational tool, we must remember that lasting motivation must come from *within* the child. Motivational techniques such as coercion, threats, and bribing are only temporary. Our job as parents is to help our children set goals and believe in them enough to see them accomplished, and whenever possible, use our resources to help them achieve those goals.

8

The Secret of a Close-Knit Family

- Six Characteristics of a Close-Knit Family
- Sharing Life Experiences Together
- Dealing with Difficulties in a Positive Manner
- Three Practical Ways to Share Life Together

*T*HE MUSCLES OF MY left thigh were beginning to ache. Pain shot from my knee as I pounded past the fifteen-mile marker. I had been running for two hours, and so far the enthusiasm of this being my first marathon had kept me going. But now, doubts caused by this week-old muscle pull began to creep into my mind as several runners passed me. I started to wonder if I would even make it to the finish line.

The faces of the crowd lining Scottsdale Road were a blur. I was only vaguely aware of encouraging shouts from spectators. Then the words "Way to go, Dad!" broke through the haze. My entire family—Norma, Kari, Greg, and Michael—were screaming and waving at me. As I passed them, they joined in step with me and their enthusiasm filled me with a new surge of energy. Norma and Kari ran a few steps, then said they'd meet me at the finish line, but Michael and Greg wanted to keep me company.

The pain in my leg faded as I enjoyed this special moment with my boys. I was too tired to say anything as we ran, but their company made me feel great. After three more miles, Michael, who was only nine years old, was obviously too tired to continue. I left him at a corner and told him to wait for his mother to pick him up.

Nearly two hours later, I finished the race with Greg not far behind. Exhilarated by my achievement, I claimed my T-shirt and certificate and accepted congratulations and hugs from Norma and Kari. It took me a few moments to notice that their faces were filled with concern. "I'm feeling fine," I told them, but that wasn't the problem.

Norma took me by the arm and pulled me away from our two children. "We've lost Michael," she said. "He's been lost for over two hours."

I started to think back to the thousands of people lining the streets and immediately was concerned about our little blond, blue-eyed boy. I recalled newspaper stories about a child kidnapper and molester in the area and began to wonder if Michael might have become the next victim.

We headed over to the nearest police car and filed a missing person report. As I finished the description, Greg asked if he could talk to me alone. He looked right in my eyes and said very tenderly, "Dad, if we don't find Michael, can I have his bedroom?"

Greg has always had the ability to calm us in the midst of tense situations. However, I was glad Norma didn't hear this comment, for she probably would not have taken it with such amusement. But now I was relaxed. A few minutes later, Michael found us, having walked in with some runners who were late finishing the race.

That evening, we were able to laugh together at the whole incident, and I realized that this was another example of the secret to our close-knit family. This secret is a factor common to every close-knit family that I have observed.

Dr. Nick Stinnett of the University of Nebraska supervised a study of several intimate families nationwide, families that had a great deal of happiness and parent/child satisfaction. For the purpose of the study, he focused only on families with a husband, wife, and at least one child living at home. However, the close-knit secret also applies to single-parent families or any small group for that matter.

Six Characteristics of a Close-Knit Family

Dr. Stinnett discovered that there were six consistent characteristics among these families. First, family members expressed a high degree of appreciation for each other. Several families even created projects around the house to stimulate praise. For example, one household of five had an event Dr. Stinnett called "bombardment." Every few months, the family members would meet and each would spend one minute praising every other member of the family. Sometimes the sessions were a little embarrassing, but they certainly were stimulating and inspirational.

Second, these families spent a great deal of time together. They genuinely enjoyed being together. They *worked* at doing things that involved every member of the family.

The third characteristic was that these successful families had good communication patterns. They spent time talking to each other. The key to effective communication, according to Dr. Stinnett, was that members listened and worked at understanding each other.

Fourth, the families had a strong sense of commitment. They actively promoted one another's happiness and welfare. An example of this commitment was in how these families handled themselves when things became too hectic, causing them to spend less time together. In one home, each family member made a list of his or her individual activities. The things he or she really didn't want to do or that weren't very important were scratched to provide more time for family involvement.

The fifth common ingredient was a high degree of religious orientation. These families participated in church activities together. They were committed to a spiritual lifestyle.

The final characteristic was that they had an ability to deal with crises in a positive manner. This isn't to say that they enjoyed crises, but even in the worst situations they were able to find some positive element, no matter how tiny, and focus on that.

For the remainder of this book, I want to focus on two of these factors, which I feel are the most important. Together they form the secret to developing intimate families:

1. Spending time together lays the foundation for close-knit families.
2. Close-knit families have the ability to deal with crises in a positive manner.

1. Sharing Life Experiences Together

Several years ago I used to speak to groups of four hundred to two thousand people in fifty cities annually. I began to notice that certain families in the audiences experienced unusually happy interaction among themselves. I was intrigued by this and began to do a study. I would interview the wife, husband, and children separately. Each person was asked the same question: What do you believe is the main reason you are all so close and happy as a family?

What I found amazed me. Each family member gave basically the same answer: "We do a lot of things together."

I found that these families also had one particular activity in common—camping. A minister in South Dakota echoed this idea. He told me that when he has asked each of his children separately what was the best thing they had done as a family, each one answered "camping." I'm not necessarily advocating camping. We've camped as a family for over fifteen years and we've found that *camping* is not the secret! But I believe the secret to being a close-knit family almost always can be found *in* camping.

One reason our family is so close is that we maximize our togetherness and minimize our times apart. That's not to say that we can't be alone as individuals. I work every day. My wife operates our office. Our children pursue their school or career interests. My wife enjoys swimming and going to the gym alone. I enjoy reading a book or watching a television program by myself, and I love running alone. All of us go our separate ways almost every day.

But for the most part, we try to discipline ourselves as a family to organize times when we are all together. For example, every Friday night is family night when the kids are home. We also share our church life together and visit friends' homes together. We share the entire summer together; my family travels with me to various seminars where I speak, and we plan a special vacation. We spend two weeks together at Christmas, another at Easter, and take weekends for various special activities throughout the year. Because of my profession, I am able to take off with the family for extended periods of time, but all-day outings provide the same opportunities for closeness. It just takes a little creativity to find fun things that the whole family will enjoy. But it is very possible!

The principle is also true for husbands and wives without their children. Close-knit marriages result from partners sharing numerous experiences. One summer, Norma asked me if I would take her through a wild animal park. I accepted the suggestion with enthusiasm and borrowed a car at the camp where I was speaking. When we arrived at the park, we were given a brochure that told about the animals and explained that if anything happened to the car, we were to honk the horn and a friendly ranger would come to the rescue.

About halfway through the park, our little convertible overheated. We pulled off the road and I honked the horn. No friendly ranger came to our rescue, but several wild burros wandered over and tried nibbling the convertible top. I honked again and in the rearview mirror I saw a herd of buffalo approach us. Within moments, we were surrounded.

Norma wanted me to honk the horn again, but I was afraid for fear the animals might stampede and crush the car. One of the buffaloes bent down on my side of the car and pushed his head against the window. His nostrils were steaming the window while his big, brown eyes looked to see if we had anything to eat. Norma and I held hands, trying to comfort each other. I couldn't stand to look, but kept asking, "Is he gone yet?" "No," said Norma. "Will you please honk the horn?"

"I can't. Just listen to him breathe."

"That's not him breathing. That's me!"

Gradually, the buffalo lost interest in us and moved on. Forty-five minutes after we had pulled off the road, we were able to start the car and drive through the rest of the park. It is experiences like that which we have shared as a couple or family that provide great memories. Common experiences draw people together.

Professional athletes tell me the hardest part of retirement is that they miss the camaraderie of their team. That unique bond is built through hard training and competition together over months and years. That closeness should be a part of every family.

One summer my sons and I went fishing in Washington. We found an incredible waterfall dropping into a beautiful pool. Having fished since I was in the third grade, I knew exactly how to catch the trout in this water. Michael and Greg weren't experienced, but they insisted on preparing their own lines. Greg did everything wrong. His leader was too long and thick. His hook was too large and his one egg didn't cover it. I had everything just right—a two pound leader, four feet long with a small hook. Although it was difficult, I left the boys and crawled around underneath the waterfall instead of staying at the front part of the pool, where there was no possibility of catching a fish.

I had cast my line and was trying to be perfectly still when I heard Greg scream. He had hooked a twenty-five to thirty inch steelhead. I, the "expert" fisherman in the family, had only caught one steelhead in my entire life. Greg, with his sloppily rigged line, had done the impossible.

I tried to scramble over to Greg to help him reel in his catch. But the rocks were too slippery, so I tried to coach him. He was screaming and reeling in his line too fast. I tried to tell him to slow down, but he was too excited to listen. When the fish reached the bank and Greg was ready to net it, the hook broke away from the line because he hadn't tied the hook properly. The fish flipped back into the water and swam away. Greg threw his pole up the hill, fell on the ground, and began to sob uncontrollably.

My heart sank for him. We both had visions of mounting this catch. In the years since that experience Greg has never hooked another fish like it. We still look back and grieve over it, though now we can also see the humor of it.

Another incident that brought our family closer together occurred in the mountains of California's Sequoia National Park. A small stream running over a large piece of granite about two city blocks long had created a natural, giant water slide. At the end was a dropoff into two pools of water. The boys and I immediately gave the slide a try.

After we'd each taken several turns, Greg asked if I thought he could slide down and make a little turn into a smaller pool. I looked at the slant and the angle and said, "Sure, you can do that." He took off and picked up more speed than we expected. He flew off the edge of a six-foot cliff, but from where Norma was seated, it looked like he had dropped off the mountain. He fell into a ravine, hit the granite abutment, and rolled twenty or thirty feet down into a large pool. When he hit the water, he was motionless.

Michael and I stood frozen in fear. Kari and Norma screamed that I had killed Greg. Finally I rushed down to him and heard him mumble about how his back felt broken. I was amazed he was even alive. After about twenty minutes, Greg was able to get up and walk slowly up the mountain. Within an hour, he was fine.

That experience did something to us as a family. First, *we were together.* Being together provides the basis for shared experiences that become precious memories. Second, facing difficulties draws a family much closer together. This experience particularly made us appreciate being together as we were forced to entertain the thought of life without Greg. The memories of being together on vacation when things went wrong or when we shared adventure is what *knits* the family together. As you read on, you'll see more clearly how a family becomes close-knit when it learns to deal with difficult situations.

2. Dealing with Difficulties in a Positive Manner

When we go camping, we can usually count on something going wrong: rain, mosquitoes, running out of gas, a flat tire, losing the traveler's checks, forgetting the main ingredient to a meal. When families share such conflicts, it can draw them closer together.

We have spent an enormous amount of time together as a family, and not all of our times are difficult. Many times everything runs smoothly. But when something does happen— something caused by an outside force beyond our control—we can recognize and accept it as a major factor that will draw us together.

Confronting such a crisis doesn't usually draw us together immediately. Frequently there is a lot of stress. We can easily become irritable and upset with each other. An important point to remember is that if conflict comes from within the family, if I get harsh and angry and yell at the kids or my wife or they yell at me, that may separate us, because it violates the principles we shared in chapter 1. A certain amount of anger or stress is natural in a conflict or mishap. But family members need to recognize this and not close each other's spirits. If the conflict has come from outside the family and we have not offended each other, we simply realize that in a few days or a few weeks we will look back on the experience and usually, in laughter, see how it has drawn us closer together.

We had an incredibly unifying experience one summer at a camp where I taught in southern Wisconsin. Kari and Greg assisted in the child-care section, teaching the younger kids of the parents who were attending the conference. After the first day, Kari told me, "I can't stand this camp. I want to stay in the cabin with you and Mom." Norma and I gave in and said she could stay with us, not realizing that it was against the rules for the children to stay in our unit.

The director of the camp section in which Kari and Greg were working learned about the problem and talked with Kari for a couple of hours. Finally, she asked Kari if she would be willing to give God a chance to change the circumstances and make the camp meaningful for her. Reluctantly, Kari agreed to do so.

The very next day, the whole experience turned around for her. She met one of the sharpest fellows at camp, and they became good friends during the week. She also developed close friendships with several of the girls, and she had a great experience teaching the younger kids. She learned a valuable lesson: that God can change circumstances, even in the most difficult situations.

We still laugh about that camp experience and are amazed at the complete turnaround in Kari's attitude. She saved her money to fly back to that camp again—the very camp she had wanted to leave.

After understanding the closeness that sharing difficulties can bring, it is almost disappointing when everything goes right. If something does go wrong, we realize it can be exciting, as well as stressful and discouraging. We know the benefit will emerge a few days or weeks later.

This second part of the secret to being close-knit is somewhat like a foxhole experience. Each man together fighting a common enemy will tend to be close the remaining years of their lives. How does this work? Pleasant or unpleasant memories lock us together. They provide common ground for conversation. Imagine being stuck on an elevator with five other people for two days. Each of you will experience common hunger, thirst, cramped conditions, fear, uncertainty, and so on. If reunion occurs several years later, all six of you will share and laugh about your unique experience, "Remember what happened the second day?" "Oh, yeah. That was terrible!" The more challenging, dangerous, and adventurous the experiences, the closer we tend to be with those with whom we share them.

It's very important to be together at various times throughout the year as families, so let's discuss some practical and meaningful ways of actually being together.

Three Practical Ways to Share Life Together

1. Schedule Regular Times Together

Because there is no way that we can effectively develop deep relationships with our children unless we spend meaningful time together, parents need to set aside a few minutes each month to schedule family time.

Spending time together is a decision that must be made and kept. There may be times when we don't want to be with the rest of the family or we feel we don't have time. That is when it is necessary to evaluate how we spend our time and what areas we can eliminate in order to schedule time with the family.

Sometimes we will plan a trip as a family and the day before one of the children will say he or she doesn't want to go. But because we already have agreed together that we will go, we do. As parents we have agreed to avoid saying, "I don't want to go," or "There are too many things to do. Let's plan this another time." Broken promises are a major factor in closing the spirits of our children. We must be careful to follow through when we plan times together.

2. Discover Each Person's Most Meaningful Activity

Once parents have agreed that it is important to spend time together as a family, they should discuss it with their children. If their spirits are closed, they may resist. But most children will say they would like to do things together as a family.

After each family member agrees to the concept of togetherness, the parents should ask each child to list the activities he would enjoy most. You might use the zero to ten scale, with ten being the most fun and fulfilling.

When we tried this in our home, Norma said her "ten" vacation would be at a place where there was shopping, sightseeing, a beach, and cute restaurants. Kari said almost the same thing. Greg wanted a place where he could fish, hike, and scuba dive. Michael's answer was almost the same, except he included playing ball. I said basically the same things as the boys.

We put our lists together and began to discuss places that were financially feasible where we could accommodate all of our "tens." We chose Catalina Island, just off the coast of Long Beach, California. The island has cute shops and places to eat. It has a beach and beautiful water. The boys and I can go hiking, snorkeling, scuba diving, and fishing. We went there for three or four days, two consecutive summers, and had a fantastic time together.

Below is a chart that might help you as a family nail down some specific activities or experiences that you could share together.

What Activities Can We Share
Together in Life?

- Our Church Life

    study classes

    prayer groups

    when?

    where?

    how often?

    witnessing opportunities (mission trips)

    when?

    where?

    how often?

    helping those in our community

    when?

    where?

    how often?

- Trips or Vacations

    What would my dream vacation be?

    What would it include?

What are two of my favorite activities? Write an actual picture in detail of one of these activities.

What is one activity in life that I fear or feel inadequate to face? Ask family members to help me overcome this area of fear.

3. Design Togetherness Times with Each Family Member in Mind

After learning everyone's wishes for family activities and experiences, families can design a trip, vacation, or special outing that meets the needs of all family members.

Some of our family trips were disastrous because I insisted that we travel to the Colorado mountains and camp in the wilderness next to a beautiful stream—miles from any shopping centers or restaurants. It wasn't long before we discovered that to have a meaningful family time, each person must be included—especially Mom. I could find that stream up in the mountains near a cute little village that Norma could walk to in a couple of minutes.

Our family spends one or two months every summer at the sports camp in Branson, Missouri. I'm involved in teaching and counseling while the children participate in the camp activities and are trained to be counselors in the future. There is incredible fishing and shopping nearby. It has everything we could want.

One summer, Michael and I experienced a special time at this sports camp. He had one last event in which to win a letter, archery. He was down to his last arrow and needed seven points, which meant a bull's-eye or the circle next to it. Some of his arrows had missed the entire target and landed in the woods, so he was quite discouraged. I had done well in my college archery class and was trying to encourage him and show him what to do. I felt bad for him, though, because I had this inner feeling that after all his effort, he wouldn't get the letter.

Michael pulled the arrow back, then stopped, relaxing the string. He was very nervous. I patted him on the shoulders, told him to take it easy, and said, "I know you can do it." He drew back the arrow, put it against his cheek, and let go. Bull's-eye! We both jumped up, yelled for joy, and hugged each other.

That kind of experience forms the very fiber that weaves a family into a close-knit unit. But it doesn't happen unless we recognize the value of being together and schedule times with each member's interests in mind.

Resources

Barnard, Charles P., and Ramon G. Corrales. *The Theory and Technique of Family Therapy*. Springfield, Ill.: Charles C. Thomas, 1979.

Brandt, Henry, with Phil Landrum. *I Want to Enjoy My Children*. Grand Rapids, Mich.: Zondervan Publishing House, 1975.

Campbell, D. Ross. *How to Really Love Your Child*. Wheaton, Ill.: Victor Books, 1977.

Coles, Robert. "Our Self-Centered Children l md l Heirs of the `Me' Decade." *U.S. News & World Report*. 25 February 1980. Pp. 80f.

Drescher, John M. *Seven Things Children Need*. Scottdale, Pa.: Herald Press, 1976.

Ginott, Haim. *Between Parent and Child: New Solutions to Old Problems*. New York: MacMillan Company, 1965.

Hendricks, Howard G. *Heaven Help the Home*. Wheaton, Ill.: Victor Books, 1973.

Stinnett, Nick. *In Search of Strong Families*. Lincoln, Neb., Department of Human Development and the Family, University of Nebraska, 1980.

Wright, H. Norman. *The Family That Listens*. Wheaton, Ill.: Victor Books, 1978.

Wright, H. Norman, and Rex Johnson. *Communication: Key to Your Teens*. Irvine, Calif.: Harvest House, 1978.

An interview with R. Armond Nicholi, Psychiatric Professor at Harvard Medical School, February 1982.

LOVE IS A DECISION

GARY SMALLEY
WITH JOHN TRENT

Library of Congress Cataloging-in-Publication Data

Smalley, Gary.
    Love is a Decision.

      1. Marriage—United States. 2. Marriage—Religious aspects—Christianity. I. Trent, John T.
II. Title.
HQ734.S686   1989   646.7'8   89–22414
ISBN 0-8499-0721-7
ISBN 0-8499-3362-5
ISBN 0-8499-4268-3 (pbk)
Printed in the United States of America

The material in this book is based largely on the "Love Is a Decision" Seminar, and its success is due largely to the efforts of Terry Brown, our national seminar director.

This book is gratefully dedicated to

Terry

Without knowing it, thousands of couples' lives have been enriched by his years of faithful, loyal service in coordinating the many details for the seminar. We thank God for this special servant and for the unique way he enriches everyone who knows him.

Contents

1

Planning on a Great Marriage?

It was just turning dark when I arrived at the home of a family I was staying with in Tampa, Florida. Exhausted after speaking at a seminar all day, I was looking forward to a restful, uneventful night.

I knew my hosts only slightly, but they lived in a beautiful home in a peaceful neighborhood. But then again, looks can be deceiving. In fact, I would never have expected either event that happened to me over the next few hours.

As I walked up to the front door, I reached into one pocket, then another. That's when I realized I'd left my key inside in my room, and I was locked out of the house. Ringing the doorbell wouldn't have done any good. My hosts had told me they wouldn't be home until late. So I decided to go around to the back yard and see if by chance a window or door had been left open.

As I rounded the back corner, I froze in terror. From out of the dark, a huge black form was racing toward me at breakneck speed. It was the biggest dog I'd ever seen in my life!

Ten feet from where I stood petrified with fear, the dog left the ground with a tremendous leap—and I knew I'd soon be on my way to the hospital. In milli-seconds I'd feel the pain of his teeth tearing into me.

I closed my eyes and braced myself for the collision . . . but nothing happened. At first I thought, *He's toying with me. This dog knows I'm about to die, and he wants to watch me suffer!* But after a moment more, I finally built up enough courage to open my eyes. Unbelievably, he was sitting happily at my feet, his big friendly tongue hanging out and his tail wagging. He was actually whimpering for me to reach down and pet him.

After my heart rate dropped from triple to double digits, I checked the house only to find it securely locked. It was getting late, and I was worn out. I was faced with either camping out on the back porch with my new-found canine friend or thinking of some alternative. That's when an idea hit me.

Another family I'd been introduced to lived in Tampa. Perhaps I could stay with them until my hosts returned. So I jumped into my car and drove across town to John and Kay Hammer's stately home—and into an even more surprising situation.

As I knocked on the door, I was greeted by Kay. "Hi, Gary," she said, flashing her million-dollar smile. She makes anyone she meets feel special and important. I explained my situation to her and John, and they insisted that I stay at their house for the night.

I met their charming children as they piled out of their rooms. Finally, after a little small talk in the living room, we all retired for the night.

My body must have known that my plane didn't leave until the next evening, because it overruled the alarm clock, and I slept late the next morning. By the time I got up, showered, and dressed, the kids and John had already headed off to school and work. Only Kay was left in the kitchen to play short-order cook for her unexpected house guest.

I'd already received one shock when Godzilla the Dog leaped at me, but little did I know I was about to be hit with a second shock that was even more disturbing. As we sat at the kitchen table, the smile quickly fell from her face and down into her teacup. She sat there, her head bowed, staring blankly at the table top. With very little prompting, Kay began pouring out an all-too-familiar story.

For years, this wife had felt neglected. Her husband gave the best of his week to his thriving business, and she and the children were left with emotional left-overs on the weekends. All the family responsibilities for raising four youngsters fell on her shoulders, and she was exhausted from putting out fires between her husband and the children.

At times she would plead with John to work on their disintegrating relationship, but her cries fell on deaf ears. Too consumed with building up his career, he didn't have time to worry about the way his marriage and family were breaking down.

Kay suffered through the "domestic" neglect that many wives do, but with one added heartache. She was a Christian with a genuine faith, but she knew that when her husband went to church it was more for social contacts, not spiritual growth.

Slowly, as the years went by, his insensitivity had eaten its way to the very core of their relationship—and had begun to poison her heart.

The Ruin of a National Treasure

As I sat with Kay that day, I felt like I was watching the wreck of the Exxon tanker, *Valdez.* Here was a beautiful home and a stunning family. Yet with disharmony and heartache steering at the helm, their family relationships had been guided right onto the rocks, just as that ill-fated oil tanker had been.

Day after day, the poison of a ruptured marriage poured onto their lives, covering the natural beauty of a loving family with three inches of sludge. They had tried to clean up some of the disaster (which their relationship had become), but in many ways the damage was already done. The kids were feeling the tensions at home and beginning to reflect it in their lives, and any interest they might have shown in attending church was now falling dormant.

Kay had been listening to her friends—even to Christian friends—who told her, "Quit being a *doormat,* Kay. You've already gone through too much. *God will forgive you.* Get out of this mess of a marriage, and try again with someone else." She'd even gone to her pastor at the time and to a "Christian" psychologist. Both had told her that *with her husband* she could never hope to get the ship off the rocks—their marriage was dead in the water and unsalvageable.

"I'm not rushing you to leave, and I hadn't planned on telling you any of this," she said to me at the breakfast table, embarrassed by the tears that quickly came to her eyes. "But when the children come home from school today, I'm leaving my husband. We're all moving out. . . . "

I'd like to say that John and Kay's story is unusual, but, unfortunately, it isn't. In working with couples and families for almost two decades, I've seen many such disasters. They have ruined our greatest natural treasure—our families.

From every appearance, a few rags or suction hoses wouldn't begin to repair the damage that had taken place in the Hammers' relationship. In fact, the more I listened, the more I could see why certain "advisors" had told her the landscape of their life would never be the same. From a human standpoint, it certainly did look like the better option might be to pack up and move on than try to rebuild the impossible. But God allowed something miraculous to happen over the next few hours with Kay that transformed her relationship with her husband—and my life as well.

It's been almost fourteen years since that fateful morning at John and Kay's home. And today the Hammers are not only some of our closest friends, but members of our National Board! Their relationship has changed from oil-soaked blackness to a crystal-clear reflection of Christ's love. Even more, their deep friendship and love for each other is a testimony in itself and has turned back many, many couples from the brink of divorce.

Without a clear action plan that points the way to deep waters of intimacy, and avoids the shallow rocks of marital ruin, we're inviting heartache into our homes.

What brought about the change in their lives? That's what this book is all about. The very verses and concepts I first scratched out on a sheet of notebook paper for Kay that day are the same things I've seen God use in the lives of hundreds over the years. I'll be sharing biblical principles that when applied to a relationship—even one washed up and on the rocks—can turn a mess back into a treasure. Learning specific directions for steering clear of danger can also keep a strong marriage or family from running aground. But change only begins at the place we all must start—at the same point the Hammers had to come to.

Planning to Have a Great Marriage and Family?

Whether it's a family, a school, a company, or a sports team, we cannot possibly guide our relationships safely through the waters of our day without a plan. That's the starting point. Without a clear plan of action that points out the way to the deep waters of intimacy and avoids the shallow rocks of marital ruin we're inviting heartache into our homes. It's critical that we clearly plan our lives and not let chance set their course.

There may have been a time in an earlier day when society itself delineated boundaries clearly enough to substitute for a clear purpose at home. But that's simply not true today. We're asking for a natural disaster of our own if we don't have a specific sense of direction for our families. And that's what this book is all about. It's our best effort to give you a workable, biblically based plan of action for building loving, lasting relationships.[1]

Now we know that asking you to adopt a "plan" of action for your home sounds a great deal like work, but we can assure you that the effort spent on steering your relationship into safe waters is far less work than trying to get it off the rocks would be.

Can having a clear plan of action really bring that much change? In one case, taking the time to learn and practice a plan of action turned a group of defeated individuals into an undefeated team:

The Man Who Made History

When our good friend, Norm Evans, was picked by an expansion National Football League team, they were mired in last place. The owner knew a change was needed, so he hired a new head coach. But that was nothing new. He had already hired several coaches, and hadn't changed their fortunes yet. With the way the team was currently playing, this young "upstart" he'd picked would probably be history himself within a year.

As it turned out, this particular coach *would* go into the NFL history books—but not as a failure. Today, even with ups and downs, he has been in the league longer than any other active coach—and there's a reason. He built his men into a champion team by following a clear plan of action.

The year prior to this coach's arrival, the team had a record of three wins and ten losses. Morale was down, motivation was low, and the players' efforts on the field were lack-luster. Norm remembers standing along the sideline with the other players, wondering how they were going to lose each game they played.

Then the new coach arrived in town, and he wasted no time in getting down to business. His first official act was to call a team meeting—and it was one the players would never forget.

He walked into the room, folded his arms, and stood silently in front of them for several minutes. The moments seemed to stretch into hours. He looked from player to player, and from eye to eye. Finally, he spoke in a clear, convincing voice and said, "Men, you're going to be champions of the NFL."

There was an awkward moment of silence in the room. Several of the veterans had to lower their heads to keep their smiles from breaking into laughter. *Sure, coach . . .* they thought. *Anything you say. . . .* But inside they were thinking, *Who's this guy kidding? We've always been losers in this league. Champions? We're not even challengers!* Then the coach laid out the reason he felt certain the team would be successful—a clear plan of action.

"First," he said, "we're going to give you a great game plan each week that works. I'll guarantee that you'll know more about the person you're playing against than anyone except his wife. *Second,* you're going to *practice* that plan until it becomes a natural part of you. *Third,* you're going to *learn the game plan and practice it—and win."*

Bit by bit, the next season saw the wisdom of his strategy unfold. The players learned a specific plan and then practiced it over and over until they felt a confidence in themselves and between each other that they'd never had before. Now they stood on the sidelines wondering how they were going to *win* games— not lose them. In just one short year, they were a different football team. How different?

It was exactly the reverse of the year before; they came out of the blue to win ten games and lose only three. And the next two seasons, the Miami Dolphins, under head coach Don Shula, won the 1972 and 1973 Super Bowls as the best team in pro football.

"That's a great story if you're a football team," you may say, "but the only similarity our marriage has to an NFL team is that we're always taking cheap shots at each other!" Can having a "plan" really make that much of a difference in a marriage relationship—or even with our children? It did for John and Kay.

Kay Hammer didn't know much about the pro football team in nearby Miami when we sat down that morning, but she still had something in common with them. For years, she and John had let circumstances and the emotions of the moment call all the plays in their relationship—and their lives were on the brink of a last place finish as a result. Yet like this pro team, things started to turn around in their lives once they began to follow a clear plan of action and to practice it consistently.

That morning at the Hammers' breakfast table, I scribbled out for her several biblical principles that I was only then beginning to understand and apply in my own home. The scriptural guidelines that broke through that day and gave Kay hope are the very same ones I'll be sharing with you in this book.

A Marriage Mended . . .

By applying these principles, Kay was able to see her marriage turn around in as dramatic a fashion as I've ever witnessed. Her marriage was doomed for the ashheap of divorce, but because of her willingness to follow a biblically based plan, it's alive, active, and growing today. The man she once couldn't wait to get away from is now her best friend . . . and the one with whom she wants to spend the rest of her life.

The secret doesn't just belong to John and Kay—it's available for everyone who desires to have a strong family and a fulfilling marriage. I look forward to the years ahead and get excited about what can happen in families all over this country. I'd love to see hundreds of thousands of husbands, wives, and children make a commitment to do whatever it takes to honor God by following a clear plan for family intimacy. I believe it can happen; in fact, that's the whole goal of our ministry! One of the places you can start is by putting a biblical plan for relationships into action.

To keep our relationships off the rocks, we need to follow two essential steps: we must gain *knowledge* and then *skills* at applying what we've learned. The more we *learn* and *practice* what we've learned, the more gifted we'll become at developing intimate relationships within our homes. In the chapters that follow, we're going to open God's Word and see what He says about making our relationships strong and fulfilling—beginning with the very foundation of a successful family.

Keys to Building Loving, Lasting Relationships

In the next two chapters, we're going to discover that to have any loving and lasting relationship, we must understand:

- *Honor is at the heart of all healthy relationships—and*
- *Genuine love is a decision . . . not a feeling.*

Are you tired of your feelings of love going up and down like a roller coaster? I'll share with you how you can develop a love that remains consistently strong from season to season, year to year. Contrary to popular belief, love is actually a reflection of how much we "honor" another person—for at its core genuine love is a decision, not a feeling.

Second, you'll see that love can best be put into action by mastering and practicing specific skills like:

- *Recognizing the incredible worth of a woman*

I'll spend an entire chapter helping men in particular see how incredibly valuable women are. In particular, we'll see how God seems to have designed within a woman the very talents that can make her an invaluable resource in the home.

- *Learning how to energize our mates in sixty seconds*

One key to loving relationships is the ability to step in when our loved ones are hurting or discouraged. In this section of the book you'll see a method Christ often used with His disciples and others that can help you reach out to those who are facing discouragement, frustration, or a loss of energy.

- *Keeping a major destroyer of relationships out of our homes*

There is a killer lose in many homes today. It can take the life out of a relationship. One thing that I shared with Kay was how to keep the destructive "tapeworm" of anger out of relationships, and how to re-open the spirit of a loved one who may be closed to you.

- *Understanding the tremendous value of a man*

While many couples don't realize it, a man is not a "second class citizen" when it comes to the ability to have strong, lasting relationships. In this section of the book, you'll discover how to tap into a man's God-given gift for nurturing which can form the basis of genuine love. In fact, you'll see in detail four specific skills with which each man comes "naturally" equipped. These can make a tremendous difference in his relationships. *These same four skills are ones a wife must also master to see her relationships deepen and grow as well,* and they include:

- *Providing security to see a marriage bloom and grow*

If a relationship was like a plant, then security would be the sunlight it needs to grow strong and true. In this section, you'll see not only the results of insecurity, but how to build—or re-build— trust and hope in a home.

- *Uncovering a crucial key to meaningful communication*

For everyone who has ever felt misunderstood, there is a way to communicate with our loved ones that provides the greatest understanding—and the least negative reaction. This communication method is used throughout the Scriptures for praise, correction, deeper understanding, and intimacy—and you'll see it strengthen your relationships as well.

- *Keeping courtship alive in your marriage*

Emotional, romantic times can be a constant part of a courtship—and nonexistent in a marriage. In this important aspect of intimacy, you'll see how to keep or regain the elements of courtship, even years after a wedding.

- *Opening the doorway to physical intimacy*

While many people don't realize it, one book of the Bible focuses specifically on the sexual act of marriage—Song of Solomon. Instead of this important area of marital life being a source of frustration, putting some biblical basics into practice can strengthen a couple's physical intimacy, so that this important aspect of married life is no longer a problem.

• *Discovering how to be best friends with your family*

I've spent years studying and personally interviewing "successful" families, and we've consistently found they share one major characteristic. They've all learned the secret of developing family intimacy in even the most difficult of times. We can use that same secret to draw closer to the Lord personally during difficult times as well.

Kay's life did change the day I spoke with her—or at least she had a dramatic change of heart. But her marriage didn't turn around overnight. It took consistent prayer, time, and energy as she began to learn a specific plan of action and how to put it into practice. Even so, the specific skills I laid out to improve her marriage weren't what ultimately made the lasting difference in her life. Those skills made a major impact on her husband, but in themselves they weren't enough to bring the relationship back from the brink of disaster.

Am I saying that her personal force of will and effort to change weren't enough—even when she learned several specific communication and relationship skills? That's exactly right. You see, if we set out, in our flesh or with our own "will power," to guide our relationship into safe waters, I can guarantee that the day will come when we'll fall asleep at the wheel and run aground.[2] If we want to see lasting change in our lives and the lives of our loved ones, we must learn to rely on the only Source able to guard us "day and night."

Without question, the most important section of this book —and of my life—is found in the final two chapters. It is here that Kay Hammer found the power to put into practice all the relationship skills she learned—even when she didn't feel like doing a single one emotionally. For it is only in learning to depend upon the Lord as the Author and Sustainer of any truly successful relationship, that we'll find the inner strength to make lasting changes. And these changes can come—just as they did for John and Kay—by:

• *Learning the art of tapping into the unfailing power source behind a great marriage*

Most of us expect the "gifts" of life—including our spouse and children—to be the "source" of our life and happiness. In this most important section I'll show that while husbands and wives can make great friends and lovers, they make lousy gods. Learning to plug into the only consistent source of love, peace, and joy is the only way to have the spiritual and emotional stamina to withstand the storms of life. And finally, we need to learn how to . . .

• *Turn trials in our homes into lasting benefits for our lives*

"But what if things don't change around here?" "But you never met my husband!" "But you never tried to live with my wife!" "But *your* kids weren't born with a naturally rebellious spirit!"

In every relationship, there are roadblocks that can seem to stand so high they block out any hope of our ever getting past them to intimacy and oneness. And yet in this last section of the book, *you'll see that even the problems we face can do nothing but benefit our lives.* Even more, they can provide a consistent source of deeper love and sensitivity to pass on to others.

Much of the material in this book comes mainly from the "Love Is a Decision" video and film series which, in turn, is based on much of what John Trent and I do in our conferences. It also includes concepts from other books Dr. John Trent and I have done together as well as books I have written individually. Therefore, if you've had the opportunity to read some of the other books we've written, you may recognize some of it as familiar ground. However, in this book's unique format, I've had the opportunity to rewrite and update almost all the major concepts we share at our marriage and relationships seminar. John and I are only able to do eight to ten "Love Is a Decision" seminars a year, but by providing this information for you in this way, I hope it will give you a comprehensive look at what we teach in a way no single book we've done before could ever do.

It's a scary thought that the twenty-first century is right around the corner. And with a new century breathing down our necks, it's unfortunate that most of us don't have a plan for next week, let alone a plan for the next century.

I hope you're different. I hope you'll work at learning and practicing a plan—any plan—that is based on the Scriptures and grounded in His love. If you do use this book as a guideline, it's my prayer that it will be one of the most sensible, down-to-earth books you've ever read. I also hope that once you've read it, you and those you love will never be the same.

I earnestly pray that spending time in these pages will cause you to fall more deeply in love with God and His Word. As a by-product, I hope that loving God and His Word more deeply will then give you practical tools for constructing a mirror image of God's love to reflect to your family. That building process begins in Chapter 2, where we'll discover that all relationships begin with an essential element to a fulfilling life.

2

The Foundation for All Healthy Relationships

It is winter in Washington state, and a cold, wet wind is blowing. Smoke pours from the chimney of a small, two-story white house that looks warm and cozy in the chill night air. In fact, if you were to come close and peek through the kitchen window, you'd see a scene reminiscent of a Norman Rockwell painting.

Inside are a father, a mother, and five children, seated around the kitchen table having dinner. At first glance, it seems to be a portrait of pure Americana. Like the crackling blaze in the nearby fireplace, the scene gives the illusion of emotional warmth. But if you stayed around for a bit, you'd see that looks can be deceiving. For inside is an emotional chill that can cut to the bone like the northern air whistling through the trees.

The American dream starts to disappear when the father reaches over and pops the nearest teenager on the arm with the back of his hand. The teenager fires back a smart remark, and the two begin their nightly yelling match. The rest of the children all join in with a chorus of jeers—some angry, some laughing.

That is, all except the smallest child . . . the young boy sitting across from his father. He sits wide-eyed, his little heart pounding, watching everything that's happening around the table, wondering why his mother looks so sad, and wishing things would be different tonight.

But at this home, it's always this way—the smart remarks, the challenging looks, the unbridled anger. In most homes, there is a soft side and a hard side to life. But for this little boy, there's just one side of life with his father.[1] The cold, rough side that recalls his Dad decking one of his older brothers in anger . . . but never his giving him or his mother a hug.

Before turning away from the window, we see the father jump up from his chair and slap his napkin down on his plate.

"I never get any respect around here!" he shouts. "I'm leaving!"

"Yea, go ahead! *Get outta here!*" the kids shout back, laughing and taunting their father as he stalks out of the room. But for the little boy, it's been another night of conflict and confrontation at the dinner table, and another layer of painful memories to cover his soul . . . memories that are as vivid today as they were almost forty years ago. . . .

I hope this story doesn't bring back personal memories of a hurtful home for you; but it certainly does for me. For that little boy watching wide-eyed at the dinner table, getting all the wrong messages about family relationships, was me.

Over the years, I've thought quite a bit about what happened in my home growing up. Even as a child, I knew something was very wrong. There always seemed to be something missing from our family that kept us intimate strangers—always together but forever apart. For years, however, I had no idea what it was!

Have you ever wondered at times about the missing ingredient in your own relationships? Have you ever been so hurt that you've felt like throwing up your hands in despair? Have you looked at marital or family unity like candy inside a broken gumball machine—taking nickel after nickel after nickel—but never putting intimacy within your grasp?

Join the club. Most of us—even those from very loving homes and happy marriages—have experienced times when our most important relationships were difficult or unfulfilling. Why is it that the intimacy we want so often seems to be just out of reach?

At times, some of us have felt like John and Kay Hammer in Chapter 1—that the answer to all our family's problems is close at hand. Perhaps she's staring us right in the eye, or he's sitting across the table from us or even sleeping next to us at night. If only "that child or spouse" would change and begin meeting some of our expectations, finally our family life could be all it should be!

The Age-Old Mistake

It's easy for us to get excited about *another* person's need to change. For years, I was like a husband I once heard about. In his personal devotions he was reading Proverbs 31, the section in the

Bible that gives a picture of a practically perfect wife. During the course of an average day, this far-from-average woman buys and sells land, feeds the poor, prepares scrumptious meals for the entire household, hand-sews each child's wardrobe, and basically leaps over tall buildings with a single bound.

The more he read about this godly woman, and the more virtues that piled up about her, the more frustrated this husband became with his own wife. Finally, his emotions reaching the boiling point, he picked up his Bible (making sure he kept his finger on the verse to mark his place), and stomped off to find the "source" of all his problems.

Finding her sitting at the kitchen table, he laid the Bible down in front of her and pointed his finger repeatedly at the verses he'd been reading in Proverbs.

"Honey, do you know about this section in the Bible?" It was less a question than a threat.

She glanced nonchalantly at the open Bible in his hand, recognizing the passage.

"Yes," she said, "I know about that section."

After waiting, unrewarded by any further response, he continued, "Look, I know you want to be a godly person, and if you knew about this section. . . ."

Lifting an eyebrow, she repeated more firmly, "Listen—I *know* about that section."

Then straightening up to his full stature, towering over her as she sat at the table, he said, "If you *know* about this section, how come you don't get up every morning and make me a hot meal?"

"Dear," she said, "if you want a hot meal, *light your corn-flakes on fire!*"

By most people's standards this couple might be classified in the "highly strained" category. The story still points up a key problem in many homes. For years I felt that if only my wife Norma would change, every problem in our relationship would disappear. And during all that time, Norma was feeling exactly the same way I was—with one exception. She wanted *me* to change and then marital intimacy would finally be within reach.

But a funny thing happened on our way to changing each other. As much as I pushed Norma to change, and as much as she pulled me, neither one of us ever budged an inch—and neither did our relationship. For many reasons that we'll look at later, when our best efforts go into trying to change another person, we seem to reap the worst relationship rewards.

It's like the wife who noticed the new neighbors who moved in across the street. Every evening, she peeked through the curtains and watched as the husband came home from work.

She couldn't miss the fact that nearly every night, this man would bring home flowers or a little gift for his wife. She'd run to greet him as he got out of the car, and he'd hand her a gift. Then they'd hug and kiss until they had walked inside and closed the door behind them.

God's Word contains the only genuine blueprint for successful relationships, both with Him and others.

One night, after weeks of watching this same gushy scene repeated over and over, the poor neighbor woman finally reached the breaking point. The moment her husband walked in the door, she said, "Have you noticed we have new neighbors across the street?"

As he dropped his briefcase on the floor and fell into the easy chair in front of the television, he replied, "Yeah, I've noticed we have new neighbors."

"But have you noticed what they *do* every night?"

"No, dear," he answered, "I haven't noticed."

She continued, "Every night when he comes home, he gives her a big kiss, he hugs her, and he almost always brings her a special gift." Then she added, "How come *you* don't ever do that?"

Her husband stared at her with a puzzled look on his face and said, "Honey, I can't do that. I hardly know the woman!"

This age-old tactic of trying to get one's mate, friend, child, or boss to change may win a few minor battles, but it never wins the war of unmet expectations. Nonetheless, it was the primary way I tried to improve my marriage for several years.

Looking back now, I deeply regret not having realized how fruitless this approach is. It causes so many more problems than it solves (unhealthy dependency and increased selfishness to name just two). And it forces each marriage partner to be a competitor —not a completer. There have been many times I've wished I could have those years back.

Had I been wiser, Norma and I could have been spared dozens of painful, unnecessary discussions. If only I'd been aware that God had a plan for family relationships—and a personal plan for each one of us—I could have stopped arm-twisting and started arming myself with His wisdom on the family.

The Knowledge and Skills Necessary for a Great Relationship

God's Word contains the only genuine blueprint for success-ful relationships, both with Him and with others. Yet, for years, I had been looking at the wrong set of plans. As a husband, I based most of my actions on unhealthy family patterns drawn from my past. Instead, I should have been looking to God's unchanging plan for the family where the results would have been far less frustrating and much more fulfilling.

Over the years, in speaking and counseling with thousands of couples, I've discovered I wasn't alone in coming into mar-riage without the proper knowledge and skills to nurture a grow-ing relationship. In fact, across our country, the average couple spends more than two hundred hours getting ready for the wed-ding service, and less than three hours in any type of premarital counseling or preparation.[2]

In every state in our country, it is far easier to get a marriage license than it is to get a driver's license! And yet statistics show time and again that even a small dose of training before marriage can positively affect marital satisfaction and outcome.[3]

In talking with hundreds of couples, I've found that my premarital preparation wasn't far from the norm. It consisted of one meeting with a minister who asked me two questions:

"Gary," he asked, "do you love Norma?"

"Well . . . yes," I said. (Norma was sitting right beside me
. . . what else could I say!) But now I realize that I really didn't
understand what it meant to truly love her in the way the Scriptures describe.

Then the pastor asked me a second question, "Gary, would
you lay down your life for her?"

Again I said yes, thinking he was asking if I would throw
myself in front of a truck for her, or step in front of a gunman to
take the bullet meant for her.

The truth of the matter is, when I married Norma I knew the
right words—but not the right answers. I didn't have a plan to go
by, and after marrying a sparky, enthusiastic, godly woman, it
took me about five years of applying the wrong information re-
garding relationships to knock the sparkle right out of her life.

Early in our marriage, I could tell we weren't doing well, so
I decided to try a few quick-fix remedies. As I mentioned, I tried
the "If you'd just change" tactic, and even resorted to the lecture
method of teaching her what the Scriptures say about being a
godly wife. I never used an overhead projector, but I probably
would have if I'd thought about it. Many a night, 99 percent of
my dinner table conversations were actually lectures aimed at
drilling into Norma what the Bible said *she* should do to make
"us" happy.

During all that time, I conveniently ignored the Scriptural
words of wisdom that applied to the husband—probably because
I had never taken the time to truly understand the concepts
behind the words. And to go one step deeper, without realizing it,
I was covering up my own weaknesses and feelings of inadequacy
by pointing out hers.

The Death of a Dream . . .
the Birth of a Genuine Love

Norma kept hoping that I'd "get with it," but I never did. As
she saw her hopes for a warm, fulfilling family life slipping away,
she felt resigned to a marriage that would never match her
dreams.

After nearly five years of watching our relationship grow
more and more strained, I came home one day, walked into the
kitchen, and greeted Norma with the usual, "Hi, I'm home." But
she didn't respond.

"Is anything wrong?" I asked.

I knew from the look on her face and her nonverbal expressions that I didn't need to ask the question. It was obvious that something was drastically "wrong."

Suddenly, I felt tired all over. I had been battling my conscience for years and spent untold energy to keep up a facade of closeness to those at the church. Here I was teaching and counseling each week on relationships, and in my own marriage I felt like a failure. After years of pretending, I knew I didn't need a quick "self-help" gimmick to get through to my wife. I needed the kind of total heart transplant that only God can give. And so I gently put my arm around her and asked, "Norma, what do *you* think is wrong in our relationship?"

"Oh, no, you don't," Norma said, pulling back from me, her eyes filling with tears.

"You're not going to get me to share what I'm feeling and then turn it into another lecture on what I'm doing wrong."

"Honey," I said, trying to stay as soft as I could, "I can see how you'd feel that way, and I'm very, very sorry, but could you *please* just tell me one more time? I promise you, this time you won't hear a lecture."

Reluctantly, Norma did share with me the concerns that had been building up in her heart, and while it may have been her one hundredth time to tell me, I had never heard it the way she explained it that day. Little did I know that this single conversation would become one of the most traumatic—yet one of the most significant—moments in our lives.

Norma said several important things that afternoon, but there was one thing in particular I'll never forget. I now realize that the problem she explained that day is one of the most common reasons many couples and families struggle for years to find a healthy, meaningful relationship, and yet never quite reach it. She told me:

"Gary, I feel like everything on this earth is far more important to you than I am. . . ."

"I feel that all the football games you watch on television are more important than I am, the newspaper, your hobbies, your counseling at the church. Gary, I can spend hours working in the kitchen, and you never say a word. I can even farm out the kids to a baby-sitter and have a candlelight dinner all prepared for you, and the phone will ring and you'll say, 'Oh, I'm not doing anything important. I'm just eating. Sure, I'll be right over.' Then you're gone, telling me to keep something warm for you in the oven.

"I'm not saying that your ccunseling isn't important, but many of those couples you talk to have struggled with their problems for *years!* Taking one night out to spend with your wife isn't going to bother them—but it's killing us!

"It's like I don't matter to you, but other people do. In fact, sometimes I feel that you're more polite to total strangers than you are to me. You'll say the most awful things to me, but never to anyone else, especially not people at the church. . . ."

She went on, but you get the point—and so did I. While it may have been a message that was on continuous play around our house, I was hearing the recording loud and clear for the *first* time.

Before talking with Norma, I would never have stood up in front of a group and said that my counseling or even the nonstop sporting events I watched on television were more important than my wife, but without realizing it, that's exactly what I was communicating to her.

Little did I know that for five years of marriage, I had also been violating a crucial biblical concept which lies at the heart of any strong relationship. Every time I ignored its power to build loving, lasting relationships, I was literally shutting the door to the kind of home and family I'd wanted all my life.

What is this biblical principle that I'd been ignoring for years—and that weakened my marriage as a result? It's a simple, yet incredibly powerful, principle, and it comes wrapped in a single word—"honor."[4]

Honor Is the Foundation for All Healthy Relationships

Without a doubt, the concept of honor is the single most important principle we know of for building healthy relationships. It's important for a husband and wife to begin applying it toward each other. And children to apply it toward their parents, and for parents to apply it toward their children. It even works with friend-to-friend relationships. The results of allowing "honor" to reign can be dramatic and life-changing.

Honor is not only the basis of all our earthly relationships, it's at the heart of our relationship with God (see Matthew 6:19–21,

33). Yet we know so little about it that it's almost as if there's an active cover-up going on to keep it a secret from us.[5] To give you an idea of this crucial concept, let's get a brief thumbnail sketch of what "honor" means in the Scriptures.

During biblical times, the word "honor" carried a literal meaning that has been all but lost by translation and time. For a Greek living in Christ's day, something of "honor" called to mind something "heavy, or weighty."[6] Gold, for example, was the perfect picture of something of "honor," because it was heavy and valuable at the same time.

For this same Greek, the word "dishonor" would also bring to mind a literal picture. The word for "dishonor" actually meant "mist" or "steam."[7] Why? Because the lightest, most insignificant thing the Greeks could think of was the steam rising off a pot of boiling water, or clouding a mirror on a cold winter day.

When we honor particular people we're saying in effect that who they are and what they say carries great weight with us. They're extremely valuable in our eyes. Just the opposite is true when we dishonor them. In effect, by our verbal or nonverbal statements we're saying that their words or actions make them of little value or "light-weights" in our eyes.

When the apostle Paul wanted the Corinthian believers to repent from their immoral life-styles and renew their love for Christ, he told them, "You were bought at a price [literally, with "honor"]. Therefore honor God with your body" (1 Corinthians 6:20).

Every angel in heaven and each of us who make up the heavenly hosts of believers will one day sing, "Worthy is the Lamb, who was slain, to receive power . . . wisdom . . . *honor* . . . glory . . . praise" (Revelation 5:12). In both these verses, honoring God means to recognize that nothing on earth or in heaven is as valuable, as weighty, as significant as He.

But how does the concept of honor specifically apply to a marriage relationship?

How to Bring Honor into Your Home

One of the most powerful statements in all the Bible for husbands is, "You husbands, in the same way be considerate as you live with your wives, and treat them with respect (*honor*) as the weaker partner and as heirs with you of the gracious gift of life, so that nothing will hinder your prayers" (1 Peter 3:7).

In 1 Peter 3:1-2 the apostle states the same idea about a wife's relationship with her husband. Do you want to motivate your husband spiritually? Then the apostle says for a wife to use the powerful shaping tool of "honor" by letting him see your genuine and respectful (or honoring) behavior. Finally, a verse that also communicates the mutual need for honor in a home or in any relationship is Romans 12:10. It clearly states, "Be devoted to one another in brotherly love. *Honor* one another above yourselves."

When I came face to face with the concept of "honor" in a home, I suddenly understood why a major part of my prayer life was being hindered. When it came to Norma, the person who from an earthly perspective should receive the "highest value" I could give, I put a hundred things ahead of her. Work projects were more important to me than my mate, and while it's to my shame to admit it, there were countless times that a mountain trout, a small white golf ball, numerous church meetings, close friends and acquaintances—and almost anything "interesting" on television—took the place of honor which should have been reserved for Norma.

If someone had stopped me on the street or at church and asked me if I loved my wife, I would have answered emphatically "Yes!" The problem was, you could never tell I loved Norma by her place of honor (her priority status) in comparison to a hundred more "important" things in my life.

So right there at our kitchen table, I pledged to change. I didn't realize all the implications of what I was doing, but I had a profound sense that things in the Smalley house would never be the same—and they haven't been.

First, I went alone before my Heavenly Father and asked His forgiveness for my incredible selfishness. I realized that at times many things, even good things like my ministry, had taken on more "weight" to me than my relationship with the Lord. That would have to change. I knew that the first step toward giving my wife honor had to be giving God the place of honor reserved only for Him in my life.

It was hard to admit, but I was coming to realize that the idea of honor was out of balance in my life. At that point, something interesting happened. Almost immediately, I noticed it was easier than ever before to pray and read the Scriptures.

Because I valued too many other things of this world more than my time in God's Word, I didn't naturally dive into the Bible and pray early in our marriage. In addition, I wasn't obeying the command of Scripture to give "honor" to my wife. Today, because of my decision to make God the "weightiest" Person in my life—and my commitment to give Norma the "honor" she deserves—one of the most natural things I do in the course of a day is to pray and spend time in His Word. We'll take time to focus on this important issue in a later chapter.

However, while I had come to grips with the concept of honor in my relationship with my Heavenly Father, like Peter, I couldn't stay on the mountaintop. It was time humbly to go back down in the valley to Norma and ask her to forgive me for the way I'd treated her.

"Honey," I said, "I know that we both want to give God first place in our lives. But from an earthly perspective, I want you to be above everything or everyone else in my life."

When Truth Needs a Track Record

Going to Norma was an extremely traumatic moment for me, and it would prove to be a major turning point in my life and in our marriage. But there was one problem. Norma didn't believe me that day.

I knew I had come face to face with the truth of God's Word, and that my life was going to be different as a result, but she just thought it was more empty words. So she threw out a half-convincing, "Yeah, okay," at my vow to honor her and got up from the table to continue preparing dinner.

It's not that Norma lacked faith in God or His Word. From the first time I met her almost twenty-nine years ago until today, I have always been blessed by her deep faith and commitment to Christ. What she lacked wasn't faith in God, but faith in her husband. She needed a track record of being "honored" from a husband who had never practiced it.

I have to admit that at the time, I didn't know exactly what it meant to put the concept of honor into action in our home, but I knew enough to realize that honor would have to be a daily—sometimes hourly—decision. And I had made that decision. I wasn't going to keep Norma on a starvation diet of praise and three full meals of criticism and unrealistic expectations anymore. I was going to consistently feed her with a nourishing meal of significance and high value in our home.

"Norma," I said, "I know you have every reason to doubt me, but I mean what I'm saying. I never understood this before, and I want to ask you to forgive me for making you think that everything else I'm doing is more important than you. No matter how I've acted in the past, that's not what I really believe."

Our evening discussion was over, and she wasn't dazzled by my promise of change. In fact, because of the five years she had lived with the "old Gary," it took her almost two full years of a consistent track record of honoring acts to finally believe the "new Gary" was for real.

*W*ith honor as a permanent resident in a home, there is hope we can restore our relationship with God and with our loved ones.

Norma has never failed to forgive me when I asked her, and she forgave me that day. But she was right to question whether I would actually follow through on my promises. She'd been standing in fifth or sixth place in my life for so long, it was natural for her to be skeptical. It was hard for her to believe she was finally moving to the front of the line.

If you make a decision today to increase the honor in your home, don't be disappointed if your mate doesn't do back-flips until tomorrow or the next month. Remember, he or she has been watching your actions for a long time. They have all your past press clippings cut out and pasted in their memories. And if your previous track record has been less than spectacular—as mine was—emotional scar tissue may cause them to be calloused to your present promises for several months. Hype may sell hamburgers and automobiles, but it doesn't work on your spouse the way time linked with a track record does.

With honor as a permanent resident in a home, there is hope we can restore our relationship with God and with our loved ones. Feelings that have taken years to develop don't change overnight, but persistent honor has the power to win over even the hardest of hearts—particularly as a husband or wife sees affirming actions become a consistent part of a marriage.

Putting Relationships in the Right Order

For me, that fateful conversation with my wife at the kitchen table forced me to get my spiritual and family life in order. In fact, I actually began to prioritize my life from zero to ten, zero being something of little value, ten something of highest value.

I established God and my relationship with Christ as the highest—a ten. On a consistent basis, I began looking at my spiritual life and asking the question, "One to ten, where is my spiritual life with Christ?" "How highly do I value His Word?" "Prayer?" "Sharing my faith?"

Then I placed Norma above everything else on this earth, way up in the nines. With this relationship, too, I often asked myself (and Norma), "How am I doing at making you feel like you're up in the high nines, above every one of my hobbies and friends and favorite sports teams? What can I do to keep you believing you're a high nine?"

How about you? If you were to rate the "honor" quotient of your marriage relationship right now, where would it be? Where do you think your spouse would rate it? Have you asked him or her lately?

You're probably as convinced as I am that we need to give God the honor He deserves first, and then make honor a non-negotiable item in our home, but you may still have questions about how to honor those you love in a practical way.

Let's bring honor out of the cloudland of theory right down to the cobblestone level where we live. Let me share with you three ways to bring honor off the pages of Scripture and right into your home. Each has been life-tested in my home and in the lives of thousands of people at our seminars. It all begins with practicing the "ah-h-h-h-h-h" principle on a regular basis.

Three Ways to Honor Your Loved Ones

1. The "Ah-h-h-h-h-h" Principle

As I've noted, the most fulfilling relationships in life begin with honor. In fact, the Bible says that the "fear" of the Lord—the honor and respect we give Him—is the beginning of wisdom.

The fear of the Lord is being "awe-inspired." For Moses it happened as he beheld the burning bush (Exodus 3). For Elijah the Prophet it came as he listened for the still, small voice as God's glory paraded by (1 Kings 19). And for Peter the fisherman, it was the result of watching Christ calm a rolling sea with only three words (Mark 4:39). In each case, being in God's presence produced reverence and "awe."

In fact, the fear of the Lord is being so awed that you drop your jaw and inhale a gasp, catching your breath in an audible "ah-h-h-h-h-h." It's a gasp of reverence mixed with a bit of wonder.

In short, honor is a reflex of the heart toward one who is deeply treasured. It's the conviction that you are in the presence of somebody so valuable it's "ah-h-h-h-inspiring." It's important to realize too that this life-changing attitude doesn't start with a feeling—it's a *decision;* and the *feelings* of "awe" eventually follow.

Picture it this way. Let's say you're a homemaker who has taken a well-deserved winter break from housework. It's spring now, and you've decided to pull the house back in order.

You reach into the pantry and take out a can of Johnson's Wax and begin to clean the parquet floor. You've been working an entire twenty minutes when the doorbell rings. Since you were just getting ready to take a break anyway, you cheerfully get up off the floor you've been scrubbing and head to the door.

As it opens and you look up, there stands the President of the United States in the flesh, flanked by two husky Secret Service guards.

"Hi," the president says. "I was just walking in the neighborhood and thought I'd stop in and ask you a few of your thoughts on my foreign policy."

As you stand there with your wet sponge dripping on your

fuzzy slippers, how do you respond? Can you picture the president suddenly showing up at your door to ask a question? No matter what your political viewpoint, having the main occupant of the White House suddenly appear at your doorstep would be cause for a breath-catching gasp of reverence mixed with awe—the "Ah-h-h-h-h-h" response.

Now, I agree that having the president show up at your home for a foreign policy discussion is far fetched, but every day, we see examples of the "Ah-h-h-h-h-h" principle at work. If you've ever been called to jury duty, what does the bailiff say as the judge enters the courtroom?

"Would everyone please rise? The Ah-h-h-h-honorable Judge Wapner is entering the room." It's time to stand up and show ah-h-h-h-honor because someone extremely valuable is about to enter the room.

What do the Orientals do upon meeting someone important or upon signing an important agreement? They bow to each other as a symbol of honor. The gesture means that I have decided you're important and deserve special merit and respect.

Sometimes I walk in the house and see one of my kids sitting in the easy chair watching television. Just for fun, I'll drop to my knees and say, "Unbelieeeevable! I'm actually in the same room with Michael Smalley! I can't believe that I'm living in the same house with somebody as ah-h-h-h-mazing as you!"

My kids usually howl, "Da-a-ad." But basically, that is the way you build the "Ah-h-h-h" principle into your relationship. You decide that the people around you—your spouse, your children, your friends, and your parents—are worthy of honor. They are worth an "ah-h-h-h-h-h" on a consistent basis.

Have you ever wondered why the dog is considered man's best friend? As you'll discover in Chapter 5, it's because men, in particular, are extremely motivated by the "Ah-h-h-h-h-h" principle.[8]

Think about the way the average dog greets its owner. Whether you've been gone for two weeks on vacation or ten minutes to the mini-mart, he probably falls all over himself showing his happiness at seeing you. Nonverbally, dogs honor their owners with massive doses of love and enthusiasm. In fact, I'm sure that if the dog could gasp, "ah-h-h-h-h!" when he saw you walk in, he would!

That's probably one reason why men tend to dislike cats. You can call them and they just give you that "Garfield" look of disdain, as if they were saying, "Where do you get off thinking you're valuable enough for me to come running over to you? *I'm the one who gets honored around here!*"

In the book of Proverbs, we're told that even the smallest act of "ah-h-h-h-h" can have a positive effect on a relationship. There we read, "Bright eyes gladden the heart . . ." (Proverbs 15:30, NASB).

Have you ever appeared at a surprise party for a special friend and seen their eyes "light up" when they see you? That same feeling of "I'm really special to them" is at the heart of having "bright eyes." And where do "bright eyes" come from? From a heart that is looking at someone very, very special to us—someone we're delighted to see. Someone we're ah-h-h-h-honoring.

2. Remember That "Ah-h-h-h-h-h" Is in the Eye of the Beholder

When we honor someone, we make a decision that a person is special and important. Biblically (and thankfully), honor was not always something that had to be earned. It was given as an act of grace to someone who didn't deserve it.

An example of this is the verse, "While we were still sinners, Christ died for us" (Romans 5:8). Just like our Lord, we sometimes need to make our decision to honor someone apart from our feelings about that person.

It's amazing how a person's response to something or someone can change dramatically once they've made a decision that the individual is truly valuable. That fact was never more clear to me than after what happened at a special seminar we did that was filmed for a nationwide television audience.

Jim Shaughnessy is a close friend who has been to several of our "Love Is a Decision" Seminars, and he knows that I always teach a section on honoring those we love. Without me knowing it, he planned something for this special seminar that brought about the greatest natural "Ah-h-h-h-h-h" response from a crowd I've ever witnessed.

At most of our seminars, I use a three-inch piece of sparkling crystal cut in the shape of a diamond to give people a word picture of "honor." I usually begin by asking the audience:

"How many of you believe this cut stone is a $100,000 diamond?" A chuckle will ripple through the audience as people look at the crystal. Usually, I have to talk at least one person into raising his hand just so I can continue with the point I'm making.

Truthfully, people should chuckle when they hear me put the value of that piece of crystal at $100,000. After all, it's probably not worth more than sixty dollars in any store in the country, but as far as I'm concerned I wouldn't part with it for one penny less than $100,000.

It's kind of like the farmer who crossed fifty pigs with fifty deer—and got a hundred sows and bucks! *It's we who set the value of something.* And that was a fact my friend helped me illustrate better than I could have ever dreamed.

Jim owns a very old Stradivarius violin. Just for the television special, he had it flown in—complete with its own "security guard"! As I began to talk about honor in the seminar, I brought out what looked just like any old, unstrung fiddle or violin.

"This violin is worth over $65,000," I said. I could see by the smiles and nodding of heads that people believed me about as much as they did when I would hold up my "$100,000" diamond. In fact, my holding up the violin didn't produce even one "ah-h-h-h-hdible" gasp in the entire crowd. After all, they could see with their own eyes that it was an old violin. Particularly those sitting close to the speaker's platform could see that it didn't even have any strings.

But as I talked about attaching honor to something, I told them a little bit more about what I actually held in my hand. After all, there are only about 600 violins like it left in the world, and when I angled it so that I could read the inscription inside, and then mentioned the word "Stradivarius," the effect was incredible.

A spontaneous, collective, breath-catching "ah-h-h-h" reflex rifled throughout the crowd. Just a few moments before, it was just an old violin, not worthy of any special honor, but by attaching that one word, "Stradivarius," to it, it suddenly was given a high place of honor by everyone in the room (especially by me as I hoped I wouldn't drop it!).

Remember, people make the decision that something is of high value. Does a Chevy pull up to a Mercedes at a stoplight and gaze at it enviously, wishing it could be a Mercedes? Of course not. Do you think that silver cries itself to sleep each night because it's not as valuable as gold? It doesn't care. *We're* the ones that attach value to a thing—or a person.

Someone came up with a great idea years ago. They decided to take all the old pieces of furniture sitting around in people's attics and garages and call them "antiques." Instantly, people lined up to pay exorbitant prices for all these old pieces of "junk." Then, after spending huge amounts that would make new furniture prices blush, they take home these worn relics and spend countless hours and extra dollars refinishing them!

What happened to all those old sticks of furniture to make them suddenly become antiques? Their value suddenly rose, and that happened for only one reason—we had decided they were more valuable to us. I was aware of this concept everywhere else in life, but I wasn't practicing it in my own home—the most important place for the "Ah-h-h-h-h-h" principle to take root and grow.

Let's say the husband comes home at night and the whole family meets him at the door. Instead of running past him to go out to play or to watch television, he is greeted with a collective chorus of "*Ah-h-h-h-h! Look who's here!!*"

Then, to his amazement, the wife and kids roll out a red carpet runner into the house and as he walks down it, the kids throw rose petals at his feet. Scurrying ahead of him, they usher him into his easy chair, prop up his feet, lovingly hand him his paper, and peel grapes for him, throwing them (at an angle) into his mouth to eat.

What would the average husband think if he was greeted this way when he walked in the door? He'd probably think he was in the wrong house! Honoring actions don't have to be exaggerated the way I've described above. But the attitude of honor does have to be present if our relationships are to grow and develop.

"Hold it," I can hear someone saying, "what if some people don't *deserve* our honor? How can I act in an honoring way toward them when they're not living up to what I want?"

Whether it is a husband or a wife who asks that question about the person they vowed to honor, it takes another question to answer it: Do you want your relationship to blossom instead of wither? If the answer is "blossom," then you can't avoid the issue of honor in a home.

You may be concerned that honoring an undeserving mate will make things worse rather than better. Or you may even be worried your mate will take advantage of you and use you because of your willingness to treat them with respect. However, before you react to what I'm saying and close the book, please try to understand how love and honor intermingle.

I know that God is the only being in life who is always worthy of honor, and yet in His Word we are told to honor others —all others. Children are to give "honor" to their parents. A husband should honor his wife and a wife her husband. We are to prefer "one another" in honor.

Remember, honor is an *attitude* that someone is valuable.

It is not an absolution of all a person's faults, nor a command to be less than honest with who they are. Let me give you an example:

I have a good friend whose father is an alcoholic. I know for a fact that this man "honors" his father by praying for him, encouraging him to accept Christ, and even inviting him to his home consistently.

But "honor" does not mean that he allows his alcoholic father to drive his three-year-old daughter around in his car. Neither does honor dissolve all healthy boundaries in their relationship. There is no swearing allowed, no smoking in the house, and no "teasing" the children. There are times when the father doesn't want to play by the rules—and doesn't come to the house as a result. But he knows and has even admitted—in spite of his complaints—that his son "honors" and even loves him.

"Honor" doesn't cast pearls before swine—but neither does it mean that you treat a person like a swine until he measures up to your standards.

If you're in the situation of having to "honor" a difficult person, you may want to go deeper into several books that John Trent and I have written on this subject and can also recommend.[9] Without exception, be sure to read and absorb everything I cover in Chapters 13 and 14 in this book.

The material in these chapters (on tapping into the very power source of love) will be especially helpful for you. There you will find the secret to really enjoying life in spite of difficult circumstances. The concepts found there are also absolutely crucial for working through the fear of "What if they won't change?"

There have been times when I have been motivated to honor Norma not out of my "feelings," but as an act of my will and in obedience to God's command that I do so. And consistently, once I put honor in its right place, positive, loving feelings will follow.

Is this some type of psychological trick or basis for manipulation? Hardly. It's actually a biblical principle:

In Matthew 6:21 Jesus said, ". . . for where your treasure is, there your heart will be also." In other words, when it comes to our spiritual life, what we treasure—what we place high value upon—is where our feelings reside. The same thing is true in my relationship with my spouse. If I "treasure" or honor a person, my positive, warm feelings about him or her begin to rise correspondingly.

I realize that it isn't always easy to keep one's thoughts and feelings at the "honoring" level. As a wife, you might begin to grumble about the little things your husband does that irritate you. There's the trash can that only gets taken out when you remind him for the tenth time, or the way he remembers to fill up *his* car but always forgets to check out yours. As a husband, you may be frustrated with her weight or her discipline of the children or even with the way she drives at night.

But if an attitude of dishonor is allowed to develop or turn destructive, it's a short step to attaching negative feeling to that *person,* instead of his actions. When men (or women) begin a pattern of consistently dishonoring their spouses—even if it's only in their minds—within a matter of a few weeks they can lose nearly all their loving feelings for them.

That's when you begin to hear the comments, "Why did I pick this guy?" or "Of all the fish in the sea, I got stuck with her!" That's also where small acts of irritation—like squeezing the toothpaste tube from the wrong end—can end up being "grounds" for divorce.

But the opposite is true as well. Time and again, when honor begins to take root in a home, within a matter of a few days or weeks, your feelings will start to change. Your husband may seem like a beat-up old violin, but the moment you begin treating him like a Stradivarius, your world and his can change for the better.

There is a third way to keep honor inside your home. We must concentrate on keeping dishonoring acts—even minor ones—outside of our experience.

3. It's Worth the Hard Work to Keep Dishonoring Actions at Arm's Length

It takes time for honor to take root in our lives, and before it does, all of us are capable of the type of thing I used to do. It violated this crucial principle.

As is typical of all small children, every now and then they need a little "motivation" to behave. Ours were no exception. When the need arose for discipline, I'd often take my thumb and middle finger and "flick" them on the head.

"Greg," I'd say, and flick him on the head, "turn off the television!" or "Michael," flick, "stop bothering the dog."

One night we were in a restaurant, and the kids were acting up. As usual, I reached across the table and flicked my daughter on the head to get her to stop pestering her brother.

"*Gary,*" Norma said, in an icy tone, "we're in a restaurant. Is this any kind of place to flick your daughter?"

Her reaction startled me. After all, flicking my kids had become such a habit, I never stopped to think it was dishonoring, so I turned to my daughter and asked, "Kari, how does it make you feel when I flick you?"

"Daddy, I don't like you flicking me." Without an invitation to comment, my two boys quickly agreed.

"Yeah, Dad. We don't like you flicking us *either.*" Norma didn't say anything at this point because I had never flicked her.

Right there I decided to quit flicking the kids, but I knew that since it was a habit, I'd need some incentive to remind me not to dishonor them. So, after thinking about it for a minute, I said, "I'll tell you what, kids. I don't want to dishonor you any more by flicking you. Will you forgive me?" They nodded their heads.

"To show you how serious I am about wanting to stop, I'll make a deal with you. From now on, anytime I flick you I'll give you a dollar right on the spot."

Their immediate response after looking at each other, was, "Flick on, Dad, flick on!"

Let's start making a mental list of what we do that can dishonor our family or friends. Here's our current list of the top ten dishonoring acts we have reported to us all over the country. They're not in a particular "dishonoring" order, but all of them can be killers of meaningful relationships.

The Top Ten Dishonoring Acts in a Home

- Ignoring or degrading another person's opinions, advice, or beliefs (especially criticizing another person's faith)
- Burying oneself in the television or newspaper when another person is trying to communicate with us
- Creating jokes about another person's weak areas or shortcomings (Sarcasm or cutting jokes act like powerful emotional word pictures and do lasting harm in a relationship.)[10]

- Making regular verbal attacks on loved ones: criticizing harshly, being judgmental, delivering uncaring lectures
- Treating in-laws or other relatives as unimportant in one's planning and communication
- Ignoring or simply not expressing appreciation for kind deeds done for us
- Distasteful habits that are practiced in front of the family —even after we are asked to stop
- Overcommiting ourselves to other projects or people so that everything outside the home seems more important than those inside the home
- Power struggles that leave one person feeling that he or she is a child or is being harshly dominated
- An unwillingness to admit that we are wrong or ask forgiveness

I don't want my wife or children to feel any less loved than God would have them be in my home, and that means that honor must become an everyday activity in my life—like shaving or taking time out for meals. How about you? Are you ready to turn loose the "Ah-h-h-h-h-h" Principle in your home?

In this chapter, we've talked about the decision we all need to make to honor others—that people are worth our time and energy! Now, in the next chapter, let's look at the second greatest aspect of any healthy relationship: love. *You'll discover that love is the action we take to communicate how valuable another is* and, like honor, that love is actually a *decision*.

3

Love Is a Decision

Imagine that you've pulled up a chair next to me as I sit facing Kay Hammer, the woman whose story began this book. Like me, you can sense the tension around the table as it soon becomes obvious that the only thing standing between her and the door are the words that will be shared during the next few hours.

What do you say to a woman who was clinging to the end of her rope when it came to her willingness to hang on to her marriage? As you sit with me, you'd hear me tell her that she should try once more to hold her marriage together, but you'd also hear reason after reason why she should leave John. You would hear me tell her how important it is that God be given every opportunity to keep them together—and sharing the latest research that shows the life-long emotional pain that children and spouses suffer after divorce.[1]

Kay listened and agreed to stay with John after our conversation. But I never realized that things were about to get much worse for her and her husband, not better. In fact, he did something a few weeks later that even caused her Christian friends to say to her, "Kay, *leave* him. You shouldn't take that from anybody. . . ."

At first it took an hourly decision to stay, but with each day, Kay became more committed to do what we share in Chapter 13 and especially Chapter 14. She made a decision to respond to her husband out of the fullness of her love for Christ—not the empty feelings she had about her marriage. And the difference in her attitude instantly began to show. But a severe test was coming of how much Kay was willing to seek God's love first, and then reflect it back to her husband. For a few weeks later, he ripped away the most important thing to her in a moment's notice.

Almost Too Much to Take

John couldn't help but notice the change that had come over his wife. Like many mates who see the first blush of change—he tested her to see how real it was.

For two years, Kay's life-line of support had been her Bible Study Fellowship group. These ladies had prayed for her and encouraged her on those hopeless mornings when she was ready to toss in the towel. As a group leader, the highlight of Kay's year was the annual "leaders' retreat" coming up.

She had already paid her money and arranged for babysitting for the children. Kay was less than twenty-four hours away from heading to the airport and the retreat when John came home from the office.

"Where are *you* going?" he demanded, looking around at the suitcases she'd packed.

"To the Bible study leaders' retreat," Kay said. "You know that I leave tomorrow."

"Well, I've changed my mind," John announced. "I don't want you to go. In fact, I think you're spending way too much time with this group. I want you out of that leadership program right now."

Can you imagine the choice she had to make? To stand against her husband and go to the retreat would be to play the same chorus of "I'll do it *my* way" that she had sung unsuccessfully for years. On the other hand, to follow his leadership—and cut herself off from her primary source of fellowship and spiritual support—seemed equally wrong.

What was she to do? This wasn't a situation where she could change the channel and have her decision go away. She could tell John was waiting for her response. What's more, she knew that this was a major test of her "decision" to show him honor, no matter what the circumstances. Just then the phone rang, and she was saved from having to respond to him on the spot.

It was a friend calling to ask if she and John could come to dinner that night with a noted pastor who was speaking in town—a man named Ray Stedman. John and Kay ended up going to the dinner, and as soon as she could, Kay drew Dr. Stedman aside and explained her situation.

"What should I do?" she asked. "What can I say to my husband that will get him to change his mind about my going to the retreat and being in leadership?"

Kay would never forget what this wise pastor told her:

"Kay," he said, "your first responsibility is to seek the Lord, then your family, and *then* a ministry. I'm not going to talk to you about a way to manipulate John to change his mind. If your husband tells you to get out of Bible Study Fellowship, then when I leave tonight you tell him that you're getting out!"

At the time, she thought someone had tossed four gallons of ice water right in her face. She sat with her mouth open wondering, *How could he say such a thing?* Yet as the evening wore on, she realized that what he said was right. For years, she had tried with varying degrees of success to manipulate her way in and out of things—and now she was being asked to change. It was like hearing an army trumpet sound general quarters. The pastor's words called out that she was in the midst of a spiritual battle— not just a battle with her husband.

When they got home from dinner, Kay's normal response would have been, "There is not enough money in this *world* that could keep me home from this retreat. We already agreed that I could go, and you're breaking that promise!"

But instead, her response was based on a decision that God was in control of her life. "If John doesn't want me to go," she said, "then God must not want me to go this time."

"Father," she prayed, "I don't understand why, but I feel like this is a test. So, Lord, please help me find a reason for my not going."

As she looked at her plane tickets lying on the piano, tears filled her eyes. Yet, in spite of the pain, with all her heart she knew what she was doing was right. It was one of the most difficult things she'd ever done in her life, but she walked up the stairs and told her husband that she would skip the retreat, that she would drop out of her leadership position.

We live in days and times where words like "sacrifice" and "commitment" are four-letter words. I realize that, to many people, Kay's decision to love and honor her husband's wishes might seem unenlightened or even terribly wrong. After all, *she had her rights.* But as Kay was to find out, it was in laying down her rights that she finally broke through to her husband.

In simple terms what Kay literally did was make love a decision. *Genuine love is honor put into action regardless of the cost.* It comes from a heart overflowing with love for God, freeing us to seek another person's best interests. Kay knew that only by loving God first and foremost could she ever hope to pull off loving John

—especially after what he had done. Every "instinct" she had told her to lash out. Yet in spite of her "instincts," her love would be based on a decision to honor her husband—not her emotions.

Let me admit that there are situations where either the husband or wife is emotionally unhealthy. In no way am I saying that we are to give a "blanket" yes to a spouse who commands us to do something against the law or in direct violation to God's law. (For a look at the balance between unconditional love and dealing with an emotionally destructive person, we recommend Dr. James Dobson's *Love Must Be Tough*). But Kay believed this was her chance to prove to John what was more important: her husband or her retreat. Perhaps that's why she determined more than ever that her love for Christ would be the basis of her love for her husband. And that's what led to . . . the rest of the story.

The Rest of the Story

Several months passed, and John and Kay were invited to a large Christian conference held in the auditorium at Indiana University. At the conclusion of the seminar, the speaker did something unusual. He opened up several microphones for people in the audience to come up and share what God had been doing in their lives. That's when it happened.

Kay suddenly looked over and noticed that John was getting up from his seat and heading to the front of the auditorium. He waited his turn in line and then stepped up to the microphone.

"Ladies and gentlemen," he said to a group of over a thousand people. "*I just want you to know that I'm here tonight because my wife First Peter three'ed me into coming!*"

The entire place came unglued with laughter as his words sank in. Indeed, as the verse says, Kay's commitment to trust God had won over her husband "without a word" by her godly actions (1 Peter 3:1–6).

"I'm going to tell you all something Kay doesn't know," John continued. "We had this guy named Gary Smalley come to our house and I don't know what he told my wife—but things haven't been the same since. Basically, I'm here tonight because my wife has worn me out with her love.

"I've got to confess that there have been days when I actually sat in my office, thinking up something I was going to tell her to do when I got home *just to see if she would do it*—and she did!

Watching the reality of this woman's love for God is the reason I'm standing up here tonight. . . ." And there was more to come.

John changed so much that soon *he* was in the leadership program of the *Men's* Bible Study Fellowship. And then came the day of *their* men's leadership retreat. Kay drove her husband to where the bus would take him and several others on a weekend retreat. John had never been on a men's retreat, and he was like a schoolboy going to summer camp for the first time.

Genuine love is honor put into action regardless of the cost.

While she never said anything at the bus station, Kay couldn't help thinking about the retreat she had given up months earlier. And as she drove off, the emotions of the moment finally hit her. She was thankful for the changes in her husband's life, but the hurt of being denied an opportunity to go to her own leaders' retreat brought tears to her eyes—until the phone rang.

Kay had barely gotten back home when John called.

"We're at a truck stop picking up some other people for the retreat," he said, "and I just had to call you."

With his voice choking with emotion, he said, "Kay, I've been thinking back to a time I told you you couldn't go to a retreat. Could you forgive me for asking you to give up something I knew was really important to you? I'm so sorry I asked you to step down from your leadership group. I never should have asked what I did, and I never will again. Can you find it in your heart to forgive me? . . ."

Kay has been to many retreats since the one she missed over thirteen years ago—but none have held as much meaning as the one she never attended. Later, she would say in reflecting on that unforgettable call, "*I gave up a retreat—but I gained back a husband!*"

Over the years, John and Kay have developed a rock-solid love for Christ and each other. This couple whose relationship at one time was dead in the water, held fast by the rocks of insensitivity and bitter arguments, now help countless couples fight back from the brink of divorce. And they do this by sharing the reality of their own story—and by helping others see that genuine love is a decision, not a feeling.

Moving Honor into a Home by Loving Actions

I realize that there are times when love needs to be tough and set firm boundaries with a loved one. But what turned around John and Kay's life was a principle that is true in any home. *The most effective way to open the door to needed changes in a relationship is to honor a loved one. And once we've made that decision to honor, love is the action we take no matter how we feel.*

Genuine love is honor put into action, regardless of the cost. It comes from a heart overflowing with affection for God, freeing us to seek another person's best interest.

In a nutshell, that definition is an outline of this book. We've already seen in Chapter 2 that honor is at the foundation of all healthy relationships. Now we've seen that out of our decision to honor flows loving actions *regardless of our feelings—regardless of the cost.*

Now in the chapters that follow, you'll learn the ten areas that took me all day to teach Kay, and that I've spent fifteen years refining and researching ever since. Each one is a *specific loving action* that expresses the honor and the decision to love that we've made.

The very first loving action that is so essential in any home or relationship is recognizing the incredible worth of a woman. Every woman has two tremendous tendencies that we'll uncover for you. What's more, you'll see that there are three questions any husband can ask his wife that can reveal her built-in marriage manual.

4

The Incredible
Worth of a Woman

One of the greatest joys I have in teaching the "Love Is a Decision" Seminar is sharing with men how incredibly valuable women are. Why? One major reason is that I've spent time learning and asking questions from women. That includes twenty-five years of marriage, and interviewing over 30,000 women at conferences and in counseling sessions across the country. I've seen, first hand, the tremendous relationship skills that God has woven into the fabric of their lives.

But a few years ago, I had an experience that gave me a whole new appreciation for their incredible worth. For on a wind-blown afternoon, one woman's "intuitive" senses quite possibly saved my life, and the lives of several others as well.

A River Gone Wild. . . .

It was mid-May, and time for our annual "staff retreat" where we do more retreating than staffing. We did have one legitimate reason for spending the weekend fishing. We were in the process of interviewing Steve Lyon, now an invaluable associate on our staff, and we decided that spending a weekend quizzing him at our favorite fishing spot was just the place to get to know him—and a few trophy-sized trout at the same time.

We were on our way to Lee's Ferry, located just below Lake Powell on the Colorado River. Lying at the mouth of the Grand Canyon, it offers great fishing and some of the most spectacular scenery in the world.

Early the first morning, we waited at the dock for our two guides. Soon, a truck rumbled up, two figures bouncing in the front seat as it rolled to a stop. The door opened and out stepped a tall, weather-beaten man of about forty. Beside him was his wife, a petite woman only half his size. What I would discover later that day was that anything she lacked in size, she would more than make up for in fishing skill—and her natural female "instincts."

Beautiful canyon walls rose literally two and three hundred feet straight up from the edge of the water as we began a tour of the Grand Canyon at water level. It took our boats nearly an hour traveling upstream to reach the dam which stood as a towering marker to "the end of the line." We shut our engines down and quietly began to drift with the current, letting out line behind us as we trolled for speckled and rainbow trout.

The early morning passed with little success. Then lunch time rolled around and we beached the boats about halfway back to the dock. It had been a fairly calm morning, but by the time we got back to the boats, the wind had changed from a whisper to a stiff breeze. I remember thinking, *We won't catch a thing until these gusts die down.* But they didn't.

With each passing minute, the wind grew stronger and more steady. The once glassy surface of the river was beginning to roll as the water churned with a thousand tiny waves. But we were all seasoned campers and fishermen. *What's a little wind?* I thought.

As we got back in the boats, I noticed our two guides talking. I couldn't hear the words they were saying, but it was obvious they were in the midst of a heated discussion. Finally, the man shrugged his shoulders, nodded his head, and marched over to us with some unwelcome news.

"I'm sorry, guys, but we're going to have to pack it in for right now. I can't explain it, but my wife really feels strongly that this isn't just a minor front coming in—and I've learned to listen to her on these waters. So we're heading back."

It was a good thing we listened to her when we did. Almost instantly the wind began to howl, and the waves were beginning to form whitecaps. Within minutes, we lost the ability to communicate from boat to boat as the fury of a desert windstorm drowned out even the most desperate attempts to shout instructions.

We were all on our own to make it back. By now the wind was blowing with such a galelike force that if we had turned sideways to the current, we would have easily been swamped by the angry swells. The only hope we had of making it back on top of the water was to point the boats directly downstream into the wind, meet the waves head on, and speed full throttle to dock and safety.

For thirty minutes (they seemed like a life-time), our three boats fought a river gone wild. A major storm had turned the narrow Canyon walls into a wind-tunnel. I had no idea at the time what was going on in the other two boats, but I knew that prayer kept ours afloat.

Finally, after stopping to bail out water at one point, all three boats had docked safely with all hands accounted for. I learned later from my two sons, who were in the guide's wife's boat, that she had handled herself beautifully. In fact, she was the first one back to the dock. At one point, a gust of wind caught the front end of the boat and began to flip it over backwards, but her cool-headed reaction, at the very least, saved everyone from an icy swim. At most, she saved my sons' lives.

I walked away from that trip with another reason why women are so incredibly valuable. I know for a fact that if our guide hadn't listened to his wife, we would have been in major trouble.

It's struck me several times since that incident how much I've profited from learning the valuable character traits and natural talents that God has built into my wife. Far from an attempt to erase all differences between the sexes, I feel strongly that God placed the differences there for a purpose.

In this chapter, we'll look at several areas of natural, complementing strengths in men and women. I hope one result for every man will be that he finds new reasons for treasuring and valuing his wife, and I hope that one result for every woman will be to find yet another reason to thank God for the natural gifts she brings to those she loves.

Meeting Our Missing Part

It was a wise and loving God who said, "It is not good for the man to be alone" (Genesis 2:18a). But was a woman designed merely to provide a man with companionship—or does it go deeper than that?

Most people are familiar with the passage that talks about God creating woman and His words, "I will make (him, Adam) a helper suitable for him" (Genesis 2:18b). The Hebrew word for "helper" actually means "completer." The word is used throughout the Old Testament to talk about God being our "helper," the One who "completes what is lacking," or "does for us what we cannot do for ourselves."[1]

One of the things that should increase the "honor" a husband gives to his wife is realizing that God created her to help him in areas he isn't naturally equipped to handle. In other words, a wife is designed to bring strengths to the relationship that the husband does not naturally have himself.

Over the years, I've noted a number of ways in which men and women are different, but there are four areas in particular, I've seen a woman's natural gifts act like missing parts needed to complete a man. That first missing piece comes with a special language that a woman speaks which cannot only strengthen a marriage—it can literally be a life-saving gift to some husbands.

1. Two Languages in the Same Home

One study of little four-year-old boys and girls recorded every noise that came out of their mouths over a period of time.[2] The study concluded that 100 percent of the sounds made by little girls had something to do with literal words. They spent a great deal of time talking to each other, and almost an equal amount of time talking to themselves.

For little boys, however, the figure was only 60 percent words. The remaining 40 percent were simply noises and sound effects (like Bzzzzzzzz!, Zooooooooom! Baaammmmm!). In short, the tendency in even little girls is to use more words than little boys, and that early difference in language skills holds up throughout each age level.

Not only are women more verbal, but they often speak a different language than men do. I'm not talking about homes where English and Spanish, or Japanese and English are spoken, but about a much more common family environment where "Womaneise" and "Maneise" are spoken!

In roughly 80 percent of all homes, men primarily relate to their wives using what we call a *language of the head* while women tend to speak a *language of the heart*.

Typically, men tend to be logical, factual, and detail-oriented. In general, when a man runs out of facts to talk about in a conversation, he often stops talking! Usually, men don't have as much of a need to share as deeply or consistently as do their wives. Nor do they have the need to speak the same number of words their wives do. Some studies have shown that the average woman speaks roughly 25,000 words a day, while the average man speaks only 12,500! What this can mean in a marriage is that a woman is often left holding her cup out for meaningful conversation day after day and drawing it back with only a few drops to nourish her.

On the other hand, women often speak a *language of the heart.* In most cases, they love to share thoughts, feelings, goals, and dreams. A woman's natural skills at communicating often will make her wonderfully sensitive to small things others are thinking, saying, or feeling. And her desire for deep relationships usually exceeds what the average man desires.

It's almost as if men are two-humped camels. They can take a little conversation and then go for days across even the most difficult terrain without any need for more "watering" words, but a woman covering the same distances needs a daily allotment of water to survive and flourish—and often double that ration of "watering" words during difficult periods in her life.

Why should a man be interested in having his wife help him learn to speak her "language of the heart"? For one thing, it can actually help him live longer.

In his provocative book, *The Language of the Heart,* Dr. James J. Lynch presents compelling evidence that effective communication skills can do wonders for a person's cardiovascular health.[3] Whether we realize it or not, each time we engage in conversation, whether we are under stress or not, our blood pressure increases. However, when the conversation is stressful—*and especially when we hold our words inside*—our blood pressure can go to extremely high levels. This can be a dangerous situation, especially for people with a history of heart problems such as hypertension.

When a man learns to bridge both worlds—by speaking the language of the head and the language of the heart—it can make tremendously positive changes in his own life and the lives of those with whom he lives and works. Not only that, it can decrease the unnecessary stress that accompanies poor marital or business conversation. In the end, our hearts will thank us for the decreased workloads, and those around us will be thankful for the increased depth and feeling we have added to our communication.

But how does a woman actually help her husband bridge the "language" barrier in a home? If a man opens his eyes to several natural characteristics of his wife, he'll see that her natural strengths can complete him because. . . .

2. Women Tend to Relate on Multiple Levels

When most women are asked to describe the mental capacity of men, their response is, "He has a one-track mind." In a sense, that's pretty close—and not just in the area of sexual relationships. We men usually do concentrate on one thing at a time. It's as if our minds are like the inside of a battleship, with many different decks and compartments. When we leave one deck, we close the water-tight door to the last compartment and busy ourselves with what's close at hand.

Many a wife knows that if she leaves the house for an hour with her husband "in charge" of the kids, she's likely to come back and not see them anywhere in sight.

That's one reason why a wife, when she asks her husband if he thought about her at work that day, is likely to hear:

"Did I think about you today? Well . . . I mean . . . I'm sure I *must* have thought about you sometime!" Take heart, ladies; it's probably not that he doesn't love you, it's just a reflection of his tendency to "compartmentalize" his thinking. A man tends to remain in one world at work that centers around the office or job-site, and when he leaves that one, he enters another that revolves around the family.

A woman's mind, though, is like the war room on that battleship. It's the nerve center, equipped with fancy electronic devices that allow it to monitor all the vital signs on every deck of the house at the same time. Because of the way her mind has been designed, its radar is constantly on and sweeping in all directions.

What this means is that the average woman misses very little about her environment, no matter how crowded it is. That same "radar" system that is so sensitive in Norma is what alerted our fishing guide's wife to the coming windstorm. And it's also the same system that makes it very difficult for the average woman to relax completely if her husband is watching the kids.

Many a wife knows that if she leaves the house for an hour with her husband "in charge" of the kids, she's likely to come back and not see them anywhere in sight. Then when she asks her husband (who's now in front of the television set) where they are, he's liable to say, "Oh, I don't know . . . they're around here somewhere. . . . I think they went down to the pond to play," as he turns back to his game.

She, on the other hand, usually knows exactly what's going on with the kids, no matter what time of day it is, or what part of the house they are in. It doesn't matter if she lives in a three-story Victorian mansion. She can be in the basement when her radar goes off, but she knows the kids are in the attic fighting.

Greg and Mike literally thought that Mom had the house wired when they were out. Invariably, they'd be as quiet as church mice doing something they shouldn't, and still Norma's radar would go off, and she'd catch them.

A woman misses very little about her environment, which is probably the basis for that mysterious gift some have called intuition. We feel strongly that it's more than a natural "hunch." It's just one more way in which a woman can complete her husband—and another reason a man should honor and value his wife.

3. *Women Have the Unique Skill of Personalizing Their Environment*

Another tremendous strength a woman has is to become personally involved with everything around her. For example, have you ever wondered why the average wife doesn't care that much about watching a football game with you? Most of the time, it's because she doesn't *know* any of the players. There's nothing "personal" going on down on the field. (Now, this may not be true when she is in the stands sitting with you and some friends, but for many women, the battling going on down on the field is not as interesting as who you meet coming and going to the game.)

One way to get a woman to be more interested in a sporting event is to "personalize" it. Take a few moments and share some information with her about one of the players ("Honey, see that guy who just caught the ball? He's the guy I told you about who's been really struggling with his wife and kids . . . "). Then she'll feel more a part of the game and what's going on because she has an emotional tie to it.

How strong is a woman's need for an "emotional" attachment to someone? One indication is the fact that in this country alone, over ten million romance novels will be purchased this year, and 97 percent of them will be bought by women. Why? At least in part because these stories offer a picture of intimacy and deep personal relationships that, unfortunately, many find too infrequently in their own lives.

If a man isn't aware of his wife's tendency to "personalize" almost everything around her, it can lead to friction in a home. That's because for most women, the cat is not just an "animal," but their first baby. The wallpaper isn't just "something to cover the walls," but a reflection of who she is.

As you may have noticed, many men tend to take certain things in their surroundings for granted. For example, the car they drive. Recently, a story appeared in *Reader's Digest* that I really enjoyed.

There was a man with several daughters who owned an old, decapitated convertible. For years, every woman in the house urged him to get rid of the "pile of junk" and even refused to ride in it with him in public. Then one day it happened. He walked out from work, and the car had been stolen.

The man's wife and daughters were celebrating that night that his eyesore of a car had been stolen when the phone rang. The party was over—the police had found the car.

"We found your car only about ten blocks from where they took it," the policeman said. "We don't know who did it, but they left a note saying, '*You can have it back. We'd rather walk!*'"

For a man, a car can often be in the worst of shape because, "It's just transportation" to him, but for a woman, if her car isn't washed it can often leave her feeling incomplete. Why is that? In part, it's because it's usually easier for a man to separate himself from his surroundings than it is for a woman.

This is especially true of the house or apartment you live in. To a man, the home is a place of rest. To a woman, it's an extension of herself.

That's why a woman may feel "trashy" if the trash hasn't been taken out; she may feel dirty if the floors aren't cleaned and the carpet not vacuumed; she may even feel broken down if the fence isn't fixed or the door is falling off the hinges. Each of these things is a part of her; when they aren't right, she feels as if something's not right with her.

Why is this something that can benefit or "complete" a man? In part, it's because a woman's natural sensitivity to her surroundings makes her alert to the things that surround us—and especially the people in her world.

It's like having a quality control expert in the home who can spot lurking problems with her "early warning" system. In addition, her heightened awareness of those around her rarely causes her to make a crucial relationship mistake many men make at the office—and at home.

4. Women Are Generally More Concerned about People Than They Are about Projects.

For the most part, men are conquerors. That means at least some of the time they tend to be less concerned about people and feelings than they are about "getting the job done." This is quite natural for men, because we tend to derive our sense of worth from what we do. The better "job" we do, the better we feel about ourselves.

Women, on the other hand, primarily derive their feelings of worth from those to whom they're related. If a woman is married, she looks to her husband more than any other earthly individual for her personal sense of value and worth.

That natural concern for deep and loving relationships that a woman has can certainly be shared by a man—but it can also be more easily set aside by him as well. Take hunting for example.

The average man can load up his high-powered rifle, go hunting, and blow away one of God's beautiful creatures. Then he can cut off its head, stuff it, hang it on a wall, gather his neighbors around, and triumphantly say, "I did that!" He's conquered something!

But generally women have already made much too deep an emotional attachment to Thumper and Bambi in the movie theater to execute one of their real-life counterparts out in the wild. When those sweet little animals die, a part of the woman is hurt as well.

You can even see this difference between the sexes when men and women go shopping. When the average man hears the average woman say, "Honey, let's go shopping and find a new blouse for me," he hears the word "shopping." But what she usually means is

"Shooooppppppiiiiinnnng!"

Once a man hears her words, "Let's get a blouse," he is like a bloodhound who has just had an escaped prisoner's scent held in front of his nose. Once he's gotten a "whiff" of what he's going to the mall to hunt for, then it's off to sniff out a new blouse (any blouse), bag it, get back home, and lay on the porch as quickly as possible.

Since men are often more "conquer"-oriented than women, they usually tend to concentrate on the completion of a project—regardless of the personal costs. But because a woman's sense of value is so closely tied to all the relationships around her, she's often gifted in helping a man be more sensitive to what's really important beyond the immediate goal.

Take Brian, for example. For several Saturday mornings, his goal was to get up as early as he could, mow the yard, do his chores, shower, and get in front of the television set just before kickoff of the first football game of the day. As he attacked his objective of getting the yard done and getting in front of the television, he wasn't always concentrating on how to build a strong relationship with his six-year-old son, Mark.

Mark would get up with his father each Saturday and desperately try to help him with the yard. But try as he might, he could never keep up with his father on any of the chores. That was especially true when it came to "helping" his father dump all the grass from the catch bag into the trash can.

"Son, that's enough," Brian would finally say in frustration after having to pick up yet another pile of spilled yard clippings. "I don't need that kind of help right now. Why don't you go inside and see if you can help your mother? *Now.*"

Brian's wife watched each week as little Mark would walk out the door to help his Dad with his chest sticking out—and walk back in a short time later crest-fallen. As a loving wife, she brought what was happening to his attention.

At an appropriate time, she used a word picture[4] to explain to him the way he was killing his son's spirit in his "quest" to quickly mow the yard. He was sacrificing his relationship with his son for a football game that could easily be video-taped and played when his son was in bed. Fortunately, Brian was wise enough to accept her correction. He even expressed appreciation to his wife for what she said:

"Thanks, Honey. Now that you mention it, I've got to admit that I have been pushing Mark aside these past few weeks. I'm not sure why I get so caught up in getting something done my way, but I'm going to learn. My son is a lot more important to me than how quickly I get the chores done—no matter what game is on."

In Brian's home, a sensitive woman received extra honor that night because of her willingness to point out his steamroller tendencies to put projects in front of people. But that's not the only reason he's thankful for the woman God has given him. There's one more reason that outshines them all. Namely, in every marriage, right under a man's roof, is one of the most priceless things God has given him—one that he can tap into almost any time to help him in his responsibility to develop a close-knit family.

The Incredible Worth of a Woman: She Has a Built-In Marriage Manual

Do you know the main reason why men are held back from a promotion at work? Is it a lack of technical skill? Rarely. A lack of education? Occasionally. But the primary reason men fail to be promoted is their lack of relationship skills.[5]

What most men don't realize is that they have the world's greatest instructors in relationships living right under their roofs. A wife is a gold mine of relational skills. If a man wants to take advantage of the "missing part" of the nature that has affected every "Adam" since the beginning, all he has to do is look into the eyes of his wife—and learn to *tap into her built-in marriage manual.*

In talking personally with women in over sixty cities (where we've done our conferences these past five years), I've always asked for—but never found—a woman who was an exception to this rule. Namely, I have never met a woman who by her God-given nature didn't possess a built-in relationship manual.

So here's how a husband can tap into this rich source of relational skills to improve his own marriage—and his skills with his children and others as a result. First, a man needs to realize that his wife comes equipped with two tremendous inner strengths:

1. She has a strong, innate desire for a good and healthy relationship; and

2. She has the natural ability to recognize a great relationship.

These two underlying qualities are the basis for three important questions that a man can use to pull out of a woman her built-in relationship manual.

Three Questions That Can Help a Man Tap into a Woman's Built-In Marriage Manual

Three simple but life-changing questions are all it takes. For the sake of argument, let's say Bob is going to ask Julie these questions:

Julie, I realize that one way God equipped you as a helper was to complete me in the relational side of life. So let's begin with our marriage . . .

Question #1: On a scale from one to ten, with zero being terrible and ten being a great marriage, where would you like our relationship to be?

Naturally, almost every woman (and man, too!) answers that they'd like to consistently be around a nine or a ten. After all, how many of us are into misery? Bob would then go on to question two:

Question #2: On a scale from one to ten, overall, where would you rate our marriage today?

In most cases, a man will rate the marriage two to three points *higher* than his wife will, so don't let the initial difference in perception shock you. Remember, the average woman is much more in tune with the state of the relationship than the average man.

Be sure and give her time to think and share. Use the "quick listen" method described in Chapter 9 to reassure her that you value her opinion and want to understand her as much as possible.

Whether you agree with your wife or not, it's important to honor her by giving her your full attention. The goal is to understand her and to be open to what she may say.

The next question is the crucial one. In fact, in some ways it doesn't matter what she answers to Question Two, for the most important question is this third one—the one that can flip open the pages to her natural marriage and relationship manual.

Question #3: *As you look at our relationship, what are some specific things we could do over the next six weeks that would move us closer to a ten?*

I have yet to find a woman who cannot paint the answer to that question in brilliant detail. However, I have met numerous men who can't even find the paintbrush!

In some cases, your wife may be reluctant to answer this question, fearing she'll hurt your feelings—or even worse, that you'll hurt *her* feelings by your defensive response. That's why it's important to patiently give her the time to talk and to consistently reassure her about the security of your relationship—no matter what she says or where she rates things. If she feels secure in your love, almost without exception she'll be able to open up with many helpful specifics on how you can more effectively steward the gift of the marriage and family God has given you.

For any of us who are serious about effectively loving those who mean the most to us, honor must characterize our relationships. Nowhere is that more true than for the man who is serious about being a Christlike lover to his wife.

Let me state something clearly. *Valuing his wife's differences, and even tapping into her built-in marriage manual, does not transfer leadership or responsibility away from the husband and place it onto the wife.* Biblically, there is no escape clause from the man being the head of the home—the man is the fact-finder when it comes to building a strong relationship. But to be the type of loving leader God intended, allowing a wife to fulfill her God-given function as a loving "completer," is a must. It can help a man replace insensitivity with sensitivity, and lording it over others with genuine love for them. It can also help men become the observant servant leaders they were always meant to be.

By appreciating the unique and wonderful way God has created a woman, we can add a richness and joy to our marriage that virtually everyone wants, but very few have. The secret is in learning to honor a woman as someone unmatched in God's creation, made especially by Him as a completer, to do things for a man he could never do for himself.

Yet what do you do when your "completer" becomes discouraged or loses energy in your relationship? Or what happens when you do? In the next chapter, we'll see a second loving action that can be a tremendous help to a home. It involves learning a practical method of energizing your mate in as little as sixty seconds.

5

Energizing Your Mate in Sixty Seconds

My wife Norma has always loved zoos. Regardless of what type of zoo, or how many times she's been through it, she always thrills at the opportunity to go again. On the other hand, having been through dozens of zoos over the years, I rarely get excited about going through another one. But one day on a speaking trip to the Midwest, Norma picked up a brochure advertising a "Wild Animal Park" that actually attracted my attention.

When she saw I wasn't immediately saying "no," her face lit up. Her voice was full of excitement as she read me the brochure and said, "Gary, I know you'll like this one. Will you come with me? *Please.*" Once again, we were off to one of Norma's favorite places in life.

Before we could actually go, there was one minor problem we had to overcome. The brochure described this park as a "drive-through zoo" and we didn't have a car. So with a phone call, I arranged with my close friend and now ministry associate, Terry Brown, to borrow his car for the afternoon. He graciously agreed and delivered to us his tiny Fiat convertible within the hour, and we were on our way to the park.

As we drove up to the main gate, they said convertibles were allowed, but that we would have to keep the top up. The friendly park ranger also gave us some advice on how to feed the animals, when not to feed them, and a strong warning about the one place in the park where we had to keep the windows rolled up. This area was called a "danger zone" because of the very large or very wild animals living there. Emphatically, we were told:

"If anything happens to your car in this section of the park, just pull off the road and honk your horn and a friendly ranger will come and rescue you."

It sounded safe enough to me, so we began our self-guided

tour of the drive-through zoo. Once inside, we quickly discovered that the animals living there were particularly friendly. The giant birds tried to stick their heads inside the car looking for food. One giraffe did manage to stick his twenty-inch gray tongue inside the car and tried to slurp Norma's sandwich out of her lap. At this point I readily agreed with her that this was far better than a "regular" zoo.

Then it happened. Halfway through the park, we finally came to the well-marked "danger zone," and right when we were in the middle of no-man's land, Norma asked, "What's that coming out from under the hood?" Well, it was steam from our overheating radiator, and it was beginning to form an unwelcome white cloud!

"Oh no," I groaned. Glancing at the temperature gauge for the first time, I noticed that it was way beyond the "hot" reading on the gauge and nearing the "melt down" zone.

Great, I thought. *We've only been gone an hour and already I've ruined my friend's car.*

I started to pull over, but Norma cried out,

"You can't pull over here! Didn't you see that sign? *This is a danger zone!*"

"But honey, I can't wreck this man's car. I've *got* to pull over!"

"But not here!" she pleaded. "What if we're both trampled to death or eaten alive? Who'll take care of the children? . . ."

"Now, don't worry," I said as gently as I could. "It says right here in the brochure that if we have any trouble in a danger zone, all we have to do is honk the horn and a friendly ranger will come right over and rescue us!"

Norma frowned, but with the way the car was acting, it was obvious we didn't have any choice. So we pulled over, and I started honking the horn. . . . and honking. . . . and honking. . . .

I honked for forty-five minutes, and no friendly ranger ever came and rescued us. Basically, the guide at the gate had lied to us. We could have been eaten, trampled, or both. But what happened between Norma and me during this time illustrates one of the most important principles I've ever discovered when it comes to developing loving, lasting relationships.

"Don't Look Now, but. . . ."

While all my honking didn't alert a single ranger, it did notify every furry resident of the "danger zone" that we were there—and that we might have (or become) lunch. First, the wild burros ambled up and began nibbling at the top of my friend's convertible. I finally had to get out of the car and yell and chase them away to convince them that hay would be better than our fabric top. I had just gotten back inside the car when I made the mistake of looking into the rear view mirror.

"Norma," I said in my calmest voice, "don't look now, but you're never going to believe what's coming!"

An entire herd of huge, shaggy buffalo were walking out of the woods and soon surrounded our little Fiat. One of them, on my side of the car, wandered over, knelt down, and put his head right up against my window. With those great big brown eyes and a huge head about four inches from my face (the steam coming out of his nose began fogging my window), it was obvious he was saying nonverbally, "Got anything in there for me?"

Then he started pushing on the window, rocking the car as he did. During the whole ordeal, neither of us looked up, hoping our ignoring them would make them go away.

"Listen to that thing breathe!" I said.

"That's not him breathing," Norma said. "*That's me!*"

Finally, our hairy friends wandered off, and our car cooled down enough for us to drive to the main gate for help.

As funny as it seems now, that hour trapped in the car together was actually a very tense situation. In fact, if it had been several years earlier, one or both of us might have responded in a very different way. We could have easily used that tense situation to explode and so weaken our relationship, rather than relying on an important principle that could strengthen it.

Norma could have said to me, "Gary, I can't handle this! I don't care if this thing explodes, get this car moving!" or I could have easily said to her, "Be quiet! You're going to see a wild animal inside this car if you don't hush up!"

Either of us could have done and said things to each other in the "heat of battle" that we would have later regretted; and if we had blown up, it would have drained away the positive feelings and energy we'd stored up in our marriage for weeks as quickly as the water draining from our radiator.

On this trip, however, things were different. They were different because we had finally begun to understand and practice an incredibly important concept in the Scriptures.

We never know when we're going to find ourselves in a frustrating situation with someone we love. During these times, when a high-intensity predicament is threatening to drain the positive energy right out of our relationships, most of us take one of two roads. We either choose to react and blast those near us or we choose to respond in a way that actually helps to strengthen our marriage. It all begins with learning how to energize your mate during a stressful situation in as little as sixty seconds.

Energizing Your Mate in Sixty Seconds

What is the biblical principle that kept our emotions in check during this difficult time? It's really an incredible power that is right at our fingertips—the ability to be gentle and to tenderly touch each other.

> *What is the biblical principle that kept our emotions in check during this difficult time?—*
> *The ability to be gentle and to tenderly touch each other.*

For years I had known intellectually that "a soft answer turns away anger" (Proverbs 15:1), and that a key fruit of the spirit was "gentleness" (Galatians 5:23). But I had never applied either principle in my most important relationships. Now, if softness as a way to energize a person sounds too easy to you, how often do you feel gentle in the middle of catastrophe?

Most people's basic bent during times of stress is to lash out or lecture—or both— especially if the predicament is somebody else's fault. But tenderness, above and beyond the call of our human nature, is a transformer, an energizer of those around us.

Since I wasn't fortunate enough to have a father who knew how to be tender to his wife, I wasn't aware that softness during stressful times was even an option until several years into my marriage. And that's when I learned that one of a person's greatest needs is to be comforted, especially during those moments in life when the roof falls in.

A Creative Way to Add a Skylight to Your Home. . . .

One afternoon I was very late coming home from boating with my son Greg. I had taken the car, which left Norma with only our mini-motor home for transportation. She waited and waited, but when I was several hours later than I had predicted, she decided to take our mini-motor home to the grocery store.

Granted, our motor home is not the easiest thing to handle in the world. I'd already had my share of close calls when it came time to park or back the vehicle out. But Norma re-defined the word "close-call" as she tried to back the camper out of the driveway.

She had almost made it out from under the carport when she turned the wheel the wrong way and sheared off an entire section of the roof. And if that wasn't bad enough, the falling roof bounced off the hood of the camper, scraping away paint and leaving a deep dent in its wake.

When I pulled into the driveway an hour later, I couldn't believe my eyes. Looking at the gaping hole in the roof, my first response was to look at the sky to see if the tornado was still around, but one look at our mobile home told me that it was Mother Norma, not Mother Nature, who had caused this catastrophe.

I instantly felt like ordering her out of the house and asking her questions like, "Where did you get your driver's license? From a gumball machine at Shop-Mart?!"

Instead, I sat in my car, frozen, with my hands on the steering wheel, praying, "Lord, you have to give me strength.

Every fiber in my body wants to lecture my wife now and not be gentle with her. This is one of those pressure situations, and I know I have a choice. Lord, help me figure out what I'm going to do." Turning to my son Greg I asked him, "What do you think I ought to do?"

Greg said, "Dad, why don't you do what you teach?"

"That's a good idea," I said.

But all the while I was praying for the strength to be tender. Being tender at such a moment is definitely not natural. You have to take off the comfortable old nature of lectures and anger, and put on the new nature of tenderness. This can be excruciatingly difficult (Ephesians 4:22–24).

Finally, I got out of the car and walked toward the piece of roof lying in the driveway, but just as I got up to the camper, Norma came flying around the side of the house.

I fought off the voice ringing in my mind, *Lecture her! Lecture her!* and I did what didn't feel "natural" at the time. I simply held her in my arms and gently patted her on the back. I hadn't spoken one word when finally, Norma pulled away and said, "Oh, look what I did! I wrecked the motor home and knocked off the roof," she said. Then she added, "And I told the neighbors across the street what I did, and they're watching to see how you're going to respond."

Thankfully, I hadn't given the neighbors anything to gossip about by exploding at Norma. I just put my arms around her again and gently called her by my favorite affectionate name for her:

"Norm, listen. You know I love you. You're more important to me than campers and roofs. I know you didn't do this on purpose, and you're feeling really bad about it."

At that very moment, I could feel Norma relaxing. What's more, I immediately felt better myself as my own anger drained out of me to be replaced by feelings of tenderness. While it's hard to explain, I could tell that instead of being pulled apart, we were actually growing *stronger* as a result of the trial.

After a few more minutes of talking and holding her, Norma went on with whatever she was doing, and I went out to the garage to lay my hands on the few tools I had. After taking a deep breath, I said to Greg, "Well, I'd better get at it."

Just then, from out of nowhere, a friend from my church pulled up into our driveway. This wasn't just any ordinary friend. He was a local contractor pulling up in his pickup filled with hammers, saws, lumber, nails, paint, and a long ladder. He jumped out and said, "OK, Gary. Let's get at it!"

"Where did you come from?" I asked in disbelief.

Apparently our good neighbors across the street weren't only watching my reactions to Norma. They had also been calling everyone around town to talk about our hole in the roof. Ironically, my friend had been one of the first to hear the news. With his expert help, and without exaggeration, we had our impromptu skylight patched and re-painted within two hours.

As I went to bed that night with Norma snuggled up next to me, I was amazed that I had actually done something right for a change, during a stressful situation. What would I have normally done? I could have zapped the life right out of her emotionally with angry words and lectures, and it would have taken days for us to feel our way back to each other.

If I hadn't known about the power of gentleness, I'm sure I would have acted as I had in the past and blown up. This time I didn't, and amazingly, it made all the difference. The old Gary Smalley might have lost it. The new one followed a biblical blueprint for turning away anger, and it made even a stressful event a time of closeness.

I learned an important lesson that day; it's one I've seen repeated time and time again in my life and in the lives of others. Simply put, that lesson is:

Remaining tender during a trial is one of the most powerful ways to build an intimate relationship (James 1:19, 20).

The power of tenderness is outlined and illustrated from one end of the New Testament to the other. However, from my perspective, Ephesians 4 does the best job of explaining it. In this section of Scripture:

• Verse 15 introduces the concept of gentleness by challenging us to grow up in all aspects "into Jesus Christ." We're to grow up in love and to become mature. That's what each of us wants I'm sure—to be mature, caring people who can encourage those around us.

• Then verses 22 and 23 tell us that to become complete in Christ, we're to take off our "old self," which is the opposite of godliness, and then put on our "new self." Now the question is, what is it we take off and what do we put on in its place?

• While there are certainly many aspects of our fallen nature that need to be exchanged for godly characteristics, verse 29 gives us one specific we can begin to put into practice today. Without pulling any punches, it says we are not to let "any unwholesome word proceed out of our mouth." Unwholesome words popping out of our mouths are a reflection of our old nature, and they need to be replaced with their opposite—words that are tender, gentle, and nurturing.

The verse continues with the encouragement to speak only words that are "good for edification according to the need of the moment, that it may give grace to those who hear." These are words that build up or strengthen others, words that bring energy and life to people.

Let's look at several practical ways to energize your mate, children, and friends on a daily basis by learning to replace angry, deflating lectures with tender, strengthening words.

Lectures and Tenderness Don't Mix

Let's say a woman is losing emotional energy and reaches the end of her rope. In frustration, she might say to her husband:

"Oooh, I've had it around this house. *Look at this mess.* Nobody ever picks up anything around here. I've got to have some help!"

Now that's a clear sign of a woman who is losing energy. The problem is, her husband may hear only the words, "I need help," and not the feelings or issues behind her frustration. Once a man hears the words, "I need help," his natural desire is to solve the problem at hand. Instantly, he's capable of taking over and saying something like this:

"Honey, I'm really glad you brought this up. You know, if you could just get organized around here, you wouldn't be so frustrated. It's about time you got a system of housework like we have at the office. And by the way, are you still taking those vitamin pills we spent all that money for? Are you getting your rest on a regular basis?"

Or worse yet, we men are capable of hitting below the belt and saying something like, *"Honey, do you think you're being disorganized is an indication that you're not spending enough time in God's Word on a regular basis?"*

Lectures are so natural. Particularly when they make us conquering males feel like we're solving a problem. The real problem, though, is that we've missed the deeper message *behind* her words. In fact, if we do give her a management-effectiveness course on cleaning the house, she tends to resent us, not applaud us. That often leads to a man saying something like:

"Well, what's wrong with you? If you don't want my help, then why did you ask me!"

The problem is, *she never was asking for help in the first place!* At least not the type of help that comes from lectures and object lessons. It only sounded that way because he focused on the words alone. Like many women, this wife was sharing her underlying feelings, her hurt, and her need for support, but what she expressed was her frustration. What a woman needs during times of expressed frustration is not a husband's mouth, but his shoulder. She really needs to be comforted and encouraged. She needs energizing—with a nice dose of meaningful touching tossed in.

We need to understand that when someone is going through a trial, they sometimes express that emotional draining of energy through their anger, discouragement, hurt feelings, or anxiety. The last thing a friend, spouse, or child who's hurting wants from us is a lecture, especially one that's delivered in harshness and anger.

Not only females resist or react to lectures or harsh words. Let's say it's been a very frustrating day at the office and a typical man walks in complaining, "This job doesn't pay enough for what they make me go through." In most cases, he's sharing his frustration—not issuing an invitation to be criticized. Not many men would enjoy hearing their wives say, "Yeah, they *don't* pay you enough, all right. You need to get a real job that pays more so we can make ends meet. In fact, I'll tell you what kind of job you *ought* to get. . . ."

The same thing is true with children. Teenagers rarely appreciate coming home after flunking a test and being met with angry, challenging words. I'm not saying that you can't confront a person in love over areas of error in his or her life, but at the *moment of vulnerability,* and particularly in the midst of the crisis itself, what a person needs first is tenderness.

Tenderness acts as a firebreak to an advancing forest fire. Fire-fighters get ahead of the fire, then clear a wide trail free of all "flammable" material. The fire may roar up to the firebreak, but it can't jump across and keep burning. That's one tremendous benefit of tenderness.

It takes work to "strip" an area clear of emotional kindling —particularly when a fiery trial is closing in on us. But we can head off the negative emotions that are coming and keep from getting "burned" if we do. Or, as we mentioned, we can add more fuel to the already burning fire—in the form of lectures.

*K*indness is communicating that someone is valuable through our actions.

To use another word picture, lectures act as an electronic suction device that can suck out all our energy, leaving us emotionally, spiritually, and physically drained. I've sat in numerous counseling sessions where a man was criticizing his wife or vice versa, and you can almost hear the suction machine roaring, pulling the life right out of their relationship.

Lectures may seem right, and occasionally they are an appropriate response to a person, but tender, honoring, "edifying" words can head off an argument before it breaks out in our relationship.

Making Tenderness a Habit in Your Home

Okay, I hear what you're saying: "I'd like to be more tender-hearted. But it's still a little abstract. How about several concrete suggestions on how to practice this new gentle habit?"

Ephesians 4:32 is your instruction booklet for becoming a tenderhearted person. In these verses are two powerful ways to be tenderhearted. The first is, "Be kind . . . to one another," then, "forgiving each other, just as God in Christ forgave you."

In other words, when it comes to being tender, kindness, gentleness, and forgiveness are like battery packs. They are what gives tenderness its punch. Let's look at each of these steps more closely.

Have you ever wondered what being "kind" to someone really means? *Kindness is communicating that someone is valuable through our actions.* There are ways to be kind—like visiting friends at the hospital or going to their home after the loss of a loved one. In these cases, kindness is usually best spoken without a word—by a hug, or a gentle act or touch. Our presence alone says, "I'm so sorry; you're very special to me; I'm praying for you." Combine a "kind" act with a tender touch, and the results can be life-changing.

Recently John Trent and I were on a radio program in California talking about the importance of being "tenderhearted," when a man called in and told us an incredible story about the power of silent tenderness.

A few years back, the caller had had a major heart attack. Though he was only in his early fifties at the time, it was so serious, the doctors at the hospital told his wife to notify the family he probably wouldn't live for more than a few days.

When his seventy-year-old father was called, he flew cross-country to be at what he thought was his son's deathbed. The fact that his father had come at all was a tremendous encouragement to his son. In all his life, he had never once heard the words, "I love you," from his father. Deep down, he always felt he was loved, but for years, he had longed to actually hear the words that would prove he was valuable to his father.

"My father never did come right out and say he loved me," he said. "But after he came out to see me in the hospital, I knew he did—and all because of one thing he did when I was lying in that hospital bed."

"What was it he did?" we asked, glued to our headphones.

"When I was in the hospital," the man continued, "my dad walked in and without saying a word, he took my hand and gently held it for over half an hour. He was tender with me for the first time I can ever remember. He still couldn't bring himself to *say,* 'I love you,' but I know now he really did."

We all teared up just listening to the emotion in his voice as he told us his story. As powerful a story as this was, it was "the rest of the story" that hit us the hardest, for the man went on to tell us that he miraculously recovered from his heart attack. But three days after he had come to visit his son in the hospital, the seventy-year-old *father* passed away!

This man shared with us and the entire listening audience, "If my father had never shown me his love by that one tender act, I don't think I would ever have truly known how much he loved me, but that one act of gentleness spoke more to me than anything he could have said. . . ."

His father's actions communicated kindness in its purest form. Without words—simply by his gentle touch—he shouted out the concept of tenderness in words that will forever ring in his son's heart.

Tenderness and Timing

Often the time to give someone a gentle word of encouragement or a meaningful touch is obvious. Sometimes, though, especially for people like me who do not come from a "high touch" background, it's hard to recognize the not-so-obvious times we need to be tender. What do we do then?

I'll never forget what one woman told me:

"If my husband would only put his arms around me and hold me when I'm feeling blue, and not give me a nonstop lecture or pep-talk about 'counting it all joy,' it would transform our marriage."

"Have you ever *told* him what you need?" I asked.

"Are you kidding? He'd be embarrassed and so would I," she laughed.

"This may come as a surprise to you," I said, "but he probably doesn't know how to be tender with you. He's been trained to lecture. Perhaps he needs some training in what genuine tenderness is."

"That makes sense to me," she said. "Many times when I'm crying and upset, he'll ask, 'What do you want me to *do?*' And I just flare up and say, '*If I have to tell you what to do, then that would ruin it!*'"

A husband should ask his wife, and a wife her husband, to define "tenderness" in their own terms. How he should hold her for her to feel safe and loved—when is the best time for her to be soft and sympathetic with him? A wife or husband shouldn't expect his or her mate to be a mind-reader when it comes to meeting the very important needs in this area.

Most of us aren't good emotional mind-readers anyway, and too few of us come from comforting backgrounds so we don't know the nonverbal signals that say, "Please hold me." While attempting to talk about being tender may seem awkward at first, just being willing to talk about this much needed area tends to bring energy and life to a relationship.

Using Tenderness as an Important Protective Tool for Your Children

We've talked about the need both a woman and man have for tenderness—a willingness to decrease our lectures and increase our tender expressions of love, but if gentleness is a key to marital growth, it is equally powerful when practiced between parent and child.

I know a man who had a very strained relationship with his teenage daughter. Recently, she had been dating a boy he did not care for, and her father had been extremely cutting in expressing his feelings. In fact, every time he brought up the subject (and everything they talked about seemed somehow to lead into it), their exchanges became loud and dishonoring.

At our seminar, he realized for the first time how important tenderness was, and how little of it he was showing to his daughter. He decided that he had to begin putting on the new nature of encouraging words. He still disapproved of the boy his daughter was dating—but he didn't have to blast his daughter at close range every night with angry words just to vent his frustration.

That very night at the seminar, he prayed to be more gentle with his daughter—and the opportunity to put his prayer into practice came to pass. After he got home from the seminar, he walked upstairs to get ready for bed. He passed by his daughter's room and heard her crying as she talked over the phone. It was the boyfriend he disliked so much calling, and it was obvious that they were breaking up over the phone.

Inside, this father felt like jumping for joy. He couldn't think of anything better than what was happening, but something stopped him as he began to enter his daughter's room and pull out the standard "I told you he was a jerk" lecture. As he heard his daughter crying as she hung up the phone, he remembered his vow to God to bring tenderness into his home.

He walked slowly into her room and gently sat down on her bed. She lay with her head buried in her pillow. When she realized he was sitting next to her, she instantly bristled—figuring she knew what was coming, but her father said nothing. Instead, he quietly held her as she cried. When she finally stopped, she looked up at him and said, "Daddy, thank you for just being here with me."

As my friend walked out of his daughter's room, his emotions hit like a sheet of ice water. He realized that he had been so distant from his daughter for so long, it had been years since she had called him "Daddy."

The Master's Use of Tenderness

Our children, our spouse, our close friends, and each of us have a physical and emotional need for tenderness, expressed as words or as meaningful touches. Kindness comes from *honoring* that need in the lives of our loved ones and demonstrating that *love* by doing all we can to fulfill it.

The main reason I've mentioned tenderness and kindness as the second act of love is its great importance in communicating value to others. One of the loudest cries we hear among men, women, and children is the desperate plea for tenderness and gentleness from people who love them.

Jesus was the master at using tenderness to express high value to others. Remember how He greeted the children who came to Him? Mobbed by onlookers and protected by His disciples, Jesus could have easily waved to them from a distance or just ignored them altogether. He did neither. Jesus touched and blessed the children (Matthew 19:13).

His tenderness in dealing with others was graphically displayed when a leper came to Him, described in Luke as a man "with leprosy. . . . Jesus reached out his hand and touched the man" (Matthew 8:3).

To touch a leper in Jesus' day was to flirt with contracting the most terrifying terminal illness known to the biblical world. To have leprosy was to die shunned and untouched, driven away from civilization until finally, mercifully, you died. People in

Jesus' day would literally not get within a stone's throw of a leper—and Jewish law allowed stones to be thrown at a leper if he or she did come any closer.[1]

Yet even before Jesus spoke to the leper, He reached out His hand and touched him. Can't you imagine the people around Jesus recoiling from the sight? *No one* would touch a leper. Yet Jesus, in His wisdom, knew the man's heart, and his need for both spiritual cleansing and physical tenderness (see Matthew 8:1–3 and Luke 5:12).

When Tenderness Is Tied to Forgiveness

I've mentioned several aspects of being "tenderhearted." The first is kindness, and the second is meaningful touch. There is a third element of tenderness, though, that can have incredible power in relationships, namely *forgiving* one another.

It was years before I discovered what "forgiveness" means in the original language, but its meaning has always stayed with me. The literal picture behind the word "forgiveness" is untying a knot.[2] In the confines of everyday life, we can all get tied up in knots because of what others (especially our spouses) have said or done to us.

Part of forgiving someone is actually helping them become untied from their frustrations. No matter if the offense was big or small, forgiveness is saying, "I want this person free! Released! Untied!" For those who want to give encouragement and energy to their spouse or someone else, it can have incredible results.

A doctor friend of mine told me a story about a man who was dying in a nearby hospital. He was very, very ill, and the doctors could give him only hours to live. To all around him he seemed to have given up the fight, but that afternoon, this man's brother appeared in his room. The brother was the same one with whom he had never gotten along and who had always been rough and unkind to him growing up.

"I . . . I just come to ask if you will forgive me for the way I have treated you," the man's brother blurted out. Then he did an extraordinary thing. The rough brother took his dying brother's hand and told him he loved him.

At first when the brother sat and held the sick man's hand, it was rigid and stiff from the years of resentment he'd harbored against his brother. But remarkably, in the moments that followed those extraordinary words, his hand relaxed and the strength of his grip increased.

A moment before, he had felt so weak he did not think he could make it through the night. Yet after that visit, the sick brother steadily recuperated. The doctor couldn't pin-point any single thing that led to his rapid recovery. He told me that there could have been a number of physiological reasons for the man's strange and quick recovery. However, he felt sure that his brother's appearance and this man's recovery were not accidental. Namely, his brother's touch—and especially his words of forgiveness—were an important part in giving this man the energy to have a fighting chance to live.[3]

Are you still hesitating at knocking down old walls of anger and putting in a doorway of tenderness to your home—a door that opens to energizing words, gentle touching, and courageous forgiving? Then start this way.

Begin by spending time listening to your spouse, your child, or your friend—without any lectures. Then, the next time they show signs of losing energy in the midst of a discouraging or pressure-packed time, walk over and, without a word, put your arm around them or gently put your hand on their shoulder.

If you must say something, just say something like, "I can see you're really hurting, and I want you to know that I'm very sorry," or "I'm not sure if I can help you in what you're going through, but I love you, and if you're up to it, you can tell me how you're feeling." Particularly if tenderness hasn't been a hallmark of your relationships, you'll be amazed at how quickly being soft with people in this way can bring positive results.

I often tell people it doesn't take great wisdom to energize a person, but it does take sixty seconds. That's the amount of time it takes to walk over and gently hold someone we love. A few seconds invested in being tender can not only help our relationships —it can become catching in a home as well. But the amazing part of tenderness is that it works wonders even when we're not near our loved ones.

Once, while I was on a speaking trip, my schedule put me out of town on Mother's Day. I called Norma on that special day, telling her how sorry I was not to be there.

"How's your day been?" I asked.

"It's been a horrible day. Mike and Greg have been terrible to me, and everything's gone wrong." Resisting the temptation to tell her "exactly" what to do to make things "right," I simply listened. Soon, she slowed down, and I could tell she felt a bit better.

So I said, "Oh, I wish I was there with you." I said, "I'd just give you a great big hug, ummmmmmm! In fact," I said, "put your arms around yourself and give yourself a big hug for me. Ummmmmmmm!"

Now I didn't expect her to say, "Oh, you're such a wonderful husband. Thanks for being so tender." Wives usually don't say that when they're hurting. You've got to do this by faith because there may be times when they say, "Aw, you don't mean that!"

Just as I was getting off the phone, I heard the sound of a door opening, and Norma gasping in delight, "Ohhhh, Greg! They're so beautiful!"

"What's so beautiful?" I asked.

"Greggy brought me flowers for Mother's Day!"

"Hey, that's great," I said. Then it dawned on me.

"Say, Norma. Let me talk to Greg a minute."

Once my son was on the phone, I asked him where he got the flowers.

"Oh, I ordered them from a florist."

At that time he was only about thirteen years old, so I said, "But how did you pay for them?"

He said, "Oh, I just used your charge card, Dad."

Let's just say, I tried to remember all about showing tenderness to my son when I got home.

Tenderness is catching when it's communicated in a home —whether it's shared by an encouraging word, a gentle touch, or with an act of forgiveness. And the result between loved ones is energy—and another important way to build a loving, lasting relationship.

It takes practice and relying on God's strength to put on this important aspect of our new nature, but it's worth every ounce of effort we put into harnessing the power of tenderness to energize our loved ones.

As I mentioned earlier, energizing your mate by being gentle and tender is an important act of love, but it doesn't stand alone. It's just one of several ways we can put honor into action and show others how much we love them.

In the next chapter, I'm going to discuss an unbelievably powerful emotion that all of us have, yet few of us master. It's as much a part of our human makeup as our instinct for survival. It shapes the course of human events just as a roaring river carves canyons in sandstone. In addition, it has the potential to make our lives more meaningful and our relationships more fulfilling—or it can literally destroy the very things that are most precious to us.

Understanding it, like understanding the importance of tenderness, is absolutely essential if we want to honor God and others. Let's discover the secrets to mastering what may be the most powerful of all human emotions.

6

A Closed Spirit: Overcoming a Major Destroyer of Relationships

Late one night, while I was sound asleep, the phone rang. It was a man calling long distance who had gotten my number from a close friend. As I was struggling to wake up, he said, "Gary, I'm sorry to call so late, but my wife has left me. Actually, she's thrown me out of the house! She's so hostile toward me, it shocked me. I really didn't see it coming. We've been married almost twenty-five years, and now she's put me out on the street!"

As he continued, he asked, "Could you help me get back together with my wife?"

He sounded so desperate over the phone, I decided to help him if I could. So I asked, "Before I know if I can do anything to help you, I need to talk to your wife."

He immediately shot back, "That's impossible. She's not talking to me. She's not even talking to anyone who knows me. Gary, I don't think you understand. She *hates* me. You have no idea how much she hates me. She has a court order against me right now so that I can't even get into my own home!"

Having talked with many people in similar situations, I replied, "Well, I'll tell you what. I've never been turned down yet by a woman I've called. This could be the first time, but I'm willing to give it a try if you are."

After a brief pause, he said, "Well . . . I have nothing to lose, but please call me back the minute you talk to her and let me know what happens."

The next morning, I did call his wife. When she answered, I said, "Hello, I'm Gary Smalley. Your husband called me last night and really wanted some help, but I told him that in order to do anything for him, I would need to talk to someone who knows him as well as his wife. I was wondering. Could you just spend a couple of minutes with me, helping me understand your husband and why it was so difficult to live with him?"

Instantly she said, "Ohhhhh, I hate that man so much! I don't want to talk about him. In fact, even thinking about him upsets me."

I said, "It must have been horrible living with a man like that."

"You have no *idea* how horrible it was to live with that guy," she steamed. "He was so controlling, it was like I had to get *permission* to go to the bathroom!"

"How did you endure that kind of treatment for so many years?" I asked, trying everything I could just to keep her on the phone!

"I don't know how I managed, and now you're getting me to talk about him—and I don't want to talk about him!"

In the end, she did share several specific things this man had done—beginning with their honeymoon. Many were small, inconsiderate actions that had piled up hurt feelings until molehills became mountains.

After talking with her for only five minutes, I thanked her profusely for sharing her thoughts and time with me and hung up. Immediately I called her husband.

"Did you talk with her?" he asked.

"Yes," I said, "and you're right. *You are in big trouble!*"

Over the years, I could number in the hundreds the husbands who have called or written with a similar story. In each case, the man never "realized" that he was in such bad shape until his marital world came crashing down around him.

While there are unique situations with each person that has called, I can think of one common element in every case. In fact, it's one of the major destroyers of families—*unresolved anger.* Anger, though, is such a "normal" human emotion. How can it be so devastating to a relationship?

Opening the Door to a Major Destroyer of Families

Recently, a close friend told me about a rock star who brought home a cute little lion cub to raise on his ranch in Tennessee. Of course, he had to hire a lawyer to convince the local zoning board to give him a special permit to own a wild animal as a "pet," but with money being no object, he managed to get that detail taken care of quickly enough.

For several years his "tame" lion was quite a hit with his house guests. It never acted like a dangerous predator, only like a big, playful pet. Then one day without warning, a parent's worst nightmare became this man's reality.

His little two-year-old son was playing near the lion cage. The parents heard his screams for help from inside the house, but there was nothing they could do. The lion had broken out of his cage and brutally mauled the little boy before running off into the woods. In a terrible tragedy, the man's son died before they could even get him to the hospital.

I'm sure this man loved his son, and having raised the lion from a cub, he probably never consciously thought that it would one day rob his child of life. But all the reasoning in the world on why it was "safe" to keep a wild animal around the house couldn't erase that animal's nature. For centuries, people have learned the hard way about the dark side of a lion's nature. By allowing a predator into his home, the man was setting the stage for a potential tragedy.

I can't think of a single person I've met who would willingly expose a child or spouse to the fury of a full-grown lion, but I know of many husbands and wives who are letting another deadly killer walk right through their front door without a fight —*unhealthy, unresolved anger.*

Anger can rip the heart right out of a relationship. Without exaggeration, every hour that anger is allowed to stay in a person's life, it acts like an emotional time bomb ticking down to detonation. Like a terrorist bomb placed in an innocent looking shopping bag, it cares nothing for whom it hurts or eventually kills.

"But everyone gets angry. Even Jesus got 'angry' at the people in the temple," some may say. While this is certainly true, there is a major difference between righteous anger (that can have a "corrective" effect on error), and the kind of unhealthy anger that grows wild and, unchallenged, leads to destructive conflicts.

Like that rock star's lion, anger inside a person can never be made a "tame" emotion. Even "righteous anger" can become corrupted if a person is not very, very careful.

The man who called me in the middle of the night learned a crucial skill needed in any healthy relationship. In his case it proved to be a life-saving skill. He realized that by letting anger build up in his wife's life—anger that he was directly responsible for provoking—he had *closed her spirit* toward him.[1]

Like that innocent looking lion cub, he had let his insensitive acts pile up until they finally broke full force on the relationship. What he learned, however, actually helped him begin to repair the damage. He learned how to reopen his wife's closed spirit by getting the anger out of her life—and it made a dramatic change in his situation.

> *. . . we'll never be successful in our most important relationships until we learn how to drain the anger out of another person's life.*

Unfortunately, my late night friend is not unique. Parents can sometimes leave anger in a child's life when he or she is young, closing the child's spirit to them tightly. These same parents then see that deep-seated anger turns into resistance and rebelliousness in their teenagers. Employers can even close the spirit of their employees and soon meet resistance and a stiffening will in them.

Even though anger is potentially destructive, it can be dealt with, even in cases that may seem humanly impossible. That's what we're going to talk about in this chapter. We don't have to live in continual disharmony with others. We can literally be in harmony with those around us the majority of the time.

But we'll never be successful in our most important relationships until we learn to drain the anger out of another person's life. It's absolutely crucial that we learn how to "open" a person's closed spirit and get back in harmony with them again.

That begins as we learn the skills of putting unresolved anger out of our homes.

Putting Unresolved Anger out of a Home

First, let me define what I mean by unhealthy anger. *Selfish anger is the negative emotion we feel when a person or situation has failed to meet our needs, blocked our goals, or fallen short of our expectations.* It's what we feel when we've placed our needs, wants, and desires ahead of anyone else's. Then we become frustrated if those around us don't react the way we want them to. Let me illustrate more clearly what I mean by "negative" anger by giving a hypothetical example from my own home.

If I walk through the door one night and blast Norma for being five minutes late with dinner, I'd be absolutely wrong. It certainly isn't a sin for her to have dinner ready a few minutes late, and so to "let her have it" only demonstrates I was more interested in my own stomach than her welfare. That's the real problem with anger; it puts "me" ahead of everyone else and shows its displeasure whenever "I" don't get my way.

To clarify even further, there are two things we need to keep in balance. *First,* there is a "righteous" anger that stands up against sin. In Ephesians 4, there is a clear command to be angry over the things that would grieve God's heart (often the kinds of things that fill our newspapers and evening news). ". . . *But in your anger do not sin*" (Ephesians 4:26). Biblically, two wrongs never equal one right. Even if we become righteously angry over some anger-producing situation in our life or the lives of others, we are never justified in reacting in a sinful way.

Second, try as we might by logical reason, we will not always be able to avoid an immediate emotion. If someone accidentally steps on our foot or cuts in front of us on the freeway, our instantaneous reaction may be anger. There's nothing wrong or sinful about anger at this point. But when we let anger remain in our lives, or when we take its energy and direct it toward another person to hurt them, we move from a normal, healthy feeling to a destructive one.

Apply what Martin Luther used to say to negative thoughts: "You can't keep the birds from flying over your head . . . but you can keep them from building a nest in your hair!" We may not be able to keep anger from cropping up as an instantaneous and instinctive reaction to some pain or problem, but we can make a decision to keep it from staying in our lives and poisoning our attitudes or the attitudes of our loved ones.

Putting Healthy Limits on an Unhealthy Emotion

Let's go back to the couple with whom we started this chapter. From the time they were first married, this husband never placed any boundaries around his anger. Whenever his wife blocked any of his goals, or slowed him down in any way, he blasted her without regard to the emotional impact of his words.

One could say that his wife should have been more "spiritually mature" and should not have been hurt by his angry outbursts, but in real life, after a constant stream of angry words and actions over the years, she began to wilt under his treatment. This wife didn't realize that it is possible to be free from anger on our own, as you'll see in Chapters 13 and 14, and her husband didn't realize two things about anger in a home that can cripple a relationship.

1. Anger Eats Away at a Person's Health

Inside the brain, the decision you make to harbor negative feelings toward others can set off a series of physical events you would do well to avoid. When a person becomes angry, his body goes on "full alert." When the inner brain gets the message that there's a stressful situation out there, it doesn't ask questions—it reacts. Your body can easily release as many chemicals and disrupt as many bodily functions when you are angry with your spouse as if you're being attacked by a wild animal.[2]

After several years of living with an angry man, the woman in our story began manifesting several of the symptoms of a person with deep-seated anger locked inside them: early morning awakening, depression, tension, grinding teeth, an unexplainable sense of dread, jumpiness, and increased irritability.[3] None of these negative outworkings of anger is physically helpful. In fact, unresolved anger actually pulls a person's resistance to illness down.

When a person's body is constantly tense and on edge (for unrighteous anger never fully lets a person relax—even in his sleep), this tension will inevitably begin to wear the person down. That's when really undesirable things begin to happen physiologically, such as clinical depression, colitis, bleeding ulcers, anxiety attacks, lowered resistance to colds and flu, and heart and respiratory failure. Several researchers even believe that some types of cancer result from the mega-doses of stress that unhealthy anger carries with it.[4]

Perhaps all these physical manifestations of anger are behind the first commandment with a promise, "Honor your father and mother, so that you may live long . . . "(Exodus 20:12). Anger, however, doesn't just contribute to a poor grade on a health report card. It can also keep us "in the dark" when it comes to loving God and others.

2. *The Greatest Problem of All*

In 1 John 2:9–11, the apostle says that continual anger toward another results in losing the ability to live in God's light. Being angry with our brother pushes us into darkness—completely isolated from the light of His love. When we live with anger—or provoke it in the hearts of others—we pull a veil of darkness across our eyes that blinds us to the damage we're doing to others.

In part, this is why so many angry men or women don't "wake up" to the damage they've done to a home until the very walls of the family are falling down around them. The anger they have spewed out at members of their family has doubled back and blinded them to God's love and that of others.

Walking consistently in darkness prevents us from being lovingly sensitive toward others. It also kills any interest we have in studying God's Word and puts an icy chill on our desire to pray. Further, it robs us of any desire to please and honor Him or to experience His joy, contentment, and peace.

I've met a number of people who, after years of attending church and seeking God, have still not found peace. And after getting to know them better, the major reason for their failure in many cases is deep-seated anger.[5] They are unwilling to forgive or seek forgiveness, and as a result they hide pockets of darkness inside their lives—black holes in their souls that can expand throughout the years.

Anger does tremendous damage to a person physically and spiritually—and that's not all. It also goes to the emotional heart of a relationship and can bury any feelings of warmth or attachment in its icy darkness as well.

How can we tell that anger has begun to attack our relationship, pushing it into darkness? Our loved ones will begin to withdraw from us on every level—physical, emotional, and spiritual. That withdrawal is something I call a *closed spirit*. Left unchecked, this spirit can drain every bit of sparkle and vitality out of our families and leave them empty, wounded, and alone.

Recognizing a Person's Spirit

Let me get more specific about what I mean about a person's "spirit." It can be explained this way. When you meet someone for the first time, you interact with him on three levels—first with your spirit, then with your soul, and finally with your body.

Imagine with me that I walk up to a person at one of our seminars and meet him for the first time. Before ever we spoke a word, the first thing that would "touch" would be our *spirit*. I'm defining the "spirit" of a person as the innermost, intangible part of our being that tells us if there is any natural connection or friction between us. It's also that part of us that relates to God at times when words aren't enough.

Next, is the *soul* (the Greek word for soul is "psyche"). The soul is made up of three inseparable parts: the intellect, the will, and the emotions. When we communicate with a person, we engage at all three of these levels. For example, with the person I met at the seminar, we would no doubt exchange words when we meet. Later, if we come to know each other better, we would exchange ideas or even dreams. In that way, our "souls" would have touched or interacted.[6]

If our relationship entered the third level, and if it were appropriate, we could physically touch. For example, you and I would probably shake hands if we met for the first time. Now we've had a complete relationship—body, soul, and spirit. Granted, at this point it's a shallow relationship, but at least it has all the elements of a "total" relationship.

In our seminar, I use my hand to illustrate the open and closed spirit concept. To make sure you understand this principle, hold out your own hand right now.

Look at the palm of your hand, with the fingers spread wide apart. Let's say that the fingers wiggling around freely are the spirit of a person. They're the first thing to reach out and touch others. The semicircular ridge where the fingers meet the palm of the hand could represent the soul where people meet intellectually. And the very center of the palm could stand for the body.

When you are happy and all is well in your relationship with your mate, child, or friend, those fingers are wiggling and happy. The palm is open and exposed—ready to reach out and even to lovingly hold someone else's hand. An open hand could have represented the woman whose story we told at the beginning of this chapter. When she first married, she was open and eager for love.

If I offend a person or provoke him to anger, however, that open hand can begin to close. Take time to give yourself a living object lesson. Close your hand slowly and notice what happens. The spirit begins to close over the soul and the body. If it is allowed to tighten up all the way, what do you have? A closed fist—the world-wide symbol of anger and defiance. In short, you have what that man had when he called me in the middle of the night—a wife who was so deeply hurt and so "closed" to him that she lashed back with the force of a rock-hard fist.

As long as everything is healthy in a relationship, the hand is open, the fingers wiggling and happy. The spirit is open and responsive. But hurtful words and actions—allowed to grow into a bitter spirit—can one day lead to our being shut out of someone's life completely.

How Do We Close a Person's Spirit?

While there are probably hundreds of ways to offend someone—and close his or her spirit—we consistently see several that top the list. To repeat just a few, we can close a person's spirit by—

- Speaking harsh words
- Belittling a person's opinions
- Being unwilling to admit that we're wrong
- Taking a person for granted
- Making jokes or sarcastic comments at the other person's expense
- Not trusting a person
- Forcing a person to do something he's uncomfortable with
- Being rude to that person in front of others
- Ignoring a person's genuine needs as unimportant or not nearly as valuable as our own

That's just a sample of the "hit list" of actions that can close a person's spirit.[7] Our loved ones could probably make up their own list. We may not even be aware of what we do to deposit anger into their lives. When it comes to relationships, an important rule of thumb is, *whatever dishonors another person usually closes his spirit.*

While it wasn't my intended goal, I got an early start in closing Norma's spirit. When we were first married, I spoke at a number of youth groups. We were still in college, and we had no children, so Norma always went along with me to these meetings.

I thought I was quite funny at the time, and I would crack jokes at Norma's expense, totally unaware of how it was affecting her spirit. I would say things like, "Oh, it sure is great being married to Norma. She treats me just like a god! Every morning she serves me burnt offerings."

That would get big laughs. So then I'd follow up with something like, "Being married to Norma is just like being married to an angel—she's always up in the air harping about something and she never has an earthly thing to wear!"

And if I was really on a roll, I could always tell the kids about the time I pulled up to the airport with Norma and a sky cap asked, "Can I help you with your bag?" And I said, "No, thanks, she can walk." Later, in the car, you can guess what would happen.

Norma would often say, "I really didn't appreciate your jokes, Gary." To which I'd impatiently wave my hand, and say, "Oh, lighten up. You're *sooooo* sensitive!" I didn't realize it at the time, but each sarcastic comment was beginning to close her spirit to me.

Once again, part of the problem lies with the differences between men and women. Men are usually not aware that God has created most women with a highly sensitive spirit to sarcasm and criticism. I know I wasn't aware of this very important natural difference—particularly during that first important year of marriage.

My Own Valentine's Day Massacre

Six months or so after our wedding, Valentine's Day rolled around. It was our first Valentine's Day as a married couple and Norma had spent hours preparing a fancy meal just for me. In her mind as she was laboring over a hot stove, she was thinking thoughts like . . .

"It's Valentine's Day, and my new husband is going to be coming through the door any minute. He'll have a romantic card for me, and then we'll enjoy a memorable time together!"

What I did was certainly memorable—but it produced the kind of memory I'd like to forget. I called at two o'clock in the afternoon and said "Hon', I forgot to tell you something this morning. I've got a basketball game I'm going to play in tonight."

I could sense the surprise in her voice as she responded, "But this is Valentine's Day!"

"I know, I know, but this game is *really* important."

Then Norma said,

"But I've already made this special dinner, and I've got the new tablecloth on, and candles set out, and . . . and . . ."

"Norma, I have to go to this game. I gave some of the guys my *word* that I'd be there." (Which meant that I wasn't about to embarrass myself by calling up my friends and telling them I had to stay home with my wife instead of playing basketball.)

For a long time, there was only silence on the other end of the phone. Although I'm ashamed of it now, do you know what I thought at the time? *Oh, no. I have a strong-willed woman on my hands!* I mistook a closing spirit for a strong will.

Right then I decided I might as well take advantage of this tailor-made opportunity to straighten her out. So, in a controlled, but firm, voice, I said, "Now, Norma, you know that I'm going into the ministry, *right*? One of the very important things that the Bible says is the wife should submit to her husband . . . ."

I'm sure you know how well my lecture went over. Her spirit began to close on me that very moment because of my total insensitivity—only I didn't realize it at the time. I was so blinded by my own self-interest, I couldn't see the negative writing on the walls of her life, though I would one day be forced to read it.

Bit by bit, month by month, I did more and more of these "little," insensitive things until I knocked the sparkle right out of her precious eyes. It's difficult for me, even after all these years, to think about how unaware I was of her spirit—and how insensitive and wrong I was.

The tragedy is, the more a man steps on the spirit of his wife, the more resistant she becomes toward him. The more resistant she becomes to him, the more he closes his spirit toward her. Soon, you have a vicious circle of two people in the same home who have made a public vow to love each other—now living under a private pledge to have a closed fist, not an open hand. As

I close my spirit to another person, what happens? It closes up my soul and my body as well.

"But how do I know that I'm actually closing someone's spirit?" The state of a child's spirit is the easiest to recognize, because children are not as practiced at hiding their real emotions. When children become closed to us in their souls, they disagree with everything we say, lose their desire to be "with the family," and seem to love to argue. Physically, they stop touching us, or they even resist our touch under any and all circumstances. They may even turn their backs on us when they see us.

To us, our remark may mean nothing. We may not even remember it. To us, our words may seem as light as a pebble. If I dropped a pebble on my spouse's or child's foot, I might think it should bounce right off without their notice. But for our loved ones, what is a "pebble" to us might be a ten-pound weight. And we just dropped it right on their barefoot toes!

Common Marks of a Closed Spirit

Because it's difficult for many of us to recognize when we've closed a family member's spirit, it's worth taking a moment to learn four common warning signs.

Warning sign number one *is a feeling of tension between you that you can't explain away.* That may be the spirit closing.

Warning sign number two *is an argumentative attitude.* They may resist discussing just about anything. They might avoid you, never ask for your advice, or criticize you for little or no reason. Before long, you can say the moon comes up at night and the sun in the day, and they'll find a way to disagree.

Some of us have worked for a boss who has deeply offended us. We know what it's like to disagree with anything he says—even before he says anything! If I have my spirit closed toward someone, I can have negative thoughts whenever I see that person.

The same thing happens when you step on the spirit of your children. Typically, they become resistant. It's the basic attitude of a persistently strong-willed child. Almost all toddlers (and most other kids of various ages) can go through "stages" of being strong-willed. If you win the battle early, then you can avoid facing many battles later in life.[8]

There is a major difference, though, in a child who is going through the normal "stages" of challenging mom and dad, and one who is retaliating out of anger by being stubborn or "resistant." You can tell a closed-fist child to take the trash out, and he won't be "typically" slow about it—he'll be blatantly defiant. "No, I'm *not* going to do it. You do it yourself or make someone else do it."

Warning sign number three *is a loss of physical intimacy.* Hugs and kisses? Forget it; your loved one probably won't want to get within a block of you. Almost all children go through times when "hugging" mom and dad isn't "cool" (or "hot," or "rad"). But even during these times, if parents are persistent and creative, they can fill up their child's "touch" bank with quick hugs and playful wrestling (with the guys). If, on the other hand, his or her spirit is closed to you, it'll be like an armed guard in front of the bank!

Close a spouse's spirit, and watch the romantic feelings all but evaporate. I've had a number of women tell me that emotionally they felt like prostitutes when their spirit was closed to their husbands and they were involved sexually anyway.

I've heard husbands growl, "That woman is totally uninterested or unresponsive!" Yet he may be the primary cause of her low level of sexual response as the one closing her spirit. Physical intimacy for a woman is spirit, soul, and body, not just body alone. All three levels have to be interrelated, otherwise any sexual response, for both men and women, is, at best, mechanical and, at worst, dysfunctional.

Warning sign number four is *negative nonverbal signals.* If a person's spirit is closing toward you, his facial expressions may even be more negative than his words. Physically, he may pull away from you, leave the door to his room shut consistently for "privacy," or even turn his back on you in the middle of a conversation. If your children resent being at home—especially being alone with you—that too may be a sign of a closed spirit.

A Window of Hope

My purpose in writing about a closed spirit is not to heap guilt on spouses or parents who may find themselves battling a fist rather than an opened palm. It is, rather, to give people hope. As I have tried to share in detail, things I've done to both my wife and children have closed their spirits to me for a short time, but the key to maintaining strong relationships over the years is to be able to reopen a loved one's closed spirit. It reminds me of what I had to do with my oldest son, Greg, when he was just a young boy.

Five Attitudes That Can
Help to Open a Loved One's Heart

In my parenting book, *The Key to Your Child's Heart,* I tell about my son Greg when he was about five or six years old. At the time, I worked for a large Christian organization, and I was often on the phone with pastors across the country. This also meant that I would have to take calls at home from a number of Christian leaders at times, so I made a rule in our home that couldn't be violated—nobody screams when I'm on the phone!

One evening I was in my bedroom on a long-distance phone call to a distinguished senior pastor. Suddenly, my son, Greg, let out a blood-curdling scream from the bathroom. He came running into the bedroom, screaming so loudly that I couldn't hear the person on the other end of the line.

"Hush!" I signaled to him emphatically, putting my hand over the mouthpiece of the phone, "Can't you see I'm on the phone?"

But Greg continued screaming, so I quickly ended my phone conversation, telling the person I'd have to call him back later.

When I hung up the phone, I grabbed Greg by the arm. "Why are you screaming and running around the house?" I demanded. "Couldn't you see I was on the phone?"

Without waiting for an answer, I hustled him down the hall and said, "You get into your bedroom right now." Still crying, Greg hurried into his room. Once we were inside, I picked up the little ruler that the kids had all helped to decorate (they affectionately named it the "teacher"). For breaking my inviolate rule, I swatted him on the bottom.

It was our practice after a spanking to hold the child and hug away any resentment, but this time, something took place that startled me.

"Come here so I can hug you," I said.

"No," he said, still crying, and the look in his eyes said, "I hate you." He backed away from me to let me know that he didn't want me to touch him at all.

Then after all that had happened, it hit me.

"Greg, why were you crying?"

With his little voice heaving with his sobs, he said, "I fell in the bathroom and hurt my ear and when you pushed me on the bed, I hurt it again."

He was hurt. That's why he was crying! Why hadn't I asked him earlier? Now I not only felt awful, I also felt like a child abuser. I knew I had closed Greg's spirit tightly at that moment, and if I didn't do something, it could leave an emotional scar on our relationship.

Convicted to my very heart, I got down on my knees.

"Greggy," I said in the softest voice I could. "I'm so sorry that I didn't ask you what was wrong or why you were screaming. You didn't deserve a spanking. I'm the one that deserves to be spanked." I held out the little stick to him, but he dropped it and backed up. It was obvious that he still didn't want any part of me.

So I said, "Greg, I was so wrong. Maybe you can't do it right now, but I wonder if you could forgive me? Would you?" Then it was as if his little heart melted, and he rushed into my arms. I fell back onto the bed with him in my arms and just held him tightly as his sobs slowly turned into regular breathing.

After a long time, I asked him again to be sure, "Greg, are you sure you've forgiven Daddy?"

He just patted me and said, "Oh, Daddy, we all make mistakes."

Do you know what that told me about Greg? It told me that Greg was opening his spirit to me. He was touching me. We were talking. His feelings were coming back. His body, soul, and spirit were reopening.

What was happening between us as we held each other was the result of five attitudes that work together to help open the spirit of a person. Let me state clearly, *these are not steps.* You can't mechanically go down the list and expect to wipe away every hurt or draw out all the anger in a relationship. With Greg, it took only a half-hour to reopen his spirit and put us back into harmony. With Norma, it took almost two years of consistently applying these attitudes to reverse all the closing of her spirit I had done.

The important thing is not the time it takes, but the decision and commitment to do whatever it takes to come back into harmony with a person *to release as much anger as possible.* For years now, I have practiced these same attitudes with my wife and each of my children. They have been a tremendous help in making sure anger is drained out of our home each day. I know they can be an encouragement in your home as well.

Five Attitudes to Reopen a Person's Spirit

1. Become soft and tender with the person

Proverbs says, "A gentle answer turns away wrath" (Proverbs 15:1). My whole problem with Greg started when I became harsh and unreasoning. Things began to turn around when my tone of voice softened along with my spirit. My attitude, nonverbals, and voice said I cared about him. Sometimes softness alone can open a person's spirit. That's the whole message of Chapter 5.

2. Understand, as much as possible, what the other person has gone through (remember, listen to what is said; do not react to the words used)

I would have cried if I had fallen in the bathtub, too. Then to get a spanking on top of that? So I showed Greg by my words, as best I could, that I understood what he felt. I talked with him about how awful it must have been, all the time being careful not to "react" to something he said defensively.

3. Acknowledge that the person is hurting, and be sure to admit any wrong in provoking anger

"Greg," I said, "I was so wrong." As a parent (or a spouse), it can be very hard to say those words at times, but as it did with Greg, it can work wonders. Admitting we are wrong (when we clearly are) is like drilling a hole in our loved one's "anger bucket" and allowing that unhealthy emotion to drain away. Once they hear us admit it, the anger has a way to escape from their lives.

Sometimes we may not think we are wrong, but our attitude might be. Or, it may be the way we've done something that's offensive. If my attitude is harsh and angry when I tell my wife about a legitimate problem, I'm still wrong. ". . . Man's anger (or that of a woman) does not bring about the righteous life that God desires" (James 1:20). Stopping short of admitting we were wrong leaves a dangerous gap between you and your child or mate that may not mend quickly—or at all.

4. Touch the other person gently

If you step on your mate's spirit at ten o'clock at night (or in the morning) and then you get into bed and expect to be amorous, what's likely to happen? Your spouse may move way over to the other side of the bed. That's when you'll hear that she has a headache, it's the wrong year, or she just doesn't want to be touched. The nonverbal message, "No touchie the toes," may mean, "My spirit is closing to you."

If you try to touch someone with a closed spirit, you will find out just how deep the hurt is. If a woman has only been touched in anger or to meet her husband's sexual needs, she may resent *any* touch and pull away, or be stiff and unbending. But persistent softness—expressed in meaningful touches apart from any demands for sex—can go a long way toward draining anger and negative feelings from a relationship.

5. Seek forgiveness—and wait for a response

Say something like, "Could you forgive me? I've disappointed you so many times. I know I don't deserve to be forgiven, but could you try?" or "I don't want you all tied up in knots, not responding to me at all. I know I have a million miles to go before I get everything together in my life, but I love you very much, and I ask you to forgive me. Will you forgive me?"

Try to get a positive response from the person before you quit, but if you need to, start with the first loving attitude of being soft and work your way back down to forgiveness again. Remember, too, *don't just respond to your loved one's words.* In the heat of battle, or if you've deeply hurt someone, that person may say something in retaliation to hurt you: "That's right," they might respond. "You *don't* deserve to be forgiven. I really don't know how I live with you when you mess up so often."

For many people, men in particular, hearing words that may hit below the belt can set off a defensive lecture—or even be an invitation to another round of angry retaliation. But those men and women who are wise enough to reopen a person's spirit have to learn to listen beyond the words to the hurt feelings behind the words.

There have been times when I felt something Norma said to me was unfair, even though I was trying to be soft and ask her to forgive me. Perhaps she misinterpreted my motives or even questioned my character in the process, but when you're asking another person to forgive you, it's not the time to get into a lecture on the precise wording of the problem. Your focus should be on draining away the anger and not on compounding it.

The senior pastor at our home church is an exceptional individual. One of the many things we've learned from Darryl DelHousaye is a biblical admonition on dealing with anger. I've found it to be universally true in relationships. Time and again, Darryl has said from the pulpit, concerning anger and the need for forgiveness, "Biblically, the stronger person always initiates the peace." Are you willing to be the "strong" one who seeks to set things right in a relationship? Sometimes it takes a strong act of the will not to react to someone's words. Remember—in most cases it was hasty reactions that helped to close that person's spirit in the first place.

*B*iblically, the stronger person always initiates the peace.

Untying Our Own Knots

There is an important reason why forgiveness plays such a pivotal part in opening a person's spirit. It has to do with the very way the Bible defines the word. In the original biblical language, remember, the word for forgiveness means "to release, set free, to untie."

With that picture in mind, when we say or do something offensive to other people, we are actually helping, emotionally and spiritually, to tie them in knots. Perhaps what we've done has come as the result of knots someone else has left in our lives.

Do you know why most "difficult" people are so ill-natured, people who don't like themselves, who are resentful, or who feel rejected? Such people battle forgiving others—or feeling forgiven themselves. The way they tell us that they're tied up is through their negative, obnoxious actions. That's one reason why the

Scriptures say we are to love our enemies. Their negative tions are warning signals that their lives are tied up in knots.

What about my own knots, though? someone may be thinking. *How can I get the knots out of another person's life when I'm all tied up myself?* In the Lord's Prayer, Christ answers this important question.

If we could paraphrase a few verses, using the literal definition of forgiveness, it could read like this: "If you are willing to untie the knots of the one who offended you, then God will untie your own knots (forgive you). If you refuse to untie their knotted lives, then God won't untie yours." One major reason why forgiveness is so necessary is that anger blocks the working of God's spirit.

Can you see now that leaving someone angry is allowing them to be in "darkness" and tied up in "knots"? Not only are we damaging a person emotionally when we provoke anger in them, but we are also cutting them off from God's light. There is, however, an antidote to unhealthy anger.

If we are attaching value and honor to the people around us, then we will do our best never to do anything that ties them up in knots. If we do, we will try to untie them. "Do not let the sun go down on your anger" (Ephesians 4:26 RSV).

In Chapters 13 and 15, we'll share specifically about untying the knots that may be in your life. For now, though, keeping harmony in a home comes from understanding the attitudes that can reopen a loved one's life and love to us.

Never . . . Never Give Up

There is one final question we must raise. What if we try our best, and they still don't respond?

Gently persist . . . gently persist . . . gently, lovingly persist.

Near the end of his life, Winston Churchill was asked to give a commencement speech at a noted university in England. His car arrived late, and the jam-packed crowd suddenly hushed as one of the greatest men in British history made his way slowly, painfully to the podium.

Churchill's speech lasted less than two minutes—but it drew a standing ovation. It comprised only twelve words, but it has inspired decades of men and women ever since. What he said is the best advice I can give you when it comes to being persistent in love to open a spouse's or child's spirit. What did he say?

With his deep, gruff, resonating voice, he said, "Never give up. . . Never, never, give up. . . Never, never, never give up."

End of speech, but not the end of the message. If the man who called me at midnight had given up on being persistent in love, he would have sent a wife and family away tied up in knots and still in darkness.

I'm not sure if I have ever heard a more hostile woman than the one I called that morning. Yet a little less than a year later, she called me back and said, "Gary, I just wanted you to know that I'm back together with my husband. . . ."

I'll have to admit I was floored when I received her call. From every human angle, their relationship was dead in the water that fateful evening when she locked her husband out of the house. Obviously she had thought the same thing.

"A year ago," she said, "if you had even *suggested* that there was a possibility we would be back together—that I would even *like* him, much less love him again—I wouldn't have believed you. The amazing thing," she continued, "is that I do love him again. I actually want to be around him. That fascinates me all by itself. . . ."

What happened to bring about such a change? Because this man recognized that he had let anger ruin his home—and learned how to drain it out of his wife's life—he reopened her spirit, and he did one thing more. His commitment to allow God to change him and his attitude toward his family made him never, never give up—even when she said she hated him and never wanted to see him again.

If I had given up any one of a hundred times of working to get the anger out of Norma or one of my children's lives, I probably wouldn't be writing this book now—or enjoying the strong relationships we have at home. What I and my friend learned about opening a person's spirit can work for you too—as it has in my family—to help us all avoid a major destroyer of families.

Now we head into one of my favorite subjects: the tremendous value of a man. For God has given a man exactly what he needs to be a great lover and leader of his home. We men come to the marriage relationship equipped to contribute four essential ingredients that lie at the heart of a rock-solid relationship. Let's discover what those ingredients are.

7

The Tremendous
Value of a Man

Just picture the scene. Norma and I are getting ready to begin one of our evening marriage encounter groups—an important part of the early work we did on a church staff. Everyone has been walking around, smiling, drinking coffee, catching up on small talk. Now they're all settling comfortably into the chairs we've arranged around the living room. Then, suddenly, the peaceful atmosphere is shattered.

With a bang, the front screen door swings open. In walks one of the couples from the group. The husband darts ahead of his wife and takes over the couch. Without a word, he crosses his arms and glares at everybody. His wife's eyes are red and puffy, and she walks right past him and sits down across the room, next to one of the other wives.

Only a few seconds had passed, and the evening had gone from easygoing to explosive! Since I was the leader of the group, I decided to get started, thinking that would help.

I opened with a prayer, then looked at the man again. He was still sitting with his arms tightly crossed, looking like Mount St. Helens just before it erupted. Thinking it might relieve some of the tension, I started off with him.

"How's it going this week?" I asked.

"*Terrible!*" he snarled.

"Okay," I said. "What's so terrible?"

"If you really want to know," he replied, leaning forward in his chair and looking me right in the eye, "I've been thinking about getting out of this marriage group.

"No—I'll tell you what," he continued, raising his volume level up a notch, "I've got a better idea. What I'm really thinking about is getting out of my marriage! I *can't stand* that woman over there, and I don't know if I can live with her any longer." His words ripped through the air as he sat back in his chair, a look of defiance on his face.

It was interesting to see what happened the instant he stopped talking. All the women immediately glared at him, and then went over to comfort his wife, and every man in the room instantly did the same thing, only for him. We all looked at each other and thought, *What do we do now?*

As the leader of the group, I knew I had to take charge, so I said, "Why don't we close in prayer?" And that's exactly what I did. It was probably the shortest marriage group meeting on record. As everyone filed into the kitchen, I was able to pull the man aside and asked, "Listen, why don't we get together for lunch tomorrow before you do something drastic?"

Reluctantly, he agreed.

The next day, as we talked at a restaurant downtown, we both discovered something fascinating. In fact, it's something I've used to strengthen my own marriage and have shared with hundreds of men since.

Self-Inflicted Wounds in a Relationship

"Why do you want to leave your wife? What bothers you the most about her?" I asked.

"Gary, there isn't enough time over lunch for me to tell you everything that gripes me. It'd take all afternoon!"

"Just try to hit the high points then," I said. In a few minutes, he had shared five things about her that were particularly irritating.

"She's a sloppy housekeeper . . . she's on the phone all the time . . . she's with her mother constantly . . . she won't take any trips with me . . . she never initiates when it comes to sex."

As the list piled up, his attitude became harder and harder. I threw up a quick prayer for wisdom and then I did something I'd never done before. I began by taking each one of his "gripes" in order and asking him specific questions about them. Questions like: "When it comes to her housekeeping, do you ever encourage her? For instance, do you ever praise her for the good things she does around the house?"

"No," he replied. "She never *does* anything good around the house for me to compliment."

"At least give me an example of what you might say to her when her housekeeping skills don't measure up to where you want them," I went on.

"Well," he said, his tone softening just a little, "the other day I got up and started vacuuming the house at six o'clock in the morning. When I started down the hallway toward our bedroom, she got out of bed and said 'What are you doing?' and I said, 'I'm sick and tired of living in this pig pen! We're cleaning up this place, and we're doing it *now!*'"

"Do you think that motivates her to keep the house clean?" I asked.

"No, I guess it doesn't. But that still doesn't solve the problem of her being a slob," he retorted. Ignoring his barbs, I continued through his list, asking questions.

"After work and on weekends, how much time do you spend actually talking to your wife about something important to her?"

"Well, frankly there's not a lot of time left over in my week. I've got a crushing schedule at the office. I play racquetball three days a week, and then we have to fit in *your* group which takes another night," he said, making sure I knew how much effort he was expending just to be in the group. "And I've got to do something to relax on the weekends, so I usually play golf with some of the guys from work. . . ."

"Do you spend any time talking to her during dinner?" I asked.

Reluctantly he replied, "I usually watch television during dinner. Basically, that's the only time I have to catch the news. But Gary, you've got to understand. In my line of work it's crucial for me to know what's going on, nationally and internationally, to see how it might affect my business."

I said, "Okay, the news may be important, but do you spend *any* time with her during the week, just the two of you, talking together about your lives? About what's important to her, not just your business?"

"No," he said in an emotionless voice, "not really."

I said, "Then it's no wonder she's on the phone day and night and always over at her mother's. A woman comes equipped with a tremendous need for meaningful communication—particularly with her husband. If that need is blocked, she'll find someone else to talk to."

"Oh," he said, a series of tiny lights beginning to switch on inside his mind, "I never thought of it that way."

"You've got your own company now, but in the past have you ever worked for a guy who was very critical?" I asked.

"You bet I have," he said, without pausing even a moment to think about it.

"I had one boss I really hated. He was the kind of guy who couldn't *wait* to come into my office to criticize me. He'd point out anything that was going wrong or even could go wrong in my department. Then he'd yell at me to 'Shape up! Do this! Do that!' After his tirade in front of all the other people I worked with, he'd go back in his office and drink coffee while I worked my head off."

God has built into every man the natural ability to be the very loving leader his family needs.

I said, "How did that make you feel?"

"How did it make me *feel?* I hated working with him," he answered. "I couldn't wait until the end of the day just to get away from him."

"Would you like to go on a vacation with him?" I asked.

"A *vacation?* Are you kidding?" he said incredulously. "That'd be the *last* thing I'd want to do."

I said, "Don, do you realize that you're treating your wife the same way that boss treated you?"

His eyes widened, and he sat straight up in his chair as he took in what I said.

"It's no wonder your wife doesn't want to go on a trip with you, or even to respond to you physically. The way you've been treating her, it's as if she's living night and day with your former boss."

After a long silence, he grudgingly said, "You've got a point there."

We went through all five areas he'd mentioned and made an amazing discovery. With each and every problem he had with his wife, he was at least partially responsible for creating the very attitudes and actions that were so irritating to him.

"What do I do now?" he asked, plaintively.

It's not that this man's negative contributions to his marriage in any way justified his wife's negative behavior, but in many ways, his behavior helped support her actions. Basically, he had no idea he was adding to the very things he didn't want to see in his home. Now that he realized it, he didn't know how to begin to change.

Would you describe this man as a lover? Not really. Would you describe him as a nurturer? Not likely. Could he (and did he) become both? Definitely.

Unlocking a Man's Natural Strength

I am convinced that most men, if they have a plan and know what to do, are willing to take the steps to build a loving, lasting relationship.[1] The problem is that the average man doesn't know intuitively what it takes to do so—nor does he realize the incredible benefits that a strong relationship at home brings to nearly every area of his life.[2]

Remember the women's "built-in marriage manual" we talked about in Chapter 4? In that chapter, we shared how by nature, God seems to equip a woman from birth with important skills a man tends to lack. In part, that is the reason for the special title she bears as a man's "completer" and "helper" (Genesis 2:18).

For some people, a woman's natural edge in relationships can be used as ammunition for blasting men and a man's place in the home. Some people have even read some of my earlier books and felt that I was jumping on the "men-bashing" bandwagon. However, I'd like to set the record straight.

While it is true a man doesn't speak as many words or may not be as naturally sensitive as a woman, that doesn't mean he is incapable of being a great lover in the home. In fact, it seems that *God has built into every man the natural ability to be the very loving leader his family needs.*

Saying that God has designed a man to be the lover in a home may sound a bit strange after all we've said about a man's conquering, logical, fact-driven nature, but that very nature is the foundation for my conviction.

Why? Because the kind of love that lasts, the kind that can grow and thrive apart from feelings, is the kind that comes from a decision. And as I mentioned in Chapter 3, *love*—stripped to its core—is just that, *a factual decision that doesn't have to depend on our feelings.*

There are times in life when we may not feel like doing something that's important, but we still need to do it. We need to give our two-year-old the medicine she needs when she flatly refuses to take it. Or we may have to stay up late to finish the report that has to be done on time—no matter how it bends our schedule or robs us of sleep. Or perhaps it's getting up an hour early each day to exercise and spend time in the Word and in prayer. Whatever the situation, there are times when all our "natural" instincts may say "no," but God's Word or another person's best interest demands we say "yes."

When it comes to family relationships, that same hard-driving, conquering nature that can cause a man to get ahead in his profession, can cause one of two results at home. In many cases, it can create emotional strain and tension if a man tries to blast through his family relationships like so many projects at work. Take that same drive and harness it by giving a man a specific plan of action for the home—and it can be the driving force to bring about the very relationship a woman longs for.

If the truth be known, that man in my marriage group came into his marriage with tremendous *liabilities.* He didn't have a loving father as a child, and the two communication skills his parents modeled for him were anger and silence. Yet, though he didn't know it at the time, in spite of the poor example he'd grown up with, he still possessed a God-given *ability* on which he could draw—anytime—to develop a strong marriage. Namely, once he knew what it took to have a fulfilling relationship, he could tap into his natural drive and desire to "win" and use it to strengthen his marriage.

It's hard for many women to understand how in an intimate relationship, a man is often more motivated to communicate if he puts facts in front of feelings. Normally, a woman will feel something, and then do it. For example, she'll feel an emotional need for communication, and then seek out her husband to meet that need. That's simply not the case with most men.

Usually a man is not driven by an emotional need to relate. Rather, he'll be much more motivated to do something relational (like spending a half-hour in conversation) once he's made a factual decision that it's right. For a man, actions are primarily what dictate feelings, not the reverse.

In large part, I feel that a man's unique ability to blend fact and feeling is a major gift God has given him in order to carry out his responsibility of being the loving leader in a home. When a man is given the right information, told what is right to do and how to do it, he can draw on his natural force of will to make a decision that *stays* while his feelings may come and go.

A Biblical Blueprint for
Loving Leadership in a Home

For a man, the first place he should check when it comes to building a strong family is a blueprint found in Ephesians 5. In this important chapter, the man is called to be the "head" of his wife—the primary lover—just as Christ is the head of the church and the lover of the church.

Nowhere does it say that a man is to "lord it over" his wife. In fact, Christ specifically commands that "lording it over" another person has no place in a Christian's relationships. Rather, the Scriptures tell me I am to love my wife as Jesus loves His church.

How did Christ lead in love? By serving, by committing Himself to our best interest, and by doing so regardless of the cost. The greatest among us are simply following a pattern Christ set down—namely serving those He loved and for whom He laid down His life.

Yet let's take the command for a man to be a loving leader in the home, and move it down to the shoe-leather level. What does it mean to be the "leader" in a home?

When it comes to "leadership" and headship in the home, one very specific guideline is found in verses 28–29, ". . . husbands ought to love their wives, as their own bodies . . . . (for) no one ever hated his own body, but he *feeds* and *cares* for it, just as Christ also does the church" (emphasis added).

If we are following the biblical pattern for family leadership, we men are to nurture and cherish our wives (and children). We do so just as we nurture and cherish our own bodies—and as Christ nurtures and cherishes the church.

When a husband makes that first important decision to truly honor those entrusted to him, he takes the first step toward being the loving *nurturer* God meant him to be. As a result he can see his relationship begin to blossom before his eyes and grow.

Growing a Strong Marriage

What does it actually mean to "nurture" one's wife?

The Greek word for "nurturer" means "husbandman."[3] For those of us who haven't grown up on a farm, that's a tiller of the soil, a professional gardener. A nurturer is one who helps things grow, who provides a "greenhouse" atmosphere where the plants are shielded and protected.

In short, that's what I'm called to be as a husband. Like the top gardener at your local nursery, I am responsible for understanding what ingredients cause my marriage to grow and flower —and then for providing them on a consistent basis. The psalmist puts it this way. "Blessed are all who fear the Lord. . . . Your wife shall be like a fruitful vine within your house; your sons like olive shoots around your table . . ." (Psalm 128:3).

Can you imagine what would happen if that gardener at your local nursery went by guesswork when it came to caring for his plants? No wonder in many marriages we see a "Under New Management" or "Gone Out of Business" sign up in the front yard. No less skill is required of the "head" of a marriage. He is called to be a skilled nurseryman, a caretaker of sorts. He is to be the first one to recognize and supply the ingredients needed for growth and well-being in the family and the first to spot and pull any weeds that threaten to do it harm.

In short, *my role as a "nurturer" is to be a fact-finder.* I should interview each member of my family with my fact-finder mind to see what needs should be met that day and then discover how best to meet them. When I do, I nurture, cover and protect them—and get the privilege of watching them grow. In my own life, one word picture has helped to cement this concept of nurturing in my memory.

A Man Has a Natural,
Relational "Green Thumb"

After we bought our first little home in Rockford, Illinois, I decided to plant a victory garden. I had heard that the ashes from burned leaves helped the soil, so I gathered a huge pile of leaves from all over the yard. My leaf pile burned all night long, and that's not all. At one point the wind shifted and I nearly burned down my neighbor's garage as well.

Barely escaping disaster, the next day I spread out all the ashes in the back part of the yard where I was planning my garden. I didn't really know what I was doing, but it looked great! The earth was dark and moist, and a few weeks later, the results were even better than I expected. Whatever we planted came up looking like the pictures on the seed packet covers.

Everything grew. In fact, the pumpkins became so enthusiastic about the soil that they grew along the fence and up into a tree and hung down everywhere like Christmas ornaments. After my one experience of gardening in Rockford, I felt that I was gifted with a permanently green thumb. However, one day I discovered that the green on my thumb was disappearing ink.

We had moved a thousand miles away, and I decided to unleash my gardening talents on the Lone Star state. From the first spade of soil I turned, I could tell things were going to be different in Waco, Texas. There the ground was a white, rocky, clayish dirt, not the deep brown I had been used to in Rockford.

Without consulting any of the local nurserymen or gardening books, I simply made the decision that what the soil must need was additional fertilizer. With that in mind, I went out and bought the biggest sack I could find with a label that said "For Gardens" on it. The picture on the sack looked just like the results I'd gotten in Rockford, so I figured this was exactly what I needed in Waco.

Spring came around, we put all the seed into the ground, and sure enough everything came up just like in the pictures. After a short time, the picture began to change radically. The beans started browning around the edge, the tomatoes were rotten in the middle, when we picked them, and our carrots were always spongy and wilted. It was obvious something was very wrong with this garden, but I didn't know exactly what to do.

Take Time to Talk to Your Garden . . .

At the time, I didn't realize that by dumping loads of fertilizer on soil that was already high in nitrogen, I was burning up my plants! Do you know what would have helped immeasurably, were it possible?

If only my garden could talk back to me, it could have let me know exactly what I was doing wrong—and what I could do to correct things. It may seem a little far-fetched, but I could say to my garden for example, "Good morning, down there, how are y'all doing?" And right off, the beans would speak up.

"How are we all doing down here? *We're dying!* That's how we're doing!"

"Come again?" I'd ask.

"We're dying down here! We're choking to death!"

"Hey, what's the problem?"

Then they'd say,

"Mr. Smalley, you know all those white things you poured around our roots? Well, now there are thousands of them, and they're killing us. Didn't you know how much nitrogen is in this soil already, and now you're dumping pounds of it all around us!"

I'd say, "No kidding? I didn't know I was hurting you. I never even thought to check the soil. What can I do to try to solve the problem?"

And they'd say, "Go down to the store and get some chemicals and neutralize this nitrogen. You've got to hurry, Mr. Smalley, we've only got a few days left!"

"Good idea! I'll take care of that." So I start to race off to the nursery when I notice my carrots, and I say to them, "Oh, look at your leaves, they're just wilting all over the place. Bless your pea-pickin' hearts!"

"Mr. Smalley," they cry out, "forget the peas. They're done for, but you can help us if while you're at the nursery, you pick up a nylon mesh to put over us to keep us cooler. Then we could really firm up."

"I never knew that!" I would say. "Listen, you sweet things you, I'll take care of everything, don't you worry."

If only I could have talked to my garden in Waco, I could have solved my green thumb problems in a few hours. Who knows? I could have even landed in a Miracle-Gro commercial. Unfortunately, my garden was for the birds—literally. Because I never took the time or had the wisdom to ask someone what the plants needed in my area, I ruined an entire summer's crop.

I suppose I could have taken a different approach to my "talking" garden. For example, I could have walked down early in the morning, taken one look, and said, "Hey, what's this mess? Look at all your leaves—they're browning out around the edges. Hey, you plants! Any more brown leaves on any of you and I'm going to jerk you up by the roots! Now shape up, all of you, and I mean *now!*"

Would my yelling at the plants have changed things around my garden? In actuality, I had caused much of the damage that my garden now displayed because I relied on wishing, not wisdom.

After almost twenty years of working with couples and families, I can testify that many husbands nurture the priceless relationships in their homes using the same principle that I employed in my gardens—*guesswork.* A husband often enters marriage with a picture of a great home in his mind, but relies on wishing, not hard work and wisdom, to see it come to reality. Unfortunately, when many men wake up to the damage they've done to their families, the summer's crop has almost been wasted and a bitter cold winter is fast setting in.

In short, that's why God calls the husband to be a wise "gardener" of his family. Each season of life, a man needs to prepare the soil of his family's lives, to protect them from the elements, and to mend the damage after any natural crisis. The better a man learns to be the nurturer in his home, the more it will look like the "picture" the Scriptures paint of a successful relationship. Wives and children, like the plants the psalmist talks about, reflect how well they've been gardened.

Going to a Plant for Lessons in Gardening

"Wait a minute," I can hear some men saying. "This nurturing business sounds like it puts all the responsibility on the man. What about the responsibility of a woman, or even the children, to make the home all it can be?"

Whenever I hear this argument, two things come to mind. First, it is true that a man is called to be the nurturer of his family, not a woman. In fact, the Scriptures never tell a woman to "love" her husband, but a man is specifically commanded to "love" his wife.

Throughout the Scriptures, a woman is pictured as the "responder" or reflector of her husband's and God's light. In the Song of Songs in the Old Testament, the bride of Solomon makes this important comment about their relationship, "Draw me after you, and let us run together!" (1:4, NASB).

Can you see the balance in this perspective? The man initiates the loving actions (drawing her after him); the woman responds (let us run together); and then the two of them grow together as a result. As we saw in Chapter 3, a woman's natural calling is to be a completer, a helper, a responder to his love. In addition, she is called to honor her husband (Romans 12:10; 1 Peter 3:1). When it comes to who wears the nurturing shoes in the family, biblically they come in men's sizes.

"But how can I know specifically what my wife needs, so that her life and our marriage blooms and grows?" you may ask. "I barely have time to finish everything I've got going at work. How am I going to learn all it takes to care for her in the way I should? Isn't that asking a lot?"

You're exactly right. It is asking a great deal to see that a marriage becomes successful. Without a doubt, a husband has a high calling in taking on the role of the nurturer in a home, but the task isn't impossible. In fact, it's far from it.

What are those nonnegotiable ingredients to a successful marriage? After years of counseling, researching, and interviewing couples throughout the world, it's apparent a healthy relationship needs at least four things.

As we've mentioned, by nature a woman tends to manifest these actions—and to desire them deeply. But if a husband understands these needs in the home (needs his wife and children have on an everyday basis), then makes the decision to apply them consistently in his marriage, it's almost impossible for healthy growth not to take place. What are these four nonnegotiable ingredients that can form a handbook for a committed nurturer—*man or woman?*

At the heart of "nurturing" our loved ones are providing . . .
   1) Deep-seated security
   2) Meaningful conversation
   3) Emotional/romantic times
   4) Positive physical touching

In almost all my books, I've talked about these four factors —and the only consistent power source that underlies each one. But as I speak, study, and talk to people across the country, my understanding of them deepens each year. These four needs are so essential that we'll take several chapters to highlight them all (and then two chapters at the end of the book in particular that talk about where we find the power to grow a love that lasts).

To begin with, let's take a look at the first ingredient in causing a husband, a wife, or child's life to bloom and grow. It's an ingredient that is so essential that with it, a family can experience fulfilling relationships. Without it, they often find nothing but frustration and constant bickering.

8

The First Aspect of Nurturing: Adding the Sunlight of Security to Your Relationships

In some counseling sessions, trying to get a couple to open up about the real issues they're struggling with is like trying to twist the lid off an old honey jar. When all else fails, there's a method that works every time. In fact, it's as effective as holding that honey jar under steaming, hot water.

All you have to do is invite God's little spies—their children —into the counseling session, and it's amazing how they can pop the lid off "hidden" problems in an instant. That's just what happened when Dr. Trent asked the young six-year-old daughter of one couple, "Honey, what makes you feel the worst when Mommy and Daddy argue?"

The little girl frowned and said in a small, hesitant voice, "It's when Daddy takes off his wedding ring and throws it away."

The husband quickly defended himself by saying that he didn't "actually" throw his ring away. Rather, it was only an unusual way of demonstrating his anger during a fight with his wife.

When this couple got into a heated argument, if he wanted to end the discussion he would take his wedding ring off and throw it across the room. As it pinged off the walls and rolled across the floor, the wife and his little girl would watch in silence. Later, someone would pick up the fallen ring and leave it on the counter. Eventually the husband would put it back on.

For this man, "throwing away" his wedding ring provided an immature emotional release from his frustration. For his wife and child, it caused a deep sense of insecurity and fear.

As the people who depended so much on him saw his ring go flying across the room, they saw their security level flying away as well. He didn't actually need to say the words that he was leaving. He let a flying gold band do the talking for him. Each time the ring flew through the air it shouted out, "If things don't go the way I want around here, I'll throw you right out of my life too."

Living Life on an Icy Street . . .

Have you ever endured an ice storm in your home town and then tried to walk down the street? It can be done but there's always the internal tension of knowing a terrible fall is right around the corner.

What many husbands and wives don't realize is that an absence of security in a relationship is like sentencing a person to live on an ice-covered sidewalk.

You're never free to truly relax in a home where insecurity has frozen the relationship in an icy state. It's impossible to enjoy a marriage when you're always fighting to keep your footing.

Unfortunately, in more and more homes across the country, it is always winter and never spring. There are months at a time when the cold January clouds of insecurity are never penetrated by the warm sunlight of security. Yet there is an antidote to living life under a dark cloud cover.

You can warm up your relationship in a dramatic way. In fact, you can actually do something *today* that is like turning the full force of a July sun right on your marriage. What is it? It's providing this first crucial aspect of nurturing our loved ones— unconditional security.

The Warmth to Thaw out a Relationship and Help It Grow

Security is like providing warm, invigorating sunlight to a plant. Leave a plant in the icy darkness of insecurity, and soon its leaves will wilt and turn brown. If a relationship has just been planted, the cold shadows of mistrust can keep any growth from ever sprouting above the surface. A plant must have sunlight if it's to ever be healthy and flourishing. In a marriage, the same thing is true.

Security results when a man and a woman say to each other, "You're so valuable to me that no matter what happens in life, I'm going to commit myself to you. You're so valuable, I'm going to spend the rest of my life proving to you my pledge to love you." In short, it's a reflection of the kind of security we have in our relationship with Christ. Look at Romans 8 for example:

"Who shall separate us from the love of Christ? . . . For I am convinced that neither death nor life, neither angels nor demons, neither the present nor the future . . . nor anything else in all creation will be able to separate us from the love of God that is in Christ Jesus our Lord" (Romans 8:35–39).

Every enduring marriage involves an unconditional commitment to an imperfect person.

God also goes to great lengths to assure us that the plans He has for us are grounded in His security and His protection. "'For I know the plans that I have for you,' declares the Lord, 'plans to prosper you and not to harm you, plans to give you a hope and a future'" (Jeremiah 29:11).

Now, that's security! And the better able we are to reflect the same level of security that we have in Christ to our loved ones, the more we bathe them in much needed sunlight. That goes for mothers who want to see their children feel confident in friendships and later in dating relationships. It's true for fathers who desire these same kids to do well in school and later in their professions. It's especially true for a husband or wife who want to live with the green leaves of a healthy marriage—not the brown leaves of a dying one.

Every enduring marriage involves an unconditional commitment to an imperfect person. This means we can gaze at each other's imperfections and say, "Those brown leaves do irritate me, but I'm going to find out what caused them, and see if I can help. No matter what shape you're in—I'll be around and help you grow." Without this kind of commitment, we're more likely to say, "I can't stand all these brown leaves. They've bothered me for years! That's it! I'm leaving."

If you're in a second marriage, I realize that talking about commitment "no matter what" can be an invitation to guilt feelings. Study after study exposes the long-term negative effects of insecurity that often follow a divorce. However, this still doesn't mean that genuine "security" is somehow out of reach in a remarriage situation.

Men and women who have, biblically and personally, dealt with their divorce and who have remarried have an equal or even greater need to build security in their present marriage. Like love, security is a decision we make on an everyday basis. (For those who may be struggling with guilt or fear from a past relationship, in Chapters 13 and 14 I'll look at ways God can use even something as traumatic as a divorce to make us more loving.)

For all of us, security is an essential prerequisite, not an emotional elective. Let's be even more specific in discussing how we can help our loved ones grow by providing the sunlight of security for their lives. There are at least three things that every man and woman can begin to do to build a secure marriage on an everyday basis.

They can start by 1) building their own "hallway of honor" in their home which in itself can help steer their mate or children away from the doorway of dishonor. Then they can 2) look to the Lord for the strength to make an unconditional commitment and sacrificial choices. Finally, 3) they can become students of their spouses' interests as a tangible way of expressing their commitment.

All are important ways to build security in a home, but the first has a dual benefit. It not only builds positive things into the relationship, it can also help to keep tremendous pain from the people we care about most.

1. A Hallway of Honor . . .

In the hallway of our patio-home, there is a plaque hanging on one wall that proclaims: "In assurance of my lifelong commitment. To Norma, Kari, Greg and Mike. Christmas 1976." Hardly a week goes by that I don't remind those four special people about those words and the commitment behind them.

I realize that words can be cheap. I've spoken with many hurting spouses and children who "believed" the words of commitment of a man or woman whose promises held as much weight as thin air. For them, their spouse walked out on the family leaving a doorway of shame, not a hallway of honor.

I fully realize the only things that will transfer the words of this plaque onto my spouse and children's hearts are my everyday actions and words over the years. Each time I match those words with my demonstrated commitment, I'm adding on to a "hallway of honoring acts" in my home. As a result, I'm leaving a daily legacy of love to my wife and children,[1] not a hurtful inheritance of emotional pain.

A marriage or family can't grow in a healthy way if security is constantly shifting in a home, but loved ones can live without perfection. In fact, the more genuine security a wife or child feels, the more room they allow a person to fail. It's a bit like the farmer who goes to his banker and says, "I've got good news and bad news . . . ."

"Give me the bad news first," the banker says.

"Well, you know all that money I borrowed to buy that farm? I'm not doing well, so I don't have any money to pay you for it."

"Oh?" the banker says.

"Second, you know that money you loaned me for all that equipment, the tractor and everything? I can't pay for that either . . . ."

"No . . ." the banker moans.

"And third, all that money you loaned me for all the seeds? I can't pay that back either. I can't pay you anything."

"Well, what is the good news, for heaven's sake?" the banker wails.

"The good news is, I still want you to be my banker!"

My family knows I'm not perfect; they know I'll lose my temper at times—and they know I'm not always as sensitive as I should be. But one thing that helps them be patient with my imperfections is the knowledge that I'm 100 percent committed to them. I "still want them to be my banker," and I'm trying hard to be the kind of father and husband I should be. With each act of commitment, they see me with hammer and nail, adding on to a hallway of honor in our home.

For your wife or husband, a plaque in your hall may not spell security. But sometimes a loving symbol of our commitment acts like a wedding ring. The ring itself doesn't commit a person to marriage, but it shows to the world that the commitment has been made.

Perhaps for your spouse, security is a special event like a romantic dinner or going to a helpful marriage seminar like Campus Crusade's "Family Life Conference."[2] It may even be something as small as sending a card or calling home from the office each day just to see how your loved one is doing.

Norma has told me often that the way I "date" our kids makes her feel secure. I make it a practice to take my daughter Kari out on a special outing about once a month to show my commitment to Norma. The children are such an extension of her that simply knowing I am spending time with each child individually makes Norma feel secure in the strength and love I hold for our family.

Again, like a wise gardener, ask your spouse, "What is security to you?" Then take careful notes of what he or she says. Security may be spelled, "Let me have a say in the financial decisions," or "Take the time to have family devotions," or "Call me each day when you have to travel."

If you understand what "security" is to them, then you can begin making deposit after deposit into their love bank. This accrues high interest in your relationship. Just begin with a few simple questions like, "On a 1 to 10 scale, one being very '*insecure*' and ten being very '*secure,*' how confident do you feel in my love?" or "What could I specifically do over the next few months that would raise the level of security in our relationship?"

By seeking to build security into your spouse through small, positive acts, you do even more than add positive marks to the marital ledger. You also can help them (and yourself) to guard against the temptation to walk through a doorway named "dishonor."

The more security and honor we build into our homes—the tighter we help to shut the doorway to temptation for our loved ones. Interestingly, it's also the tighter we close the door to temptation for ourselves.[3]

The more "single minded" we are in our commitment to Christ, the less the distractions of the world pull upon us. The more "single minded" we are in building a "hall of honor" for our loved ones through honoring acts, the less room we leave for insecurity to dwell in our homes.[4]

There's a second way to develop security in a marriage that calls for the courage to make and keep an unconditional commitment to one's spouse. That commitment is often best seen in the sacrificial choices we may have to make if necessary.

2. Sacrificial Choices Are Also a Part of Providing Security

Betty waited in a little examination room in the doctor's office, her head lowered. Here it was, only two weeks before their only daughter's wedding, and she'd had another "lock-up" with her arthritis.

Once, Betty had been a cheerleader in the West Texas town in which she grew up. But you could never tell it now. Her heart and bubbly spirit were the same, but today (at fifty-five) they were trapped inside a body that was so crippled, she couldn't walk as well as most ninety-year-olds.

The constant pain from her joints flaring up had been bad, but the "lock-ups" were worst of all. Whenever she had a reaction to one of the "experimental" medicines prescribed for her, it was as if every joint in her body froze in place, and the pain and discomfort were almost unbearable.

Betty was a brave woman, but as she sat in the privacy of the doctor's office, tears rolled down her cheeks. She thought of her marriage to Rusty and all their dreams. She remembered all the plans they'd made for their retirement years . . . that would always remain as dreams. She thought of all the places they wanted to travel . . . but now never could. In her heart she knew that her arms were so battered by arthritis she'd never even be able to hold her first grandchild—the pain would simply be too great.

The door to the room opened, and her husband walked in from talking with the doctor. Looking over at his wife, he could see her chin trembling as she fought to regain her composure.

Try as she might, she couldn't help breaking into sobs.

"Oh, Rusty, please leave me," she begged him. "I'm getting worse, not better. I'm a mess. It hurts too much for you to touch me. I'm spending every cent we've saved toward retirement fighting this thing. I'm a burden to you and the kids and you know it."

Her tall, weather-beaten husband pulled over a chair and sat down beside her. Gently, he took her hand, twisted by arthritis, and said, "Sweetheart, it doesn't hurt to smile, does it? If you'll just smile at me now and then, that's all I need. I really don't even need that. I just need you."

Real love means a sacrificial, courageous commitment— especially when the other person may not be able to give back to you. None of our family members should have to feel what that little girl did when she saw her father's wedding ring bounce off the wall. Security should never be something you take on or off as you see fit. It's an abiding conviction that all is well with our commitment and all will be well—no matter what.

Sometimes sacrificial choices must be made in a marriage —but time and again they can heighten the security level in a home. Take Bill and Brenda for example.

Brenda had always wanted to be a veterinarian. However, she and Bill only had high school educations, and neither could really afford to go back to school. But Bill wouldn't let her dream die. He decided that she would go to school, regardless of the cost.

He knew what it meant to encourage her to get the training she'd need. He was looking at long hours spent on a second job in order for them to have the money for tuition. It took seven years of grueling work and sacrifice on both their parts for Brenda to become a vet, but the day finally came when she got her diploma. That meant her diplomas now outnumbered Bill's, three to one, but he couldn't have been happier—and neither could she. Their relationship didn't suffer because he had sacrificed his time and effort for his wife; it flourished.

Why does sacrifice add so much to a growing relationship? It should be obvious to those of us who live on this side of the Cross. That symbol of sacrifice is an unforgettable word picture of God's love for a lost world—and for each one of us who love Him.

Bill was simply following a biblical pattern when he built security into his marriage through sacrifice. After coming through the winter of a tough struggle together getting Brenda's degree, their marriage experienced an Alaskan summer where there's sunlight nearly twenty-four hours a day.

We've looked at building a "hallway of honoring actions" and making sacrificial choices to add sunlight and security to a marriage. There's a third way to raise the security level in a home, and that's to practice the kind of love that gets involved in another person's life in a very special way.

3. Building Security by Going Back to School

Recently, a close friend of ours, Jim Brawner, did a survey of several hundred teenagers at perhaps the top Christian sports camp in this country, Kamp Kanakuk in Branson, Missouri.[5] One of the first questions each boy or girl responded to on the questionnaire was: "*What is one tangible way your mother and/or father demonstrate that you're important to them?*" Can you guess what the number 1 response was, by far?

"I know they think I'm important because . . . they attended my games . . . my practices . . . my concerts . . . my open-houses . . . my band competitions . . . " In other words, with a teenager, security can be spelled with four words, "*Come and watch me!*"

While many men and women may not realize it, we never really outgrow the deep need we have for our loved ones to be excitedly supportive of our interests. What this means in a marriage is that the sunlight of security can shine on a marriage when we show an active interest in our loved one's life.

This was brought home to me in a tangible way when I first met a couple who became special friends. He was a huge offensive lineman for an NFL team when we first met, and his wife was perhaps 5'4" in heels. On the basis of size alone, there probably wasn't a more oddly matched pair. But in terms of their shared interests, this couple was only a heartbeat apart.

I met them at a Pro Athlete's Outreach Conference and was fascinated with a conversation we had at lunch one day. Out of curiosity, I asked this NFL wife how much she knew about the position her husband played on his team. I expected her to say something like, "Oh, he's paid to stand in front of other people." Instead, she gave me a ten-minute presentation on offensive blocking techniques.

Taken aback by her grasp of the sport, I asked how she'd become such an expert on her husband's position on the team. That's when she gave me a real-life lesson on what it does to become one's spouse's biggest fan—by becoming a graduate student of their likes and dislikes.

She explained that when they were first married, she resented the time he spent on the practice field, she resented all the team meetings and the travel. Finally, she grew tired of feeling so negative all the time, and she decided to go on the offensive. She would stop throwing spit-balls from the back row, and get up in the front row and learn about this career that she resented so much.

She began to ask her husband all sorts of questions about playing on the line for a pro team. She even cornered a few of the assistant coaches to learn more intricate details of the game. The more she learned and read, the more of an encourager she became. That's when a funny thing happened.

As her level of encouragement and interest went up, she noticed their marriage improving. While it wasn't her goal to get anything from her husband in return, he began showing more than a passing interest in her likes and dislikes.

What this wise woman had done was to push back the dark clouds of resentment to let the sunlight of security shine on her marriage. She didn't try to "coach" her husband, but her knowledge and interest in his life said clearly, "Because you're so important to me, your interests are important to me, too."

At the end of our conversation, my huge pro-football friend made a comment I've never forgotten: "Sometime I'll have to tell you how much my wife's taught me about refinishing antiques. I wouldn't be surprised if learning about one of her big interests is where I end up after football."

For this couple, being committed to each other meant showing interest in the things they individually valued. The message came over loud and clear that because of that attitude, they felt secure in each other's love and commitment. That security level showed clearly in their lives and the quality of love between them.

Like sunlight to a plant, the warmth of genuine security can be the first element a husband or wife gives to a successful relationship. In the next chapter, we'll look closely at a second crucial ingredient if intimacy is to grow. In fact, we'll introduce you to something we can do in our marriages that can act like life-giving water to our loved ones.

9

Meaningful Conversation:
Life-giving Water
to a Relationship

Most people take rain for granted—but not farmers. One of the most powerful black-and-white pictures I've ever seen is that of a dust-bowl farmer. He had waited over a year for rain, and now at last he had a chance. His face was turned up to the sky as the desperately needed rain poured down and mingled with his tears.

Every time I see this picture, it calls to mind what happens in many homes. In a marriage, meaningful words are like those raindrops. They can bring life-giving water to the soil of a person's life. In fact, all loving and meaningful relationships need the continual intake of the water of communication, or they simply dry up.

How many couples have I counseled who after fifteen or twenty years of marriage say, "What went wrong? Why is our marriage over?" Time after time, even casual conversation will show that instead of building a spring of consistent, meaningful conversation, they let the well run dry of encouraging words.

If that is the case—if meaningful, intimate conversation is like much needed water to a relationship—why is husband/wife communication often so difficult? Why do couples often learn what *not* to talk about, rather than what *to* talk about?

All too often encouraging words fall as infrequently as a dust bowl storm. Why? There are at least four natural roadblocks to meaningful communication that typically seem to emerge after the wedding day:

Roadblock # 1: Emotional Mind-Reading—
or "Please Give Me a Clue!"

Because of a woman's natural sensitivity, nine times out of ten she will be the first one to spot a potential problem in a relationship. However, the problem can be so "obvious" to her that she can legitimately think, *Surely my husband is alert enough to see what the problem is. I'm not going to embarrass him by having to draw him a map.*

Yet, that's the very thing most men need! Give a man a road map of what issues are important to discuss, and often he'll be motivated to talk about them. But expect a husband to "sense" the subtleties (or even bold realities) of a marital or family concern, and often he won't see it as clearly.

Time and time again, I've been thankful for Norma's willingness to point out the "obvious" I've overlooked.

"Did you notice that Greg was acting a little down at the dinner table tonight?" she might ask.

"No, I didn't notice."

"Don't you think you ought to talk with him?" she'd persist.

"About what?" I'd ask. Like most men, I'm motivated to talk about facts. So far, Norma has been cluing me in on "feelings" and nonverbal behavior she's sensed that I've missed. I need "facts" to get really motivated about a conversation.

At this point, Norma could give up, throw up her hands and either go in and talk with Greg herself or chalk up another mark in the insensitivity column for me. But her love—and her knowledge of how to motivate me to communicate—doesn't let her stop here.

"Gary, I'm not sure if it's school, or the girl he's dating, or exactly what it is. But I can tell you that something is bothering Greg. Would you be willing to take your 'fact-finding' nature upstairs and *lovingly* find out how your son is doing?"

Rarely am I able to withstand Norma's call to go on the hunt for a problem to solve, and almost never has she been wrong in her sensitivity about one of the children.

The difference between mis-communication and meaningful communication often comes when a woman is willing to take the extra time to paint the obvious into a picture a man can clearly see or vice-versa. Mind-reading is never encouraged in the Scriptures, and while it may be part of an illusionist's act, it can wreak havoc in the realities of life at home.

Roadblock # 2:
"I No Speaka Your Language . . ."

In Chapter 4, you will recall we discussed the different "languages" that men and women often speak. In short, it seems that there is a "language of the heart" and a "language of the head" often spoken by women and men. Let me paint you a picture. Failing to tap into the unique conversational world of your spouse can cause this kind of frustration. It helps to illustrate a major mistake many women make in dealing with men. Namely, while trying to improve the level of meaningful communication in her home, a woman can inadvertently stifle the very thing she wants so much!

Let's say I walk into an auditorium where in a few short hours, Dr. Trent and I are going to give our "Love Is a Decision" seminar. I'm relaxed and looking forward to a great time with the couples and singles who'll be there, when all of a sudden I get one look at the room and nearly hyper-ventilate.

There's no doubt that this is the room and this is the night of the seminar—but there's also no denying that someone has made a major mistake! The chairs in the room are scattered all over, trash litters the floor, and the stage hasn't been set up. What's worse, with little time left before people begin coming early, I don't see anyone working to get things ready!

Frantically, I begin doing what I can to get the room in shape for the crowd that is bearing down on the auditorium. After ten minutes of going at a whirlwind pace, I notice a petite, bright-eyed woman sitting in a chair near the front row. Elated, I run over to her, and with a smile on my face and excitement in my voice I say, "Pardon me, but in a short time I'm going to be speaking at a conference in here, and I've got a real problem. If you don't have anything to do, could you give me a hand, please? Would you mind setting up some of these chairs while I pick up the trash and get the stage set up? Thank you so much for helping!"

She responds with a warm smile and nods her head, so I bound off like a big puppy, happy to have someone to help. The only problem is—two minutes later she's still sitting there. A little annoyed, I approach her again.

"Pardon me, Ma'am, but setting up chairs must not be your thing, so I'll tell you what. Could you help me with the stage, and I'll worry about the chairs and picking up the trash? Thank you so much for helping!" Once again she smiles and nods her head—but after another few minutes she's still sitting right in the same place.

Now I'm really irritated, and I come storming up to her and say,

"Pardon me, but . . . are you a Christian?"

I could get really angry at this woman and speak unkindly to her. That is until she opens her mouth and the words come out, *"Perdoneme, Senor. Yo no hablo Ingles. Puedo ayudarle a usted?"*

If I found out that this woman didn't speak a word of English, it would be pretty insensitive of me to stay angry at her, wouldn't it? But here's the very thing that many women do without even realizing it.

What many women fail to keep in mind is that their husbands genuinely may not see or understand the concerns that they're sharing. In many cases, they simply don't "speak-a" the language!

Getting angry and frustrated with a man to "motivate" him to a deeper level of understanding rarely works. Actually, it can make the surface soil of misunderstanding rock-hard and tougher than ever to penetrate.

Roadblock #3: Test the Soil of a Relationship to Determine Its Needed Moisture Level

As we've said, meaningful communication is like water to a growing relationship, but how do you find out how much "water" is needed in a marriage for maximum growth? Just as we found out that "security" needs are like sunlight to your spouse in the last chapter, in this chapter we'll look at what a nurturing husband or wife can do to encourage his or her partner. We'll find out how much meaningful communication he or she needs to feel fully watered. But let me make an observation.

I've asked hundreds of women in over sixty cities this question, "How much time do you need in meaningful conversation *each day* to feel really good about your relationship with your husband?" And time and again, the average woman answers that she needs at least *one hour a day* in intimate conversation to keep her marriage alive, thirst-free, and growing.

"An hour!" I can hear many men groaning. This can be a mammoth roadblock for many men. "Where am I going to find an hour a day?"

Before you panic, it's important to realize that the hour need not be spent in one block of time. Fifteen minutes in the morning as you trade places in front of the mirror getting ready for work, five minutes on the phone during the day, twenty minutes after work, fifteen minutes after the kids are down, five minutes before bed and then praying together can all be ways to bring needed moisture to your marriage.

We're not suggesting you put a stopwatch on your conversations (as one CPA friend did with the kitchen timer: "OK, Honey. We've got ten more minutes to talk. Now let's talk!") Exact time limits aren't important, but providing sufficient, consistent time to talk about important issues is.

To be accurate, I realize that an hour isn't necessarily the conversational need of every woman. One couple may be content with half an hour of talking, while another may need two hours to work through some difficult issues. Each couple must explore what best meets their needs, and consistently carve out the time from already overcrowded days to make sure their marriage stays a priority. The important thing to realize is that if communication is like life-giving water, a marriage will yellow and brown out if this necessary ingredient for growth is insufficient.

Why Try to Take the Road At All
If There Are So Many Roadblocks?

At this point you may be saying, "What's the use? We're so hopelessly different, we'll never be able to understand each other or be able to reach any kind of intimacy."

That's not true. Time and time again, we've seen the natural "incompatibility" of the two sexes become the very grounds for a great marriage. Rather than retreating into frustration, silence, or verbal explosions, why not take the time to master two specific communication skills that can re-vitalize your communication. These two particular skills help take conversations to a level many never dreamed possible.

The first of these skills is to employ the most powerful communication tool we know of in the Scriptures. We call these emotional word pictures, and without exaggeration, we've seen it turn forty-watt communication into a laser beam of words that hits both head and heart at the same time.

One Emotional Word Picture
Is Worth a Thousand Words

"An emotional word picture is a communication tool that simultaneously activates a person's emotions and intellect. In so doing, it causes another person to not just hear our words, but experience them."[2]

Some of the greatest communicators in history have used word pictures to inspire patriotism, lead nations, and direct the course of history. George Washington and Thomas Jefferson did so in our early history. Abraham Lincoln credited Harriet Beecher Stowe with the North's involvement in the Civil War, claiming that once it got a picture of what slavery was like, there was no turning back. The picture she used? *Uncle Tom's Cabin.*[3] Roosevelt and John F. Kennedy, even Ronald Reagan in more recent times, all salted their political and public speeches with word pictures. For all the good these have done, tragically, many evil leaders like Hitler and Jim Jones have also been masters at using this powerful form of communication.

Without question, the greatest use of word pictures is seen in the Scriptures. Throughout the pages of the Old and New Testament, we are taught the greatest lessons of faith the Bible has to offer through word pictures.

What could be more descriptive of what our attitude should be toward God than King David's picture, "As the deer pants for streams of water, so my soul pants for you, O God" (Psalm 42:1)? Or what could more graphically describe God's love for a stubborn, hard-hearted people than Hosea's relationship with the prostitute Gomer and how it represented God's love for the lost?

What's a clearer picture of the call to a life of faith than of an athlete, training diligently and running hard so as to win the prize (Philippians 3:14)? And, what Christian serious about caring for a lost world has ever casually glanced at the portrait of the Good Samaritan and not been convicted to reach out (Luke 10)?

There's no doubt that word pictures are a powerful way to communicate. They take our words right to another person's heart and also lock them inside their memory. For now, let's look at a few examples of word pictures illustrated in relationships. See if they don't grab your attention more than everyday words.

Let's say a woman usually finds herself saying to her husband: "I'm sick of being ignored around here. You're always watching television." To which he could reply: "Now, honey, am I *always* watching television. Did I watch TV *this morning?* Did I watch it anytime during the day *yesterday?*" (Remember, if you share feelings with a man—the language of the heart)—you're likely to get an answer back in facts—(the language of the head.)

Instead of the same overworked phrases that really don't address the real concern (which is not he is "always" watching television but her feelings of being ignored), you could use a word picture to carry your words.

The wife could ask: "Honey, can we talk sometime soon, right now or tonight if it's better, about something that's been concerning me?" When they do sit down to talk in a quiet setting, the wife could *hand her husband the remote control unit* from the television set. Instead of the standard lecture, she could say:

"Do you know how I'm feeling right now? When you watch TV, you use the remote control device to skip past something you don't like and turn to something really interesting. For the past several weeks, I've been feeling like I'm one of the channels on your set—one of the ones you skip past when you're looking for something really interesting to watch.

"In fact, when my face finally does come up on the screen, you either click the remote to the next channel or put it on 'mute.' On the few times you do leave me on the screen, I feel as if I'm talking and talking to you, but you're just staring at me as if you can't hear a word I'm saying.

"What I want to know is what it would take to have you get your finger off the mute button so I could get some 'air time' to talk about some issues that I feel are very important."

Or instead of a man saying to his wife over and over: "That's it. I've had it with you nagging me. I'll tell you when I'm going to fix the fence. *When I'm good and ready, that's when*! That is unless you keep bugging me—in which case I'll put it off even longer!"

He could use a word picture to communicate his frustration:

"Sweetheart, we've got to talk. Can I ask you a question? How would you feel if you were with the two little ones at the grocery store, and every cash register had a huge line behind it? And not only that, after you finally picked a line, the check-out lady decides to go on a break when you're two people from the front. That means you have to go all the way to the end of another long line and wait all over again, and all the time you're waiting in line, the kids are acting up and arguing with each other and embarrassing you. How would that make you feel?"

Certainly, if she'd experienced such a day at the store she'd be very frustrated, and after hearing her response, he could say:

"Well, you may not realize it, but that's exactly what's going on at work lately. With the move coming up and my having to work with so many different departments and problems, I feel as if I've had to stand in one line to order new equipment, then get in another line to get the space in the new building to put it in. Then I find out that I can't have the space, and I'm back in line, having to start all over again. All the time there are people running around pestering me with little problems and making things really frustrating.

"Finally, after standing in lines all day, I come home from work, and you tell me there's another chore you want me to do. I know that the house and the fence are important to you, but right now, I feel as if I'm standing in so many lines at work, I just can't get in the 'fence' line until we finish our move in three weeks. Can I have a 'time out' from reminders to fix the fence until the move is done at work?"

Do Word Pictures Really Motivate a Person to Change His Behavior?

Word pictures can help make the hard work of a relationship easier by providing the initial motivating factor in getting the process of change started. My own family continually uses word pictures with me because they're so powerful. Recently my daughter Kari shared a word picture with me that motivated me to change an out-of-balance attitude I had with my youngest son, Michael.

We were driving home from a vacation in our rented motor home. We had been gone for about five days, and it was about ten o'clock at night as we finally headed back to Phoenix. Everyone else was asleep when twenty-two-year-old Kari came up to sit by me. It brought back special memories of old times, as it seemed that she was always the one who would "stay up and talk to Daddy to help keep him awake" when she was a little girl. Only this time, instead of talking about her dreams or dating, she said: "Dad, there's something I want to talk to you about. . . . But it can wait until we get back home."

"No, go ahead," I said. "We've got nothing but time."

"But I don't know exactly how to explain this to you," she said.

"Why don't you try to think up a word picture?" I suggested.

"Okay," she said. I jogged her thoughts by saying, "Pick some area that's very familiar to me." We drove on in silence for a few moments as she thought up a word picture.

"Okay, I've got one," she finally announced.

"Pretend that you're giving a seminar somewhere, and it's a really big one. I mean like 2,000 people in the conference. On the first night, you're really funny and warm, and everybody's responded well. They all can't wait for the next day.

"But the next morning when the seminar starts, you're not warm or funny at all. In fact, you spend the whole time criticizing them—even when a lot of them really don't deserve it. You say things like, 'I'm fed up with all of you. You go to church and read the Bible but you don't really love your family like you should!' Or you say, 'I'm so sick of the way some of you wives hound your husbands, it's push, push, push all the time!!! And you men, why don't you grow up and be the lovers you're supposed to be?'

"What would happen to the people in the audience, Dad, if you spent the entire morning criticizing them?"

I said, "Kari, I probably wouldn't have an audience very long. Undoubtedly some of the people would get up and leave as soon as I got started—and many more would begin leaving at the first break. They'd say, 'Why am I sitting here listening to this junk? Who does he think he is? He doesn't even know my situation. . . .'"

I thought for a moment—not realizing that I was digging myself a deeper grave—and said, "You know in Proverbs it says, 'Pleasant words are a honeycomb, sweet to the soul and healing to the bones.' I pray that God will help me speak that way. I don't want to come across harsh."

Kari said, "Dad, I hate to say this to you, but this is probably more true of you than you realize. You see, Michael lives at one of those seminars every day where you are criticizing people —only he's a captive audience. He can't get up and leave like those people when you criticize him."

I couldn't have been stopped any shorter if I had just hit a brick wall with the camper. Perhaps it's because Michael is so much like me, but I have had to battle a tendency to "pick, pick, pick" on little things he does. "Mike, chew with your mouth closed. Mike, don't drink out of that. Mike, don't. . . ." At the time of this writing, it's been a year since Kari hit me with that word picture, and I have yet to forget it.

Kari's word picture literally changed my behavior on the spot, because her words turned into a laser beam and hit me right in the heart. The first thing I did when Michael woke up that morning was to ask his forgiveness. For a year now Kari's word picture has been my constant reminder that I'm to be his greatest encourager—not his strongest critic. Word pictures can be extremely effective, but just as with any skill, we have to learn the basics—and practice them.

Becoming an Expert One Step at a Time

When I first learned to ski, the instructor had to show us how to do it one step at a time. That was frustrating at first, because I saw all these expert skiers gracefully gliding down the slopes, and all the time I was feeling like a pigeon-toed duck with two left feet. He kept drilling us on different skills involved, and after a while I became so dejected that I never thought I'd be able to ski like everyone else, but I was wrong.

Deep-seated problems don't vanish instantly without consistent work by the couple and relying on God's strength for daily endurance.

Bit by bit, as I practiced what he taught, I began to wed one skill to another. Pretty soon, I could get out on the slopes and not have to think, *Plant your pole, pressure on the downhill ski, lean into the turn, turn around the pole, slide the uphill ski alongside.* After practicing time and again, it just came naturally! Now I enjoy skiing more than I ever thought I could.

It's the same way with word pictures. At first, you may feel awkward and discouraged when you try to use them. Each step may seem tedious. But keep at it! You'll get the hang of it quicker than you think. Soon you'll be a master at using them.[4]

Time and again we've seen frustrated, tense relationships transformed as committed couples have used word pictures. This change in their lives doesn't happen by magic. Deep-seated problems don't vanish instantly without consistent work from the couple and a reliance on God's strength for daily endurance. But word pictures can and do bring change—particularly as people discover this powerful pattern of "picture talk" set down in the Scriptures.

If word pictures are the most powerful method of communicating we know, there is a second aspect to communicating that any healthy home shouldn't be without. This method has saved many a conversation from deteriorating into a distasteful argument. It works by slowing down what we say—in order to quick listen!

The Effectiveness of Slowing Down to Quick Listen!

During my morning run one day, I thought of something I could do as a loving act for Norma. I decided that since we were going camping that afternoon, I'd volunteer to pack the camper. She could go to breakfast with her good friend Helen and have a great time while I got our things stowed away.

I increased my pace, and when I got home, I said, "Hey, do I have a surprise for you!"

"What's that?" Norma asked.

"What do you think about calling Helen and the two of you going out to breakfast this morning? I'll do all the packing for the trip."

"Hmmmph," she said as she turned and walked away. It was not exactly the reaction I was anticipating.

"What's wrong?" I said, following her. That's when she said something that I couldn't believe I was hearing:

"You've been thinking for a long time how you could take over the packing, haven't you?"

I was stunned. "No!" I answered emphatically.

She responded by saying, "Then why do I get the feeling you think you can pack the camper better than I'm doing it?"

"WHAT?" At that moment, I wanted to tell her *she* could go ahead and pack the camper and *I'd* go to breakfast with Helen.

When the initial anger subsided, I realized she thought I was coming from a totally different direction, but before we got into a major blowout, I decided we needed to do a little *quick listening* to straighten things out.

"Why are you reacting to me like this?" I asked.

"Because I know that secretly you don't like the way I pack the camper."

"You mean you think I made up the thing about you going to breakfast with Helen so I could get you out of the way and pack the camper. Is that right?"

"Yes, exactly."

"Norma! That wasn't it at all. I was trying to think of something loving I could do for you today."

She paused, "You're saying that you were trying to do something *nice* for me?"

"As strange as it may seem, *Yes!*"

By doing some quick listening, I was able to clarify exactly what she thought the issue was, allow her the opportunity to see that I truly understood her, and then correct the misperception in our communication. By listening rather than reacting, I was able to avoid a major confrontation.

Quick listening is simply one technique you can use to help you understand what the other person is really saying. It slows conversation to a pace that both of you can manage. Surprisingly, in our high-speed world, putting thoughts in low gear can move understanding ahead more quickly.

It's a helpful tool to use when an argument is about to erupt, and it is also very useful in everyday conversation to clarify meaning and enhance understanding. It helps you talk through problems succinctly and more clearly, and forces you to make your statements fairly. There are just three simple steps in mastering the art of quick listening.

Three Steps to "Quick" Listening

1. Try to Recognize the Issue behind the Issue

Let's say you and I are having a discussion and are having difficulty understanding one another. Using quick listening, I can honor you by giving you the opportunity to clarify what you're saying first. It lets you know that I'm genuinely concerned and interested in what you're saying—and that I'm making an effort to understand you. It relaxes you because you realize I'm more interested in comprehending what you say than conquering the discussion. It also allows me another opportunity to hear what you're trying to say.

With Norma, the issue wasn't breakfast with Helen. The issue that was at the heart of her hurt feelings was her sensitivity in thinking I was really criticizing the way she packed the camper. We could have talked all day about my words, but when we slowed the conversation down to talk about the issue *behind* the words and her reaction, we quickly came to an understanding of the real problem.

2. Restate What the Other Person Has Said in Your Own Words

After the other person has had the opportunity to summarize what they've said, I can respond, "Now let me repeat what you've said to make sure I understand." I can then verbalize what they've said to see if I've actually received the message *they* meant to communicate.

If I have it right, they'll say, "Yes, that's it." If not, they can say, "No." Then I can restate what they've said. Again, that's what I did with Norma. I had to slow things down and ask her specifically—by repeating her words—if she felt that I was criticizing her instead of helping her. It's my responsibility at that point to keep asking questions and rewording her statement until I get a "yes." When I do, it's my turn to tell her how I feel. That way we're both honored in what is said.

3. Lovingly Confine What You Say

Using too many words during an important discussion can actually break down intimate conversation. When we talk in long, rambling paragraphs instead of short concise statements, we increase the chances the listener has for reacting to what we say, without really understanding it. If we continue to add words without clarifying the issues and feelings we have, the other person can become so frustrated or bored that he'll tune us out altogether.

Learning to be brief isn't always as easy as it sounds. Not too long ago, I took an intensive two-day course in Los Angeles on how to be interviewed on television, radio, and for a newspaper. The first day I felt like a dismal failure. The instructors kept trying to get me to be brief and to the point, and I just couldn't do it.

"Now, Gary," one said, "you have to summarize the most important part of your message in one sentence." After years of being "wordy" by nature, I couldn't do it. She kept stopping the tape and making me try again and again.

"Gary, you said that in five sentences. I said *one!*" my coach would insist. "If you're going to get your message across on television, you've got to be brief. People may like to read about details, but on television or in person they won't stay with you for five sentences."

By the second day, I was doing much better. When I concentrated on what I was saying, I was amazed that I could use half as many words and say twice as much. I love to talk, so, take heart—if *I* can slow down and summarize my conversations, *anyone* can!

Often, couples need to limit their words to increase their understanding of each other. Once, while counseling a couple where the wife rarely stopped talking to listen, I had to break in on her: "I'm sorry, but if you really want your husband to spend time with you, I have to be honest." We were close enough friends for me to say, "You've got to make a decision to confine yourself to saying things with a fewer number of words. I'm getting bored listening to you, and I'm the counselor! Remember that confining your words and listening to what he has to say is one of the most loving acts you can do."

God has endowed some of us with a love for the spoken word. That's tremendous, but sometimes we can get carried away! As did the wife mentioned above, we can lose our audience of one as a result.

Quick listening has stopped numerous arguments from flaring around the Smalley household, and I know it can make a difference in your family as well. We've made a conscious decision not to let our anger stay around longer than the sun going down and to make every effort to honor one another through greater understanding.

Proverbs 14:29 says, "He who is slow to anger has great understanding, but he who is quick tempered exalts folly." One of the keys to any healthy relationship is a willingness to say, "I'm more interested in understanding what you're saying to me than in thinking of what I'm going to say once you're done talking." Quick listening is one of the best ways I know to help others discover what you're thinking—and what they're thinking as well.

In the previous chapter, we looked at how a husband or wife needs to provide security as bright sunlight in which a relationship can grow. Now we've seen that meaningful communication is like a summer rain shower to encourage such growth. These are two of the four essential elements a loving "nurturer" needs to grow a strong marriage or family.

Now let's go on to discover a third important element of a loving home. It is every bit as important as soil is to a healthy root system. At the same time, we'll be uncovering a secret to keep courtship alive in marriage for years on end.

10

Keeping Courtship Alive in Marriage

Without a doubt, this was going to be the most romantic evening of their entire marriage. Of course, they'd only been married a year, but Greg knew his surprise for Sharon would redefine the word "romance."

Unbeknownst to his wife, Greg had taken off work early to get ready for their anniversary. He knew his wife's favorite thing was to enjoy dinner at a place with a beautiful view, so he came up with the ultimate restaurant—*on top of a nearby mountain!*

Greg spent five hours carrying a table, chairs, a Coleman stove, ice, and drinks up to the pinnacle of a small peak near their home. In his mind's eye, he saw the two of them sharing a wonderful dinner together, complete with thousands of city lights sparkling below them like candles. And after a romantic dinner . . . *who knows?*

All that remained for him to do was to drive to his wife's work-place, surprise her, and make the climb to the intimate nest he'd created on top of the world. Greg had thought of everything . . . except his wife's interests and response. For from the moment he "surprised" her at work, his beautiful plan began to unravel.

First, she was so tired from a grueling day of fighting office politics that she wanted to stay home and rest—not go out for a long evening. Then when he pulled out her climbing boots, she said she was too tired to climb anything—and she wasn't really hungry anyway.

Greg didn't want to give away his carefully arranged surprise. (Besides, he knew they had an hour up-hill ahead of them just to reach the summit.) So he demanded that she "quit griping" and start climbing.

Reluctantly, she trudged up the mountain to where the wind

had kicked up and blown over most of his campsite. Then the campstove wouldn't light . . . and the ice had melted . . . and the wind kept blowing dirt all over the table . . . and he'd forgotten the forks.

Finally, dinner was served but Sharon was so tired from climbing and nearly being blown off the mountain-top, she said she'd pass on eating. In total frustration, Greg ripped off the table-cloth, sending dishes flying everywhere. This only caused her to begin to cry and him to begin to fume.

Instead of walking down the mountain arm in arm in the moonlight that night, they stumbled down the now pitch-dark trail in silence (naturally, he'd forgotten a flashlight). The ice for their drinks may have melted up on the mountain-top—but the wall of ice between them was as thick as a brick wall as they drove home!

Greg had the right idea. He was trying to add an important element to their marriage that is missing for many couples. Unfortunately, he missed some important aspects of this third important way to nurture a marriage.

Keeping Courtship Alive in Your Marriage

During courtship, romance is something that seems to overflow naturally. Let the years of marriage pass, however, and often romance slows to a thin trickle. Yet romance is an essential ingredient of a strong relationship. Most women admit it is lacking in their home, and most men confess inability and failure in supplying it.

Actually, romance is not unique to our day. It has filled stories since the beginning of time, but with our Hollywood images of intimacy, for many of us it's difficult ever to experience the real thing. While it may not seem as important as meaningful communication or keeping a person's spirit open, romance is still an essential element to building the kind of loving, lasting relationships we've been discussing.

Romance finds its place in a marriage right between the chapters that illustrate love as a decision of our will, and the sexual relationship which involves our feelings and emotions. In many ways, romance is the bridge between the two. It's an important way we express honor to our spouse, and it provides the basis for a meaningful sex life.

Poetically, we could say that romance is the flame which glows on the candle of unconditional love; it's the act of honor that soothes and refreshes a marriage like a gentle spring rain; it's the fertile soil in which passion grows. But for those of us who didn't major in poetry, what is it in plain English?

Romance is the act of keeping your courtship alive long after the wedding day. Put another way, romance is an intimate friendship, celebrated with expressions of love reserved only for each other.

---

*R*omance is the act of keeping your courtship alive long after the wedding day.

Ground Rules for Helping Romance Blossom

In some ways, romance breaks open the deepest feelings of a person. Greg had hoped that all his special efforts would show Sharon how excited he was that she was his wife. He had sought to create a natural setting that would open up her life to a deeper intimacy. Instead, his relationship took a fall from the mountain-top. Why? For the same reason that many couples struggle in keeping courtship alive in their marriage. They need to follow several practical ground-rules to keep romance on the right trail to intimacy.

The most common reason why romance dies in a relationship is that it gets inseparably linked to physical intimacy. Often this happens because that's the way television or movies paint the scene. It's as if any display of tenderness or emotional intimacy is simply a warm-up for the main act of physical intimacy, but while effective romance may *sometimes* lead to sex, our goal in being romantic shouldn't be sex.

God certainly created men to be goal-oriented initiators. He filled their bodies with a wonderful chemical that heightens their sex drive (see Chapter 11). Sometimes, though, we allow our natural enthusiasm to get the best of us and make the fundamental mistake of substituting emotional closeness with a physical experience.

If the only time I take my wife's hand is to say, "Let's go to bed," I'm ignoring her need for romantic times apart from the bedroom. For most women, it's almost as if God has wonderfully crafted them with a built-in "relational safety switch" that won't allow a few moments of pleasure to be a counterfeit for a meaningful relationship.

If romance is more than just making sure the hallway's clear to the bedroom, what is it? First, it's

Friendship, Not Foreplay

In his book, *Romancing Your Marriage,* Norm Wright quotes a couple who define romance this way:

> Romance is not a setting. . . . It's a *relationship* which can be taken into and out of a wide variety of settings.[1]

I like that! Romance is a *relationship,* not an event. It's not something we do occasionally to stoke the fires of passion. Rather, it should be an ongoing, foundational part of our relationship, something that doesn't come and go like the tide, but flows as steadily as a river. An inescapable aspect of romance is being "best friends" with your spouse.

In the Song of Solomon, Solomon praises his bride saying, "This is my lover, this my friend . . ." (5:16). During the ideal courtship, couples should have time to build their friendship to its peak. Why is friendship so closely linked to romance?

Can you think back to "your song" on the radio, your table at a favorite restaurant, your secret way of holding hands? During courtship, an entire nation may be listening to the same love song on the radio—but that same song creates a special bond between the two of you.

A key to blending friendship with romance is to take the

time to explore each other's interests and then share them together. I recently saw a cartoon that captures this idea. The scene shows a couple walking happily hand in hand, looking deeply into each other's eyes, and obviously enjoying a conversation together. The caption reads, "Romance happens when . . . he asks about her potted plants and she asks about the football scores." As unromantic as "sunflowers" and "screen passes" may seem, that cartoon really captures the essence of one important element of romance.

If you're not growing a friendship based on each other's shared interests—I can almost guarantee you that the romantic soil in your relationship is lacking the essential nutrients it needs. I learned this the hard way one summer when a "romantic" getaway did nothing but push Norma away from me.

Missing the Forest for the Trees

For years one of the things that I thought would be a "10" romantically would be to take a long camping trip to the Colorado mountains with Norma. This would be a special, two-week trip where we took scenic back roads to the most beautiful places in the state, visited historic spots, and stayed in campgrounds or even out in the wild. After years of prodding, I finally convinced my wife it would be a great experience, so we loaded up and headed for the hills.

Less than half-way through the trip, Norma was beside herself. She finally broke down and said, "I don't know how much longer I can take this. There are no malls around, no cute shops, and no restaurants. I can't handle another day of this, much less another week. Can't we camp in the mountains close to a town so we could walk to it and see some other people or shop for the kids?"

At first I was angry that she was trying to ruin my "romantic" dream vacation. I even drove nonstop from Colorado to Flagstaff, Arizona, without saying one word to her on the way home. Later, I apologized for my actions, and I realized I had never thought of asking what would be a romantic trip for *her*. I wasn't interested in what she was interested in; I had my own romantic adventure in mind, even though it was hopelessly boring for her.

Fortunately, even if we feel helpless in picking a romantic

experience, there's something a man or a woman can specifically do to help turn one's spouse into the hopeless romantic we'd like him or her to be.

What's Your Ten?

Contrary to popular opinion, close romantic times don't just happen. With our over-committed lifestyles, if we don't set our schedules, someone or something else will set them for us. Since the chances to make great memories together come and go so quickly, it's important to take advantage of opportunities for romance that come our way.

Planning is the key. I know, some of you are thinking, *But Gary! . . . Planning takes all the thrill out of it. Romance is supposed to be spontaneous!* No doubt spontaneity has its place; we'll look at that in a moment. For now, though, it's crucial we rid ourselves of the false notion that the secret to building a romantic relationship is the five o'clock phone call for a candle-light dinner at six.

By planning, what I mean is using the "twenty questions" method with your spouse. This is something we've done at seminars across the country, and it's amazing the amount of "romantic" information you can get in a short time. If you remember, Chapter 4 listed questions a husband can ask a wife that can revolutionize their relationship. Each question uses the "one to ten" scale to gauge the other's response.

The same is true here. Husbands and wives should begin blending their recipe for romance together with:

"Honey, on a scale of one to ten, what's a romantic ten to you?"

It's a good idea to have paper and pen ready, to jot down each idea that is suggested. Next, "milk" these answers for added information. By "milking" I mean try to find out as much information as possible about what your spouse has told you by asking more questions about the idea.

For instance, if your spouse says, "I think it would be a ten to go on a skiing vacation," then you could ask, "Where would you want to go? What time of the year? What kind of snow would you like best? Would you need new ski clothes? What colors and styles? Where would we eat? Where would you like to stay?

Would we meet friends there or go by ourselves? Would we do anything else besides ski?" The list could go on and on.

Each question you ask makes you a more insightful romantic. The more you know about what would be a "ten" for your spouse, the more you'll be able to understand his or her interests, and become more fully involved in them.

Not too many of us are able to schedule a week's skiing as a vacation, which leads to a very important principle we need to keep in mind. *The success of romantic times together has very little to do with how much money we spend.* If successful, romantic relationships depended on the size of our bank account, most of us wouldn't even have a nodding acquaintance! Focusing on money as the secret to sharing one another's interests will rob us of some of the most romantic times we'll ever spend.

Steve Lyon, one of our invaluable staff members, recently had no money in his pocket and an open Sunday afternoon. Sensing his wife's, Brenda's, need to get out of the house, he loaded her and their baby girl into the car and drove to a downtown civic and arts center.

Sidewalk vendors were selling trendy T-shirts, jewelry, and ice cream; couples and families sat on a plush carpet of green grass listening to a brass quartet. Fountains flowed with the gentle sounds of bubbling water, and the art museum was open free of charge. They didn't buy *anything*—not even an ice cream bar or a glass of lemonade.

Two hours later, they were relationally richer and not a penny poorer. Brenda would later say, "That was one of the most romantic times we've had in months." Surprising, isn't it? Not to a man who knew his wife's love and interest in art and who took time that could have gone into a Sunday nap to create a romantic memory in her life.

So who cares if you can't jet to the Rockies and schoosh down a mountain? Spend a Saturday morning hunting down garage sales or going for a frozen yogurt. Your romance will never be better, even if your wallet isn't bulging with money! (Later, we'll share twenty-five low-cost ideas on keeping courtship alive.)

Why not sit down with your spouse and look at the year ahead? Find out each other's romantic tens, and schedule what you can into the calendar. It's amazing what anticipation does to heighten romance! Be sure to commit to making these dates a priority. If you don't, other things or other people will crowd them out of your schedule.

At our house, we sometimes know what we'll be doing a year in advance. Most families don't plan that far ahead, but my work requires me to plan so that other things don't choke the romance out of our relationship. Norma and I talk about special times we'll have together as a family (something I discuss more fully in Chapter 12), but we make sure we reserve some special time just for the two of us.

Developing a deep level of friendship through shared interests is the first essential ingredient in a romantic relationship. Discovering each other's relational "tens" and making plans to make them happen can also make a huge difference in the quality of our romantic times together. There's a third way of keeping the courtship alive with our spouse. It's found in learning to . . .

Celebrate the Moments of Your Life

Those who are wise romantics will realize that some special date or event every year can be used to fan the romantic flame. I recall one man who did put together a very special celebration for his wife to honor her for a sacrifice she had made for him.

It was the eve of his graduation from a long, grueling master's degree program. Four years of intensive, full-time study had finally found him about to receive his diploma.

His wife planned a special party where many of their friends were to come and help him celebrate the long awaited "day of deliverance." There would be cake, refreshments, banners, streamers, a pool nearby, croquet, and other yard games. Many people had already accepted her invitation to come, and it looked like it would be a full house. Her husband, though, had other ideas. He secretly contacted each person who had received an invitation and told them he wanted to make the party a surprise in honor of *her*. Yes, there would be banners, streamers, and all the rest, but they would bear her name, not his.

He wanted to do something special to let her know how much he appreciated the years of sacrifice she'd devoted to his graduation. Working full time to put him through, and putting off her dreams of a house and family, had, in many ways, been harder on her than the long hours of study had been on him.

When the day arrived, she was busy with preparations and last minute details, still convinced that all was going according to plan. He arranged to get her away from the party site, and while she was gone, he put up a huge banner with her name on it. During that time all the guests arrived as well.

She returned to be greeted with a huge "SURPRISE!!!" and when she realized what was going on, she could barely fight back the tears. Her husband asked a few people to share what they most appreciated about her. Then he stood before them and, with tender words of love and appreciation, expressed his gratitude for all she'd done for him. When he was through, they saluted her with an iced-tea toast.

The rest of the evening was a fun-filled fiesta of laughing, catching up with one another, water volleyball, yard games, and more food than anyone could eat. It was a celebration of an experience they both shared, and by commemorating it in a special way, this husband created a lifelong, romantic memorial to his wife's love and dedication.

Birthdays, anniversaries, or holidays can become more than simply a traditional observance. They can be a personal opportunity to let your loved one know they are very special to you—in ways they'll never forget.

Creative Romance: Surprise, Surprise, Surprise!

We've seen that building a friendship around shared interests and tapping into times of special celebration, can strengthen the romantic bonds in a relationship. There's another aspect of romance that, if not overused, can also be a real help in a home, for if it's true that the element of surprise has won countless battles, it's equally true that it has won the hearts of untold lovers.

A young man in our home church recently pulled off a romantic surprise that's one of the best I've ever heard. It's something his wife-to-be will never forget, and it will make a great story for his grandchildren one day.

It was a beautiful, clear desert morning. The sun was still minutes away from its grand entrance, but it teased the Eastern sky with a hundred shades of gold. The mountains kept their silent sentinel in the cold, crisp dawn, the brilliant stars shining behind them like silver sequins on black velvet.

"WHHHOOOOOOOOSSSHH," the sound of the hot-air balloon's burner broke the desert's quiet with resounding force. In a few heartbeats, its brilliant blue and red canopy sprang to life and lifted off the ground. It floated upward, carrying a basket with Steve, Jan, and the pilot cradled inside.

Going up in a hot-air balloon was something they'd both wanted to do for a long time, and now they were in the air! In just a few moments, they were several hundred feet up, gliding along with the wind's gentle currents.

The scene was spectacular, and while Steve and Jan were busy enjoying the moment, the pilot was making sure the flight continued to go smoothly.

All at once, the incredible quiet was broken by the distinct drone of an engine. At first, Jan thought it must be the sound of a truck on the road below them, but then she realized it was getting louder. Startled, Jan looked up to see an airplane headed right for them! She was paralyzed with fear—but if she had looked at Steve or the pilot, she'd have seen them both smiling.

The plane Steve had hired to "buzz" the hot air balloon was right on time. When it turned close to them, a long tail appeared behind it revealing a message that read, in larger-than-life letters, "*I love you, Jan. Will you marry me?*"

When the words on the banner finally hit her, she was beside herself; she jumped up and down in the confines of the balloon basket like a six-year-old on Christmas morning. "Yes, I'll marry you!" she said, laughing and crying at the same time. For this couple, a special surprise was an indication that creative romance would stay a part of their relationship.

Surprising ways to say "I love you" aren't reserved for restricted air-space. They can be a note put in a lunch-box, a cassette tape with a loving greeting put in the car's tape player in secret, a frozen yogurt that arrives with you at your husband's office on a hot, summer's afternoon. Planning can make sure that romance stays a consistent part of your relationship. But surprises can make the moment a cherished one. These actions all say, *I'm thinking about you, my love for you is secure, you're important to me, we're together for life.*

But I'm Just Not Creative. . . .

I once had a friend who worked with high school students in Young Life. He was one of the funniest, most creative people I'd ever met. One day I asked him his "secret" for being creative, and he told me, "My definition of creativity is forgetting who I borrowed the idea from."

Now, that might not work in writing books, but it certainly points out that even if you're unfortunate enough to have come up with a "zero" in the ingenuity department—there's still hope. Just draw together ideas from the hopeless romantics around, forget where you borrowed them, and put them into practice!

It's not so much coming up with good ideas on your own, it's knowing where to find them and then knowing how to make them work. It's important to have a good resource for creative, romantic ideas. Let me suggest two:

Tapping into Creative Ideas for Romantic Times

The first source is your spouse. Sometimes we overlook this tremendous resource because it's so obvious. If you ask your spouse, "Honey, what's a romantic ten to you?" you can potentially receive a wealth of ideas. Most people have a list of things that will strike them as creatively romantic.

One of the cornerstones of creativity is this: *Ideas give birth to more ideas.* Something your spouse says may trigger an idea in your mind for a creative way to pull it off. Be alert to this possibility as you talk together. Whatever you do, be sure to *write down your ideas.* Try to keep your "Recipes for Romance" notebook within reach as much as possible.

The second is collecting lists of romantic ideas. These can be found in a variety of places, but several of them are right in your local Christian bookstore. *Four Hundred Creative Ways to Say I Love You* by Alice Chapin is a great resource.[2] So is a chapter entitled "Keeping Romance Alive," in *Romancing Your Marriage* by Norm Wright.[3] *Men, Do You Know Your Wife?* by Dan Carlinsky[4] is a helpful way to get to know things about your wife that will no doubt spark some creativity.

Let me add a few ideas of my own . . .

Twenty Creative, Romantic Ideas That Cost under $20

1. Dress up for a meal you bring back from your favorite fast food restaurant. Take out a tablecloth, centerpiece, and a tape

recorder of your favorite romantic music and dine to a "Golden Arches" delight.

2. Buy a half gallon of your favorite ice cream, go to the most beautiful park in town, throw a blanket on the ground, and eat the whole thing.

3. Visit a museum or art gallery. Talk with each other about the art you like and dislike. Use the "twenty questions" method to learn all you can about why your spouse likes or dislikes what you see. Concentrate on listening to the other person and learning all you can from what he or she says.

4. Go to a driving range together. Cheer each other's good shots.

5. Go bowling together. Come up with prizes you can give each other for winning games; i.e., a massage, a week's worth of doing dishes, a promise to paint the fence, etc.

6. Go on a hay-ride with four other couples, singing camp songs from a tape recorder or guitar. Plan a cookout under the stars afterward.

7. Write love notes to one another and hide them in unusual places like the freezer, a shoe, in the car's glove box, in the bathtub, in a makeup kit, or under the bed covers.

8. Go snorkeling in a lake.

9. Collect leaves and pine cones together on an autumn day. Take them home and make fall ornaments for the house.

10. Attend a free outdoor concert.

11. Buy a pass from the Forest Service, go to a National Forest, and cut your own Christmas tree.

12. Buy a modern paraphrase of the Song of Solomon and read it to one another.

13. Walk hand in hand along a nature trail.

14. Watch a sunset together.

15. Make "dough" ornaments together, bake them, and then color them with the kids.

16. Rent each other's all-time favorite movies and play a double feature at home.

17. Go to your favorite restaurant for dessert. Bring a child's baby book or your wedding album and relive some memories together.

18. Throw a party commemorating your spouse's graduation date.

19. Get the children together and make a "Why I Love Mom" and "Why I Love Dad" book, complete with text and illustrations.

20. Take your spouse out for an afternoon spent in her favorite store. Note the items under $20.00 she likes best. Return to the store the next day and buy one of those items as a gift.

Friendship, planning, surprises, and tapping into each other's creativity are all-important aspects of romance, but before we close this chapter, we need to sound one caution. Let's take a brief look at something that can kill a romantic experience faster than a duck can jump on a June bug.

Putting Romance in the Deep Freeze

Imagine the following scene. A man and woman are casually strolling arm in arm along a beautiful white sand beach. The waves gently wash ashore, and the sea-gulls dart back and forth overhead. A full moon glimmers in the night sky, and the sand seems like an endless strand of silver dust. It's a romantic ending to a perfect day, until . . .

If you look more closely, you will see the look on her face. It isn't one of peace and love. It's one of frustration and anger. Why? The setting is all right, but something he did is all wrong.

Ten minutes before, she told him she wanted to take a quiet walk on the beach and talk. He agreed to the walk which excited her—but he destroyed the romantic setting when he held her hand with one hand, and his fishing pole in the other.

"Hey, I've been casting for years," he told her. "I can talk and fish at the same time, *no problem!*"

This man broke two cardinal rules of romance. *1. Make sure the romantic activity you're involved in receives your full, undivided attention. 2. Make sure you're doing the activity for her best interests, not yours.*

Any time I send Norma flowers, or give her a card, or do something special, I'm saying, "I love you." At the moment it's spontaneous and unclouded by hidden motives, but I can quickly ruin it for her. All I have to do is ask a favor or tell her about my plans for fishing with the guys that weekend, or intimate that what I've done "deserves" a romantic response, and it's as if I walked into the house saying, "Gee, honey . . . you're sure looking bad today."

We've seen several ways in which the courtship aura can remain in a marriage. First, romance doesn't just happen "naturally" in a marriage; it's not simply an extension of physical intimacy. It takes work! Second, the winning recipe for romance is found in developing a friendship centered on shared interests—and carefully planned. Third, by using surprise, spontaneity, and creativity in romance, we can celebrate those special moments that bond us in a meaningful way. Finally, we need to make sure we give our full, undivided attention to our loved one during a romantic time. Each of these suggestions on keeping the courtship alive in our marriage can help to insure that this important area of our lives blossoms like flowers after a spring rain.

The key to being romantic, then, is to concentrate on being *relational!* When that happens, and your spouse truly senses you desire a deep, intimate friendship, then the stage is set to enjoy the wonderful pleasures of physical intimacy. Let's now examine what makes the sexual union meaningful and fulfilling for both the husband and the wife.

11

Sex Is Much More
Than Physical Intimacy

Without question, one of the most interesting topics to both men and women is sex. But does physical intimacy mean the same to a man as it does to a woman? Hardly.

What is the basic physical need of a man? In most cases, the sexual act, and then, coming in a distant second, nonsexual touching. What is the basic physical need of a woman? Meaningful communication, nonsexual touching, and then sex.

We've looked at three ways in which a man or woman can nurture a marriage and see it bloom and grow. Each one is an important part of establishing a successful relationship—but the three are incomplete without a fourth. Within the confines of marriage, God has provided a way to meet an important need in a man and woman's life—that of physical intimacy.

Meeting Each Other's Needs

Numerous studies have shown that 70 to 80 percent of a woman's physical need is simply to be touched and held.[1] Just the opposite is true for a man, especially during the first several years of marriage. For most men, until they move into their late thirties, you could paint a big "T" on their T-shirt. The "T" could represent the sex hormone "testosterone" which tends to drive a man sexually.

In laboratory studies, if researchers inject a female Rhesus monkey with the hormone testosterone, she will gather other female monkeys around her and try to reproduce. Then, once the hormone has worn off, she'll go back to her more natural behavior.

(Some men have heard about the effects of testosterone and driven straight to their local druggist to see if they can get a prescription for their wives. However, as a dangerous steroid, the physical side-effects would include her shaving and being able to out arm-wrestle her husband.)

Perhaps a word picture might help to explain the common difference between a man and a woman in the sexual area. When it comes to marital intimacy, men tend to be like microwave ovens—instantly ready to be turned on at any time, day or night, and also ready to hurry through the cooking experience. The average woman, however, is more like a crock-pot. She needs to warm up to the sexual experience and savor the process, and the thing that warms her up the most is a quality relationship.

To get an idea of your husband's sexual appetite, think about your own desire to eat. How often do you feel hungry when you're on a diet? If you're like most of us, it's three times a day—morning, afternoon, and night! The hunger drive hits a woman on a diet about as often as a man's sex drive naturally hits him—especially during the first years of marriage. That's why a man can slip into bed at 10 o'clock at night after not seeing his wife all day, reach over and touch her on the shoulder, and say, "What do you *think*?"

After a hard day at work, with the kids or both—and little or no meaningful relational time spent to prepare her—her response may well be:

"*What do I think*! You *animal*. Don't even *think* about what you're thinking!"

To most women, sex is much more than just an independent physical act. It's the culmination of a day filled with security, conversation, emotional and romantic experiences, and then, if all is right, sex. For the average man, you can reverse the order—or just skip everything that comes before sex!

In many ways, it's just as hard for the average male to initiate intimate conversations and plan romantic activities as it is for his wife to initiate sex. But these two different needs in the physical area can be met—in a fulfilling way—for both a man and a woman. This is true particularly if you're aware of several practical attitudes and actions that can help to fan passion's flame.

Meaningful Touching Outside the Bedroom Can Help the Touching Inside

Recently I read of a survey conducted among several hundred women.[2] In it, nearly 70 percent of the women responding claimed that if they were never again involved in the sexual act with their husbands, they wouldn't complain a great deal. What they would strongly miss was not being touched, held, and caressed. Every area of a woman's life is affected if she's not touched and held by the most important people in her life. As we mentioned earlier, eight to ten meaningful touches a day is really a minimum requirement for a woman to stay emotionally and physically healthy.

One man I know took his wife's need for meaningful touches so seriously that it got him in real trouble. As he was lathering up in the shower, he realized he'd forgotten a towel. Opening the shower door, he made a mad dash for the linen closet in the hallway. As he opened the closet door, he looked and saw his wife standing at the far end of the hall in the kitchen.

An impulsive thought crossed his mind, and he decided he'd give his wife one of those "meaningful hugs" she needed—right in the kitchen—and with soap and water added. So without a stitch of clothing on and dripping wet, he ran down the length of the hallway and burst into the kitchen to give her a great big bear hug—and that's when he saw the neighbor lady sitting at the kitchen table.

Proper timing might need to be taken into account when giving meaningful touches, but they are certainly one important way to grow a strong physical relationship.

Learning to Put Problems at Arm's Length

Do you know what are the two *least* talked-about areas in most marriages? Death and sex. I'm not sure what the relationship is between these two subjects, but I do know many couples don't see anything humorous about either one. Unfortunately, the lack of communication about the physical side of marriage can add to the problems a couple may have—not subtract from them.

To have a healthy sexual relationship, a couple needs to have the freedom to talk about this often "out of bounds" area, the freedom to share their likes, dislikes, expectations, and frustrations. We know of one couple who used the "word picture" method we talked about in Chapter 9 to open up this sensitive area. The method resulted in their becoming closer than ever before.

Darryl was a pro football player on a championship team that wasn't in the habit of losing. Yet when it came to the sexual area of his relationship with his wife, he felt that they were always having a disappointing season. In particular, he was frustrated about how seldom she would respond to his advances—and the negative fallout that would result from his desires being blocked.

Finally, he became so frustrated he decided to come up with a word picture to explain his feelings. So, after being rebuffed again after watching her get ready for bed, and trying to initiate an intimate time, he sat next to her and shared his word picture.

"Honey, we have *got* to talk," he said.

"Do you know how I'm feeling about our sexual life? I feel as if every night we're playing the shell game. Do you know what I mean? It's the game where there are three cups placed in a row upside down on the dresser.

"Under one of those cups is a bean, and if I can just pick the cup that has the bean under it—you'll be in the mood and we'll share some 'you know what!' But the problem is, I *never* pick the right cup. I feel like every day when I'm at practice, you shuffle the cups all around, and no matter which one I pick when I come home, it's always the wrong one. What I want to know is when are you going to quit hiding the bean?"

Darryl sat back, confident that his word picture would run loose through her mind like an all-pro running back. Certainly now that she understood his feelings, his word picture would score a touchdown for his desires. Undoubtedly, it would result in nonstop "availability" on her part. The only problem was that two can play at word pictures, and the one she shared with him in response reversed fields and scored points for her team.

"Darryl, since you asked, let me tell you the reason why we end up playing the shell game most nights. Let's say I'm your favorite fishing reel." Susan instantly had Darryl's interest when she mentioned fishing—one of his favorite activities in life.

"When we were first married, I felt that I was in beautiful shape, having come right from the factory and being wrapped up in a gift box. As soon as we were married, however, you threw me an old rod you had and took me right out and fished me in salt water. Then when you got home, you never washed me off or took care of me.

"When you first got me, you could cast me a mile because my line wasn't all knotted up, and I was oiled and well taken care of. But over the years with the way you've treated me, the reel has gotten salt-corroded and rusted, the line is all frayed, and the eyelets on the fishing rod are all bent and twisted. Now, whenever you have the impulse, you take me out of the corner of the garage where you've thrown me, and without ever taking care of me, expect me to cast as if I'm brand new.

"Can you see now why all you get is knots and backlashes when you try to cast me?"

Her husband answered, "Well, what in the world can I do?"

"You can either leave me in the garage and get the kind of response you're getting now, or you can fix me," she said. "Honey, if you would hold me and listen to me and quit lecturing me when I ask you a question—it would help me respond like a reel with a brand-new line and new eyelets."

That night, Darryl walked into a word picture that hit him harder than an NFL linebacker. For the first time he was able to "see" what the problem was in their sexual relationship in a way that he could understand.

Meaningful touching outside the bedroom can light sparks in a marriage, and meaningful communication can fan the flames.

They ended up on the back porch talking for hours about a "fishing reel." But in actuality, they were talking about the most intimate area of their marriage. Darryl learned what it would take to "maintain" Susan in a way that could actually make her excited about responding to him. On the other hand, she was able to understand how frustrating the "games" they were playing by not talking about this very important area were.

As an unexpected bonus, they both ended up sharing one of the most romantic evenings in months. Why? Because a word picture can help to take even the most difficult subject and put it at arm's length where it can be more easily seen and talked about.

Like many couples, Darryl and Susan were so close to their problems, they couldn't see the forest for the trees. What a word picture did for them was to take them up in a helicopter to where they could get their bearings, see where they first went off the trail, and find the right pathway back to sexual intimacy.

Meaningful touching outside the bedroom can light sparks in a marriage, and meaningful communication can fan the flames. If a couple cares enough to explain their needs, frustrations, and enjoyments to one another, it can help to turn their relationship around. But there's still more that a couple can do.

Purifying Our Character
Increases the Passion Level in a Home

What do you think our "lovesick" society would say is the greatest "love story" ever told? Clark Gable and Vivian Leigh in *Gone with the Wind* during the '30s? Humphrey Bogart and Ingrid Bergman in *Casablanca* during the '40s? Burt Lancaster and Deborah Kerr in *From Here to Eternity* in the '50s? Ali McGraw and Ryan O'Neal in *Love Story* during the '60s? Barbra Streisand and Robert Redford in *The Way We Were* during the '70s? Or Kelly McGillis and Tom Cruise in *Top Gun* in the '80s?

Actually none of these would be right (or even close!). The greatest love story of all times is recorded right in the Scriptures. In fact if junior high kids realized that an entire book in the Bible talks specifically and explicitly about romance, sex, and intimacy, they'd turn to it in droves. (Of course, they would have to understand a little bit about Hebrew poetry.)

How do we know this love story is the greatest? Because we're told so in the title of the book. This book announces itself as "The Song of Songs" in bold letters. For a reader of Hebrew, something significant stands out. When biblical writers wanted to address something as "the very best, the highest, without equal," they repeated it. In other words, that's why we read statements like "the King of kings" and "the Lord of lords!" in reference to Christ. He is the King above all kings and the Lord without equal.

The title's repetition of the words, "The Song of Songs," then, tells us that this is it. It's the greatest love story of all times. It begins with a strong statement of passion.

"Let him kiss me with the kisses of his mouth!" Solomon's bride says to him in the first full verse of the book. For observant readers, that's *her* initiating an intimate response and *her* asking for him to kiss her—repeatedly!

For every man who was ready to inject his wife with testosterone, here is an example of a woman who didn't need any artificial prompting to want to kiss her husband. Interested in what prompted those words of passion from Solomon's bride?

If we look at the very next verse, we're given the reason—and it might surprise us. She tells us that it wasn't his charm or his good looks; it wasn't the expensive cologne or clothes he could afford to wear as the king; it wasn't even his prestige and power. What made his bride responsive to him was his character (Song of Songs 1:3). Her passion came as a direct reflection of the positive qualities in his life.

"May he kiss me with the kisses of his mouth. . . . *For your name is like purified oil,*" she tells him.

Let's not confuse our modern-day techniques for purifying oil with the way it was done in biblical times. The process this woman is picturing involved taking several trays of different size rocks and layering them from large rocks to the smallest pebbles. By the time oil had dripped through all those layers of rocks and pebbles, all the impurities had been filtered out and only "purified" oil remained. To this bride, Solomon's life, his "name," reflected that same process of purification. All the rough edges of indifference and insensitivity had been filtered out, and his wisdom and character reflected purity of "name" and purpose.

What Solomon's wife is telling us is a truth about marital passion. The more purified my character, the more attractive I am to my spouse—and the more responsive she'll be to me as a result. Time and again I've seen this principle working in the relationships of people—for good or for bad.

I remember the case of a man who lost his job with an insurance agency primarily because he wouldn't do something that was clearly illegal. He knew if he refused to comply with the wishes of his superiors, he'd be instantly fired—but he also knew he'd lose far more if he lied.

On the day before he went in to his boss to tell him he couldn't "cooperate," he went home and told his family about what he had to do. Dinner got cold that night as he made it clear to his wife and daughters that losing his job could very well mean they would lose their house as well.

This living object lesson of standing up for the truth distinctly marked his daughters and actually brought the family even closer together in the weeks that followed. But the response from his wife startled him. Even though his dinner got cold that night, her response to him sexually was the warmest, most romantic that he'd ever experienced in fourteen years of marriage. He was totally shocked, but Solomon wouldn't have been. This man's wife had seen her husband's character ring true as a bell, and that promoted far more passion than any flowers or gifts could ever do.

Before we move on, there is another side to this principle to consider. For those who want to see the romantic spark doused with buckets of cold water—all it takes is exposing major impurities in one's character. I remember the case of another person who did this, and it came very close to ruining his marriage.

Bill was a social climber who had to have the best clothes and the best car—but he couldn't afford either. It's not that he didn't make money, it's just that he didn't make nearly as much as he spent. One day, that dishonoring fact came crashing down on his wife.

He and his wife were both working, in large part so that the children could attend an excellent Christian school nearby. With the fall semester beginning, she handed him her endorsed paycheck to cover the beginning cost of their tuition. Without telling her, he cashed the check and spent it on a "need" he had for a new suit.

He fully intended to "rob Peter to pay Paul" and pay the tuition from another account before anyone else was the wiser— but Peter came up broke. That's when the call from the school came to his wife's office. It landed like a bombshell.

It was the school secretary on the phone. Regretfully she informed the wife that her children wouldn't be able to attend class any more until their tuition was paid. The wife confronted her husband when he got home. He lied at first, still trying to cover his tell-tale tracks. Then he made up another lie to cover the first one. Soon his character looked so full of impurities to her that she didn't even want to see him—much less touch him in love. It took months of counseling about his spending problems and re-establishing a track-record of trust before she began to respond to him physically again.

The moral of the story? Our romantic relationship may never be called the "Song of Songs," but we can still sing the chorus with gusto. And a clear stanza from that very helpful song reads, "If you want to raise the passion level in your marriage—increase the purity of your character."

Passion Grows Where a National Average Doesn't

We've all read reports in newspapers or magazines that give an "average number of times" that the "average" couple has sexual relations each day/week/month/year/ or decade. I'm not really sure what the purpose of such averages are, except to increase the counseling rate.

Too many couples who struggle sexually let a phantom national average dictate their loving response. One or both spouses can be so busy chasing after a national average that they forget that the "goal" they're working so hard to achieve is just that—average.

How should couples interpret such figures? Frankly, I recommend that they don't keep track of them at all. In a normal marriage, there will be times of high sexual activity, and periods where it is very low. Trying to keep up with someone else's idea of what "average" is, is an invitation to sexual frustration, not sexual satisfaction.

What's the best marriage guide? The Owner's manual on wise living, namely the Bible. First Corinthians 7:3–5 gives us a healthy "average" to shoot for: "The husband should fulfill his marital duty to his wife, and likewise the wife to her husband. The wife's body does not belong to her alone but also to her husband. In the same way, the husband's body does not belong to him alone but also to his wife."

In other words, a desire to respond to each other in love and a consistent willingness to meet each other's legitimate needs is the best advice on when to be sexually intimate. Don't let anyone set a loving "schedule" for you from a book or newspaper. Look to the Book for the best advice on timing—and on increasing intimacy as well.

Keep "Performance" on the Stage and out of the Bedroom

There are two words that work well on the playing field but are absolute killers in the bedroom. What are they? *Performance anxiety.*

The Diagnostic Statistical Manual, Volume III, is an encyclopedia of psychological dysfunctions. In fact, it lists almost 200 pages of possible sexual problems. Do you know what one of the primary "treatment choices" is for all but a handful of these many disorders? "*Decrease* performance anxiety." In other words, if you can get acting and unrealistic expectations out of the bedroom, you can erase almost every sexual dysfunction that doesn't have a physiological basis, and you decrease performance anxiety by lowering expectations to realistic levels, focusing on genuine love, and seeking to meet the *other person's* needs, comfort, and pleasure instead of your own.

Often a man who has performance anxiety is one who judges the quality of his marriage by his sexual prowess. If, in the normal course of a marriage, he experiences some frustration in his sexual performance, fear can set in, and he can lose all confidence in this area. On the other hand, if a woman "performs" her way through the "act of marriage" by faking her real feelings or responses, genuine intimacy can be a long-forgotten experience. Couples need to stay clear of performance anxiety if they want passion to occur—and not be a memory from the past.

In a way, the sexual side of a relationship can be a barometer to the status of the marriage. In other words, if a wife is not responding to her husband sexually, 99 times out of 100 you can find the reason in their emotional or spiritual relationship. Some men may say, "Forget all these 'relationship' reasons for our sexual problems—I just married a frigid woman."

If you're one of these men, I suggest you honestly check the temperature of your relationship—the security level, the conversation, the sensitivity and romance, and the meaningful touching apart from the sexual act. In reality, *less than three per cent of all women are organically nonorgasmic or truly "frigid."* Of course, I can just hear someone saying, "It figures. I've got one of those wives in the three per cent." If that's your attitude, this is where honor needs to comes in.

Love Does Not Dishonor . . .

Dishonoring words that come up around the sexual area act like red lights to an intimate response. Take the man who would comment on his wife's need to "lose weight" just as she undressed to get into bed. Usually it's the same man who couldn't understand why she was cold and unresponsive. Or what about the woman who "teased" her husband about his sexual endurance until they had a major problem in his responding at all?

Solomon's bride knew she was deeply loved by her husband, but still she says, "Do not stare at me because I am dark . . ." (Song of Songs 1:6). Ever since Adam and Eve hid their nakedness from God and each other, there has been a natural insecurity around the sexual act. That level of insecurity can be multiplied by ten with poorly timed or insensitive words, but it's not only words that can be dishonoring and result in lowered passion. Actions can speak louder and more powerfully in this area.

Not too long ago, a man approached me as I was walking out to my car after a seminar. I could tell he was nervous.

"Gary, could I ask you just one question before you leave?" It was pushing eleven o'clock at night, following the first session of our seminar.

"I didn't want to ask this in front of anyone else," he said. "That's why I didn't come up to you inside. You see, I have a problem in my marriage. For years I've been making my wife do something when we're making love that she has hated doing, and now it's gotten so bad, she doesn't want to have anything to do with me at all. *Gary, isn't my wife supposed to submit to me, or am I reading the Bible wrong?*"

The answers to his questions were yes and yes. Yes, the Bible does say that a woman is to place herself under the loving leadership of her husband, and yes, he was reading the Bible wrong. Nowhere does it say that "submission" gives a man (or woman) the right to make a spouse do something they feel is wrong or terribly "dishonoring"—just to meet a selfish need.

I know that there are books written by Christian leaders who say that basically anything is legal in the bedroom, but I would have to disagree. As we discussed in Chapter 2, at the heart of love is a decision to honor a person—to count him or her as incredibly valuable. Forcing my wife to violate her conscience to please my sexual appetite is absolutely wrong and an invitation to sexual problems.

Regardless of the "no holds barred" pictures of pornography that are painted throughout our culture as being "acceptable," some forms of sexual behavior are dishonoring. To ask a spouse to perform a sexual act that is wrong or repulsive to him or her is to show at least a degree of insensitivity or even a lack of love.

Being "one flesh" in a marriage is a wonderful gift of a happy marriage. But it's only one part of a successful relationship. Security, meaningful communication, emotional and romantic times . . . and physical intimacy go together like pieces of a puzzle to make a nearly complete picture of a fulfilling relationship. As we'll see in the last two chapters of this book, there is still a "missing piece" when it comes to a marriage of true oneness. If a marriage is to really reach its peak, a couple must learn how to tap into the *only consistent power source* for keeping their love alive through each season of life. But before we turn to this most important aspect of intimacy, let's look at one final way to build a close-knit family.

12

Discovering the Secret to a Close-Knit Family

Not long ago, John and I were doing our "Love Is a Decision" seminar right in our hometown of Phoenix, Arizona. Whenever they can, my family makes it a point to attend the seminar, so I wasn't surprised when my oldest son, Greg, told me he was coming. What did surprise me, however, was a special request he made.

"Dad," he asked, "could I take about five minutes and share something I think is really important for the parents to hear?"

Gulp! I was honored that Greg would ask, but I also knew all too well that he is the family clown. With his light-hearted nature, he is basically capable of doing or saying anything once he gets in front of an audience. Now he'd be in front of almost a thousand people, and the possibilities for disaster were endless. Then again, how often does your son ask to join you at a family conference? So I readily agreed.

Just for safe-keeping, I did schedule his five minutes during the afternoon of the second day. That way I figured if he did say something off the wall, it would come after a day and a half of positive input from Dr. Trent and myself.

As the time grew near for him to speak, I'll have to admit I became a little nervous. *They're about to hear some inside stories about the Smalley family,* I remember thinking to myself.

Greg began by saying, "I just want you to know what a privilege it is to be here with my Dad and to share in this seminar. I really enjoy being with him during times like this, *because it's one of the few times he's sober . . . .*"

The audience roared, and of course I thought, *Yep, I shot myself in the foot all right. What's this son of mine going to say next?*

"No, no," Greg laughed, "I'm kidding. My Dad doesn't even drink."

Then he said, "I want to share with you parents for a moment." I had been talking to these people for almost two days, and for the most part they had stayed right with me. When my son began to talk, however, I could see people actually leaning forward to hear what he was going to say.

"I want to encourage you to make every effort to become best friends with your kids—and there's an important reason why. I know firsthand that it can make a big difference in their lives as they get older.

"I'm in college now, and there's temptation everywhere. I've seen many of my friends go to other people they know on campus for advice on sex, drugs, cheating, you name it! And the suggestions they are getting would make your blood turn cold. It's like the blind leading the blind! In many cases, I know why they're going to friends and getting bad advice. It's because very few of them feel that they can go to their parents to ask the hard questions.

"That seems odd to me, because I've always been able to talk to Mom and Dad. Sometimes, I'll call them at two in the morning from school to talk about something I'm struggling with. I'm never afraid to wake them up because I know they really love me, and they want to listen to what's happening in my life.

"If I wasn't confident in their friendship, I would not have been able to call them—and I know I wouldn't be open to their counsel. I can assure you that the advice you give your children will be far wiser than most of what they'll hear from people in their dorms at school. So, please, to make sure they'll listen to you when the time comes . . . do what it takes today to build a strong friendship with your children when they're young, so that they'll *want* to come to you when they're older. . . ."

I've been speaking for years, but I can't think of a time when I've grabbed an audience as Greg did that afternoon. I also don't know when I've ever been more proud of him or more humbled to be his father.

Greg struck a chord on what is one of the most crucial factors in developing and maintaining a loving relationship: *learning to be best friends with your children.* At its heart, a close-knit family is one that respects and honors each member and experiences a deep bond of intimacy.

Almost nothing strengthens a husband and wife's relationship more than when the whole family is united and best friends. The question is, "How does a family take on that kind of personality on a consistent basis?"

What's the Secret to a Close-Knit Family?

Years ago, when our kids were little, I started speaking at family retreats across the country. As I spoke, I'd pick out families who looked happy and seemed to respond well to each other. When I had the opportunity, I'd approach the husband and wife with several questions.

First, I'd ask, "You seem to enjoy each other so much and have a real love for one another! What do you think is the most important thing you do as a family that makes you so close?"

Almost without exception, each family I interviewed said, "We've made a commitment to spend quality *and* quantity time together regularly. We have separate interests, but we make sure we do things together as a family on a regular basis."

Then I'd ask, "What's the one thing you do more than any other that you feel bonds you together?" Time and time again, I'd hear an answer that I simply couldn't believe. What was the common denominator of almost every one of these "successful" families? *Camping!*

At that time, Norma and I had never camped together— by choice. But since learning this secret, we've camped together for over fifteen years. That gives me some authority to speak on the subject, and I can say with absolute conviction— camping is *not* the secret. Before I let our noncamping friends off the hook, though, I do need to say that camping is still the best method I know to *find* the real secret to a close-knit family. You'll see what I mean by looking at our very first camping experience.

Baptism by Lightning

The evidence became overwhelming—we needed to go camping. The kids were small, but old enough to travel, so we decided to give it a try. We bought a tiny, second-hand pop-up tent-trailer, packed our gear, and sped off into the sunset.

We had spent a few nights sleeping in our driveway to "test out" the trailer, but our first night of camping out was in Kentucky. There we discovered a beautiful campground with pine trees everywhere. We set up camp under the shade of the largest pine we could find. That night we built a fire, cooked hot dogs, roasted marshmallows, and had a great time together.

Soon after dark the kids fell asleep in the camper, leaving Norma and me alone to talk the evening away by a nice crackling fire. Finally, we called it a night and crawled inside with the kids. We lay there, peaceful and content. For the life of me, I couldn't think what it was that had kept me from the wonders of camping all these years—but I was soon to find out!

Without any announcement, the wind began to blow steadily. Before long, a row of dark clouds marched overhead, and a gentle rain began to fall softly on the roof. Still, it was only a tranquil "pitter-patter" on the pop-up trailer. I settled back to smell the wonderful fresh scent of rain on a summer's night, and to listen to the soothing lullaby that would send us into dreamland. . . .

Then without warning, Wham! The gentle shower turned into a violent storm. The rain began to come down in sheets, and the wind whipped up to gale force levels. Our little camper, once seemingly anchored on firm ground, began to shake and sway like a break-dancer on television. Within moments, the rain was coming down so hard that it soaked through the seams of the canvas roof and began leaking inside the trailer.

Far worse than the rain was what followed. "Round two" of the storm seemed to throw all its punches at once. Monumental lightning blasts crashed and roared all around us for a solid hour. Each bolt that darted from the sky lit up the night like a Fourth of July fireworks display. The first "near miss" lightning strike instantly blew out all the campground lights, leaving us alternating between blinding flashes of lightning and pitch-black, inky darkness.

About half-way through the thunder storm, Norma and I grabbed each other's hands. Finally, she whispered to me what we both had been fearing, "Do you think we're going to blow over?"

Knowing it was my job to remain calm and relax her, I said, "Naaaa . . . not a chance!" Truthfully, I didn't think we'd blow over. *I thought we were going to blow up!*

It's amazing what kind of thoughts go through your mind at a moment like that. I couldn't help thinking . . . *This is it! We're going home to be with the Lord tonight. When was the last time I told the kids I loved them? Who's going to take care of the dog when we don't get back? I wonder who they'll inter-view for my position at work?* I just knew that any moment, our shiny metal trailer was going to act like Ben Franklin's key on his kite and draw the next lightning blot right down on top of our heads.

Fortunately, our portable "lightning rod" didn't attract any shocking attention, and we made it through the night with little more than a lack of sleep and rain-soaked sleeping bags. Still the memories of that experience continue as vivid as the night it happened.

> *The real secret to becoming a close-knit family is shared experiences that turn into shared trials.*

Fortunately, not all our camping experiences have been as harrowing as that first one. After we'd gotten a few trips under our belt, a funny thing happened. Just like the couples we'd interviewed, we began to see a deepening bond developing in our home. Why?

Knitting Hearts Together

Going through harrowing experiences as a family draws people together like virtually nothing else. In other words, the real secret to becoming a close-knit family is *shared experiences that turn into shared trials.*

Have you ever noticed the way grown men on a football team will suddenly act like grade school kids, running around screaming and hugging each other, after a close, come-from-behind victory? Or have you ever stood at the Vietnam Memorial in Washington, D.C., and seen the closeness that veterans have there with one another after having gone through the horrors of war? The link people in those situations share is an inseparable relationship, forged from a common experience that stands the test of time.

I can think of one "trying" experience in particular that has marked my life forever—and my family's.

When our third child, Michael, was born, I have to admit I was a little upset. As terrible as it sounds, I wasn't sure I wanted another child. So, initially, I was ambivalent toward him and irritated with Norma for "talking" me into having another child.

I knew my attitude was dead wrong, but honestly, it was the way I felt at the time. During the first three years of his life, I just wasn't as close to Mike as I should have been. I wanted to feel close to him, at times I desperately tried, but nothing I did seemed to spark the emotional fires—that is until the spark of life almost went out of his life.

God's Mercy Creates an
Unforgettable Bonding Memory

We were moving to Texas, enroute from Chicago, when Mike was a little over three years old. We had been traveling all day when we decided to spend the night at a motel—with a swimming pool.

It had been a long summer's day with five people stuffed into a tiny car, and the minute the kids spotted the shimmering water, they went crazy. I had to admit the water looked pretty good to me, too. We quickly checked in, dumped our bags in the rooms, and headed for the pool.

Norma took a quick dip and then curled up on a pool-side lounge chair with a *Good Housekeeping* magazine. In no time, the rest of us were in the water, really enjoying ourselves. Kari and Greg were old enough to swim, but Michael needed a small, round inner tube to keep him afloat.

After making sure he was "seaworthy" I turned my attention to the other two, who were screaming for me to play "toss me up," a game where I threw them up in the air and let them land in the water. After a few minutes with them, I looked back over my shoulder to see how our youngest was doing.

I saw the tube floating, but I didn't see Michael. At first, I couldn't believe my eyes. I thought Norma must have gotten him out of the water. Then I saw his tiny little body lying at the bottom of the pool. The only thing moving was his blond hair waving in the water. Instantly I swam underwater, grabbing him in my arms. When we broke the surface, his eyes were dilated, and he was coughing and sputtering.

When I got him on the deck, I began shaking him to get the water out of his lungs. In retrospect, Mike was probably in more danger from me trying to help him than he ever was on the bottom of the pool! After a couple of minutes he was back to normal, with all of us doting over him like a proud mother over a new baby.

When I first looked over and saw my son lying on the bottom of the pool, I was sure we'd lost Michael. During that instantaneous moment of emotion, something took place between us that has never left our relationship. There's something about seeing your three-foot-high son in five feet of water—knowing each second he's down there more life is draining out of him—that melts your hearts together like nothing else. That is, unless it's his first words after nearly drowning.

I'll never forget what Michael said to me when he was finally fully awake and breathing. "Daddy," he said looking at me with tears in his eyes, "I could see your legs, but I couldn't reach you!"

Instantly, my feelings of ambivalence toward my son were gone. I felt closer to him than ever before—and that bond has never been broken.

It was nearly a tragic mistake on my part that I had not kept a closer eye on Michael. As we realize now, it was God's grace that allowed me to go through that traumatic experience with my son. It shook me out of my passive indifference and replaced it with a special love for a very unique and valuable son. Michael has been, is, and always will be a living memorial of God's mercy to me. Each time any of our family brings up that harrowing experience, it unites our hearts in a bond of love and commitment.

Fast-Drying Bonds of Love

None of us would plan disasters just to make our family close knit. If your family is like mine, though, *you don't have to plan them.* They just happen! Because you never know for sure when the next one's coming, you've automatically got the perfect recipe for a "crazy glue" mixture that's perfect for family bonding.

"Crazy glue" experiences are what bonds us to one another in the midst of unexpected crisis. When we're forced by circumstance to go through something trying with another person, the crazy glue gets set in place, and once it hardens the result can be life-changing.

Most of the time, being in the middle of a crisis doesn't find us saying, "Isn't this great! We're all feeling so close right now!" Normally, we're at each other's throats saying things that aren't nearly so positive. The secret is how we'll feel later.

In most cases it takes about three weeks for the "glue" of a shared crisis to set and permanent bonding to take place. Once set, though, it's usually so tight that virtually nothing can tear the memory apart. Let me give you a recent example of a family experience that has "stuck" like glue to our family's emotions.

Famous Last Words: "Trust Me"

We live in a small patio-home in a private subdivision in Phoenix. It's so private, in fact, that the homeowners' association even owns the streets! When Michael was fourteen, he asked if he could drive the car down the street a few houses and pick up some wood we could burn in our fireplace.

Since we lived on a private road, I didn't see any harm in it, so I gave him the go-ahead. But when Norma found out what I'd done, she was beside herself.

"Norma, relax," I said. "This is a private road. It's no problem. *Trust me.*"

A few moments later, we heard a tremendous "BANG!!!" Norma screamed and ran outside, with me just a step behind. When we got there, what we saw looked like something out of the new Disneyland-MGM Studio's theme park.

There was our van, looking as if the garage door had suddenly come to life and attacked it. When Mike started to pull into the driveway, he had accidentally pushed on the accelerator, not the brake. Ramming our van into the garage door made it look like a crumpled soda can. Because of poor judgment on my part, we had a pug-nosed van, one hysterical mother worried if her son was hurt, and one angry father ready to hurt his son's posterior if the accident hadn't hurt him. But there's more.

We'd only recently converted the garage into Greg's bedroom, and "typically," he was asleep inside at the time of the accident. When the van hit the garage door, it knocked a mounted fish off the wall, right onto Greg's head! Scared to death, he thought a massive earthquake had just hit Phoenix, so he jumped up and ran out of the house thinking the apocalypse had come.

At that moment, there was very little bonding going on around the Smalley household. Let's just say that as the neighbors began gathering to view the scene, not one of us felt like laughing. Several weeks later, though, something miraculous happened.

While we never thought it possible during the midst of our "van" crisis, in three weeks time we'd all calmed down, and the garage door was fixed. Today, nearly a year later, it's one of the funniest stories we re-live with each other. Who'd have thought that a smashed garage door could have provided some of the best "crazy glue" for bonding a close-knit family that we've ever experienced? The Smalley family almanac is full of stories that have "crazy glued" us together. It's no wonder we're close.

To make sure the glue sets properly in a home, it's important to remember one thing: *During difficult times, it's vital not to do or say anything that will close the spirit of others.*[1] Harsh words and calloused actions in the heat of battle are the quickest way to dilute the glue.

That afternoon, I realized I had said several things in anger to Michael that I shouldn't have, and I had to apologize to him and ask his forgiveness. It's best when level heads and open hearts work together to cement family "disasters" into positive family memories that can hold you together forever.

Once you know the "stick 'em" power of a well-handled disaster, minor family crises can actually become welcome visitors in your home. While they may knock down the door like an unwelcomed guest at first, once the crisis leaves there is an opportunity for stronger, more intimate relationships.

How do I know this for a fact? Namely, because the same principle that helps draw a family together during times of trial, works in our bonding with our Heavenly Father.

Glued to the Father

One of the most amazing things I've learned is that the same bonding that happens to families in a crisis can happen in our relationship with God when a person of faith goes through trying times.

Have you ever been through a struggle and had to depend totally on the Lord? There's nothing like the helplessness of feeling there's no one on earth to turn to. As Christians, we may often *feel* that way, but the reality is that we can always turn to the most powerful, influential Person in the whole universe and totally depend on Him. Often He allows us to experience that kind of loneliness and desperation so we'll learn lessons about His great love and faithfulness we wouldn't discover otherwise.

Walking through those valleys, you can feel a bonding with God that the "good times" just can't produce. Lessons learned about His loyal love are what inspired David to write: "The Lord is my shepherd, I shall not want. . . . *though I walk through the valley of the shadow of death, I will fear no evil; for thou art with me* . . . " (Psalm 23:1,4 KJV, italics mine). Talk about bonding! David was a man whose heart cleaved to God's because he had faced the fires and yet God saw him through.

In the same way, when disastrous things happen to each of us, we can respond in thankfulness to Him, confident the experience will make us more trusting of Him. (This principle of looking to God to find value in trials is so important, we will take an entire chapter to talk about it.)

Making positive memories out of trying times is probably one of the most powerful ways to develop a friendship I know of today. Remember when Greg stood up in front of several hundred parents and urged them to become "best friends" with their children? Reflecting on past memories is one way to do it. This is especially true if you've suffered through some family crisis that you can look back on and laugh about. This very kind of disaster was one of the worst—but funniest—experiences of my life.

Just Hanging Around

It happened a few months before Christmas. Norma asked me what I wanted her to give me that year. I told her I'd been thinking about a pair of inversion boots, the kind you buckle yourself into and then use to hang upside down to stretch out all your muscles. I told her that before I made the request official, I wanted to try something first.

Norma left for the grocery store, and, thinking this was as good a time as any to try the "invention" out, I went to the garage. I drilled some holes in an old pair of boots, placed a metal hook in each one, and put them on. Then I got out my ladder, climbed up and hung myself upside down from my son's chinning bar. Actually the boots worked fine—my muscles certainly felt as if they were being stretched like never before. But I soon realized I had created a major problem with my new invention.

The problem was, now that I was upside down—hooked to the chin-up bar—I couldn't get down! I was stuck! What's worse, I didn't have enough strength to reach up and loosen the boots to free myself. To top things off, nobody was around. I was left to hang there helplessly like a side of beef in a meat freezer. I had visions of heart failure, and Norma opening the garage door, seeing me, and thinking, *Gary sure chose a weird way to commit suicide!*

The person who finally found me was Greg, the family clown! He had heard my cries for help, opened the door, saw me hanging there, and fell on the ground howling like a hyena.

There I dangled. Dear old Dad. The one who helped to change his diapers, who played ball with him in the park for countless hours, who worked long, hard hours to put food in his mouth and clothes on his back; and all he could do was laugh while I was dying!

Finally, Kari came in and urged Greg up off the floor and tried to help me. Even together, however, they were not strong enough to get me down. By this time, I knew I was going to die. I knew I was about to have a stroke that would finish me. Norma would have to fight the insurance company for years to prove that my death wasn't "suspicious."

At long last, Kari went to get some scissors and cut the shoe strings on my boots. This was certainly helpful in getting me out of the boots, but what they had failed to do was move the ladder I'd used. As a result, I fell onto it and onto the concrete floor and cut and bruised by head and hip.

The moment I hit the floor, the kids scattered—and for good reason. I can assure you, if I had been able to move just then, I would have "laid hands" on them!

It's been several years since my "upside down" adventure, and just like our camping trips, the "crazy glue" of that shared trial has made this story one of our favorite family memories. It was a crisis that everyone in my family enjoyed, even me—after I got over the humiliation.

I have to be honest, though. That's not the end of the story. Two years later Mike and I were visiting some friends in a beautiful home in Seattle. I noticed they had a workout room with a *real* pair of inversion boots.

You know the rest of the story. I got stuck *again*. This time Mike got to do the honors of helping me down. Years after I've gone to be with the Lord, I'm sure my children and *their* children will still get together and talk—and yes, laugh—about "Dad and his boots."

Please Write on Our Walls

To add even more "bonding" glue to your memories, you can actually plan humorous things around your house that will build relationships and create happy times for your whole family as well. We know of a radio talk show host in our city who was a master at creating fun-bonding times when his children were young.

For example, when his son turned ten, he invited all the neighborhood kids over for the party—but not just *any* birthday party. He had saved for months and spent a small fortune in supplying an incredible surprise. Namely, 800 cream pies that he'd ordered for the biggest birthday pie fight that Phoenix has probably ever seen.

His son is grown now, but still recalls that party as one of the greatest highlights of his childhood—and almost every kid who participated does as well. It was terrific fun for everyone, and it created a special bond between father and son that still holds strong today. Still, that's not the extent of this creative man's talents.

As a radio celebrity, he was always being given "promotional" T-shirts when he would do commercials or "live" broadcasts. Even with giving many away to the Salvation Army, his shirt drawer soon began to bulge, and he came up with a creative idea.

When his kids were grade-school age, about once a month he'd pull out an old T-shirt that was ready for the trash (or one he'd been given that he knew he'd never wear). Then when he saw all the kids were home, he'd walk through the house yelling, "*I hope no kids are listening!* I sure hope there aren't any aggressive kids in their rooms that want to be destructive today and tear a T-shirt off of me. Because this T-shirt has a hole in it, and I'm ready to throw it away. . . ."

No sooner had he finished speaking than doors would burst open all over the house and voices screaming with delight would echo down the halls. From everywhere, his four kids would dive all over him and tear this shirt to pieces. He loved it, and they loved him for it.

How about one more example of a creative dad who knows that letting kids occasionally experience something "out of the ordinary" can build lasting, loving memories?

In every home, what is one rule that is always established as soon as a child begins testing his fine-motor skills? That's right. "Don't write on the walls." Just as in everyone else's home, this man's kids also had to obey this rule—until he decided that he'd make one "marked" exception.

One day, he and his wife were struggling over how to redecorate the guest bathroom when he came up with a very creative idea. He called the kids in (after talking to his wife, of course) and told them that whenever they brought home a friend, that child could sign his or her name on one of the bathroom walls. Of course, the wall signing had to begin by having the children put their names in what may have become the largest autograph book in Arizona.

Every other wall in the house was still "off limits" to writing, but soon this guest bath became a focal point of the entire neighborhood. It has stayed that way even now that the kids are all grown and out of the house. Today, when this man's children bring people over to their parents' home, the bathroom is still the first place they visit to have them see or "sign" the wall.

You may not know of many people who spend part of every "family reunion" all jammed into a guest bathroom . . . but now you do. This family loves to gather and look at years' worth of happy memories captured in the names of grade school, high school, and college friends of the kids—and the "grown up kids" who are the parents' friends who also insist on signing the bathroom wall! One creative idea resulted in positive memories shouting from four walls that could have just held wallpaper.

Any kind of fun time you plan, even if it's just wrestling with your kids or playing leapfrog, is something that can bind you in special and significant ways. Don't let "tradition," or fatigue, or a busy schedule, steal all the fun from your family times. It's so important.

John and I have a very close friend named Bill Butterworth who is one of the most outstanding family conference speakers in the country.[2] Often, he asks his audiences this open-ended question: "If you could add anything to your home—what would it be?"

Do you know what answer he has received as the number 1 things many people wish they had more of inside their home? You guessed it—laughter.

Such an answer might surprise you—but then again, after reading this chapter, maybe not. In particular, it shouldn't shock Christians.

A very thought-provoking book came out a few years ago called *Desiring God.*[3] For many Christians, the Christian life can be something so cold and "humorless" it almost begs kids to look for a "cheerful heart" anywhere but in their home or church. Yet that should never be the case. In this author's book, he does a very good job of illustrating that "In the knowledge of God is fullness of joy." In other words, one clear hallmark of a Christian is a joyful life.

I fully realize that joking can sometimes be hurtful. Inappropriate humor can be sarcastic or disrespectful, but let's not leave joy out of a home if we want it to be marked as distinctively Christian. Your kids will always remember you for taking the time and creativity to add a sparkle of fun to the family—even if it costs you a T-shirt or two!

The Family That Decides Together, Bonds Together

Disasters can be great ways for family bonding to take place. For the faint of heart, however, it's also possible to plan times together as a family where neither hardship nor humor are the goals. These are special times for just being together, times that allow the opportunity for relationships to develop simply because you're with someone.

Family outings such as these generally don't happen without effort—particularly in our hectic, fast-paced world. So, the best thing to do is get the family together, talk about what you enjoy doing, and plan an event or activity everyone can enjoy.

But what if you're a group of "individuals" like my family and enjoy different activities? My family solved this situation by deciding to make it a priority to spend time together. That way, when it's time to plan a family activity, we're all open to talk about it.

"Okay, gang," I say, "it's time to plan this year's vacation.

On a scale of one to ten, ten being the best, what would be a ten for you this time?" Each member then has the opportunity to share what would be a "dream activity" for them.

Kari and Norma will usually answer, "A cute beach where I can lay out in the sun, and probably cute little shops nearby." Mike and Greg typically respond, "Water, fishing, snorkeling, rock-climbing—anything adventurous." Then we put our heads together and try to come up with a place or activity that will fit our budget and still accommodate everyone's wishes as much as possible.

Sometimes, we have to make compromises, but that can be a valuable time for our kids to learn the importance of considering each others' needs and wants ahead of their own (Philippians 2:3–8). It may take time to hammer out a solution, but our commitment to doing things together as a family is a great help in urging all of us to bend enough to arrive at a decision everyone is satisfied with.

In the last few years, as our kids have moved through the teenage years, there's been stiff competition between family time and their team sports, clubs, and church trips. Sometimes, we decide *as a family* that we're already busy enough. Still, we try to plan times together as much as our schedules will allow.

It's also important to make a family decision to spend time alone with each of your children. A few years ago Greg and I went to Eastern Europe together on a speaking trip. If you want to bond with someone, just go through a few communist road blocks together as they search and re-search every stitch of you and your luggage! We'll always have the memory of staying in homes where people literally risked their lives to meet and to talk about Christ.

Taking mini-mission trips to your local Salvation Army to serve Thanksgiving dinner or help the poor can be a tremendous bonding time, or plan several years in advance to save up to visit one of your church's missionaries in the field. You can encourage and help them with a specific project or need they may have. Instead of just letting the youth leader get the advantage of all the bonding that goes on during a missions trip, go with the kids as a sponsor yourself. Usually the church is in such need of "sponsors" they may even pick up your expenses to travel with the kids! You'll lose sleep and possibly some hearing (if they're allowed to bring their tape players), but you'll never lose the closeness that can come from trips like these.

We can all waste time on television and movies, but we'll never waste one minute of time giving our children a picture of what God is accomplishing throughout the world.

Let me say clearly that it's not the distance or expense that counts but the personal contact you have with your children during the event. Over the years, Kari and I have made a habit of going out together for yogurt to talk. The warm, intimate father-daughter conversations we've had will always be dear to me.

When Greg got up to share at our conference that day, it made me very aware—and very thankful for—of all the hours we'd spent camping as a family. In many ways, we'd collected a twofold benefit. All the trials and family experiences we had have produced a loving bond with the children stronger and deeper than Norma and I could ever imagine. They've done something else as well. They've also given Norma and me more love for each other—and more positive memories to hold on to now that the kids are grown and moving away.

Whether you do all your "camping" at the nearest Marriott or deep in the heart of the Colorado Rockies, there's no substitute for quality time as a couple—or a family. A close-knit home, like our relationship with our Christ, grows and deepens as we share together moments of trial, tenderness, and laughter.

Now, finally, what I think are the most important chapters await us. I'll never write on more important subjects than the ones you'll find in Chapters 13 and 14, for they provide the insights for us to gain the desire and inner strength to do all the honoring and loving things we've written about in this book. Without these two chapters, this book would be just another "skill-building" book, but in today's world with the pressures we face—skills aren't enough. You need to be able to fully tap into the only power source for a love that lasts—if you want your love to last a lifetime.

13

Finding Fulfillment: More Than Our Cup Can Hold

One morning, a wife was desperately trying to get her husband up for church. She kept pushing and shoving him, trying to get him out of bed. "Get up, George!" she said repeatedly. "We're going to be late for church again!"

Finally, he rolled over in frustration and said, "I told you last night, I am *not* going to church and that's final. Now let me go back to sleep."

"But George," she pleaded, "it's important for you to be there." Finally, she decided to use another approach. "Okay, George. Give me two good reasons why you shouldn't go to church."

"Fine," he said, "I'll give you two reasons. Number one, I don't *like* those people. And number two, they don't like *me* down there either. That's why I'm not going."

There was a long pause as his wife thought over his answer. Finally he spoke up and said, "If you feel it's really so important I go to church, why don't you give me two reasons why I should go?"

"George," she said, "first of all you know that the Bible says it's important for you to go to church, and second, *you're the pastor!*"

Like anyone, pastors can get discouraged. I spent a number of years working at several churches, and I know what it's like to be discouraged. In fact, I know what it's like not to want to get out of bed.

When We Feel Like Never
Coming out from under the Covers

When I was thirty-five years old, there was a time I was so depressed from what I thought life had "dealt" me, that all I wanted was to crawl under the covers and never show my face again.

I blamed all my miseries on this job, and that person, and those circumstances. I can remember being so discouraged over a heart-breaking ministry situation that I lay upstairs in my daughter Kari's room, not eating for almost four days. Each of my children would come up and try to encourage me, but I'd just tell them to go away—I didn't want to face anyone or anything. Norma did her best to break me out of the doldrums as well, but for days I stayed in a darkened room, alone with my misery.

Finally, I remember telling my wife that I had made an important decision. I was getting out of the ministry. I didn't want any part of all the stress and broken promises I'd faced, and I was going to leave and get into some other kind of work.

Norma turned to me and asked, "What would you do?" That's when I realized that I didn't *know* anything else to do. I had been trained for the ministry and nothing else. I really became depressed when I thought about that! In my mind, I was on a dead-end street with no hope of ever finding a pathway that would take me away from my troubles.

During this time, I remember doing something out of desperation that turned out to be the greatest thing that has ever happened to me in my life. This period of personal darkness was the worst experience that had ever happened to me, but it turned into the greatest thing I ever experienced because of what it taught me.

I learned one biblical principle that taught me several important things I may never have learned otherwise. I discovered how to use my emotions—even the negative ones—instead of just being used by them. I learned something that led me to lasting freedom from worry, fear, anxiety, hurt feelings, and depression. I also learned how to take all the negative things that happen to me and actually find positive good and deeper love for others within the trial (I'll focus on this in detail in the next chapter).

Most of all, that terrible experience taught me the secret to experiencing continuing fulfillment in life. This is the very thing any individual or couple must discover if their marriage is to stay strong over each season of life.

Looking for Love, Peace and Joy in All the Wrong Places

What did I learn that had such a dramatic impact on my life? For years before that period of depression, I had spent a lifetime looking to any number of things to give me a sense of significance and security. But I was trying to find the right things in the wrong places.

I learned that we all have similar goals in life. If our lives were like a cup, each one of us would love to have it filled with wisdom, love, joy, and peace. We'd like to have our lives overflow with positive emotions and genuine fulfillment in life. At a very early age, we all begin to look around for what we think can fill up our cup with these positive qualities.

Unfortunately, what most of us do is to look to one of three sources, or all three, to give us the fullness of life we really want. Yet like a mirage, they shimmer with fulfillment, but offer only dust to our souls.

Looking to People to Fill Our Cup

The first place many of us tend to look is toward people. We think to ourselves, *if I'm really going to have my needs met, I've got to have another person in my life.*

Take the average single woman in her early twenties or even thirties. Often, she'll spend hours thinking and dreaming of how that "special" someone will come into her life and fill up her cup. For some women who come from a difficult family background, their personal cup may have so little love, peace, and joy that they long to finally be filled up. So in these cases, there can be a tremendous desire for a "Mr. Wonderful" to come along who can make up for the empty arms and missing love they've experienced.

In her mind's eye, this woman can come home at day's end and find "him" waiting for her. She wants someone who would hold her gently in his arms and spend hours at night in intimate conversation. She is looking for someone who is thoughtful and kind—and can fill up her cup to overflowing.

Many women enter courtship this way, but before a woman has been married a year, panic begins to set in. That's because she begins to discover almost immediately that her husband is not only failing to fill her cup—but often this "special someone" is drilling little holes in her cup by his small, insensitive actions.

Now, in addition to her cup not getting fuller, she's starting to lose whatever positive feelings with which she came into the marriage! Many women have actually told me that they experienced feelings of emotionally "drying up" when they realized that their husband would never fill their cup.

Then something happens. A light can go on in this woman's eyes as she comes to a startling realization. It isn't a husband who fills her cup. *It must be children!* Of course! God's plan. Little children running around the house. So they have little babies running around the house, and soon they discover something that all children have the capacity to do. That is, children can drill *big* holes in the cup!

Now this woman may really face a problem. Neither her husband nor her children are always filling her cup. They can be frustrating and irritating and drain away as much—or more—emotional energy than they give.

For those who look elsewhere, they'll ultimately find the same frustration in any other relationship. Friends can be a tremendous source of help and encouragement at times, but even they can disappoint us over the long haul. We can look to them as the source of positive emotions, but at times they too can punch holes in our emotional lives.

Tragically, some people have even turned to an affair to try to "fill their cup." The sweet taste of stolen waters may seem to fill up one's life, but it's actually like drinking ice-cold salt water. The burning aftertaste of sin can burn huge holes in our cup and leave us emptier and more miserable than we ever imagined.[1]

If people aren't the source that fills up our lives with the positive emotions we want so much, what is?

Looking to Places as the Source of Fulfillment

"We need a home! That's it, we need a place with a beautiful view and trees that are the envy of the neighborhood. If only we had the right place to live, *then* our cup will be full." Then we get that special home and live in it for a short while, and suddenly things begin to go wrong. In part that's true because the bigger our home, the more things there are to fix when they break.

Norma and I live in Arizona where grass front lawns are an exception, but for a period of time we thought, *We need a place that can be an oasis in the desert. We need a house that has a beautiful lawn.* Surely *that* would help our cup be full. Once we got our lawn in, though, we then discovered we were chained to it just to keep it alive.

One year I didn't water it enough, and the grass all died. The next year, I watered it too much and killed the grass again. In fact, there were numerous times when I was tempted to bulldoze the entire yard and pave it over, I was so frustrated with it!

We can put in a swimming pool, a fireplace, or even buy a mountain cabin, and those "places" don't fulfill us. Why? In part because no matter how pretty or fulfilling places look, they don't fit inside our personal cup. Instead they all have sharp edges that cut holes in our lives. What's more, the *people* we share our special places with are the same ones who continue to drain our cup as well!

But if people *and* places don't fill up the deepest part of our lives, where do we turn to finally find love, peace, and joy?

Looking to Things for Fulfillment

How about more money so that we can buy more things? Many of us feel that if we just had more money, we'd be happier in life. But study after study of people who "strike it rich" show this isn't the case.

The more money we make, the more wisdom we must have to handle it. Now I know that many of us wouldn't mind having to come up with that kind of wisdom. But to get money we normally have to pay a personal price. Thomas Carlyle once said, "For every person who can handle prosperity, there are a hundred who can handle adversity." Money alone, and all the things it can bring, can't fill up our lives with the kind of living water we desperately want.

I've met people all over the country who have little money and are miserable. And I've also met those with lots of money who are miserable. I've known people who have mountain cabins and third cars and aren't fulfilled. And some people I know barely have bus fare, but they also feel empty inside.

Most people who depend on "things" to "fill up their cup" end up looking for the one "perfect" job that will be the ticket to all their dreams. All jobs have one thing in common—work! And work doesn't always keep our cup full. It can positively drain us in terms of the people we work with, the place where we do our work, the equipment we must use, and so on.

Some of us try all our lives to get a key to a certain washroom, or a parking space with our name on it. When we get it, however, what do we have? The answer to being filled with wisdom, love, peace, and joy? Hardly. Just the opposite is too often true.

Coming up Empty in Life

At some times in each one of our lives, we run headlong into an inescapable fact. Life is not fulfilling. It's actually often unfair and exhausting. (Try reading the book of Ecclesiastes if you want a picture of someone who had everything, but everything wasn't enough.)

We can never pour enough people, places, or things into our personal cup to keep our lives filled and overflowing with the contentment we want so much. It's no wonder so many people lead lives of emotional desperation, and even consider suicide as a way out.

In fact, by focusing on people, places, and things, we not only miss the positive emotions we want . . . *we end up with the very negative emotions we've been trying all our lives to avoid!* This is true because hurt feelings, worry, anxiety, fear, unrest, uncertainty, and confusion come as a direct result of "expecting" life from a person, place, or thing.

If our ultimate goal in a marriage is saying to our spouse, "I need life from you. Will you cooperate, meet my needs, and fill up my cup?" we're asking for big problems and an empty life.

Many marriages find a husband and wife like two dry sponges, each waiting to soak up life from the other. While we're expecting wisdom, love, peace, and joy from our spouses on a daily basis, they can be sitting across the table expecting us to provide all their needs as well. Then we all come up empty, and major problems can develop.

Why do we get our feelings hurt in the course of an average week? If we're honest and look closely at our circumstances, it's because we've been expecting "life" from someone (or something) who isn't cooperating, and there's one thing more. At the heart of our desperate longing for others to fulfill our deepest needs is a grabbing selfishness that says, "Me first, me first!"

My daughter Kari is a constant source of encouragement to me—and sometimes a loving source of correction as well. I can be frustrated with her over some minor matter and begin to get angry, but she'll always stay incredibly calm. I've often asked her to help me isolate why I'm feeling angry, and she'll say, "Now, Dad, you know that this thing is not really making you angry. It's just revealing your own self-centeredness!"

As much as I hate to admit it, she's generally right! A situation or person doesn't make me angry. I choose to be angry over whatever thing is blocking my goal or frustrating my plan.

We all face the temptation to look to people, places, and things to fill our cup. We're all selfish in wanting others to cooperate in meeting our needs right now. But it's only those who are wise who realize that there is a pathway to freedom from that unfulfilled feeling.

Freedom from Unfulfilled Expectations

Anger, worry, fear, hurt feelings—we wouldn't choose these emotions for anything. Yet we often end up with such feelings starring on our team.

For years, I carried around a great deal of worry and anxiety in my life. At least a part of it came from my background. A few years ago I began to learn what it takes to be completely free from most of the destructive emotions to which I once felt chained. Fear was one of my biggest problems. Here's how it sneaked up on me.

I grew up in a home that was very permissive. Primarily this was because my mother and father lost their first child not long after my mother had given her a spanking. The spanking itself didn't have anything to do with the child's death. A splinter led to an infection and complications that a country doctor and pharmacist in the early forties couldn't heal. Because of the emotional guilt, my mother made my father promise neither one of them would ever discipline us.

This meant that I grew up in a home with no rules. Take dating, for example. Because there were no boundaries in my home, I didn't actually begin my formal dating until the third grade. I did a lot of informal dating before then, but my formal dating started in third grade.

In a climate where "anything goes," my older brothers were left to come up with any "game" they wanted to tease and scare me. One brother loved to wake me up in the middle of the night and stand me up on a chair where he and his friends would laugh at me. He also loved to take his B-B gun and say to me, "I'll give you to *three* to get going." I'd take off as fast as I could because I knew he'd shoot me if I was still in range at the count of three.

He even used to take me out to the middle of a field with his bow and arrow and shoot an arrow up in the air and say, "Scatter!" I never knew where the arrow was coming down, and I was filled with fear and anxiety as I tried to run to safety. Later, every bush became a hiding place to "scare" me. Every time my parents were away was an opportunity to make me jump in some way.

It may seem that all these things were just "childhood games," but they left fearful memories inside my life. While it's hard for me to admit, I was so filled with fear that when I was twenty-four years old I still couldn't take a shower with my eyes closed. I couldn't even stay in a house alone because I'd think I was hearing people breaking in—and I was in graduate school at seminary at the time!

Today, though, it's been almost ten years since I had a fearful thought. Why? Because I've been learning something very specific from God's Word that has taken the fear right out of my life.

Envy, jealousy, comparison. I used to struggle with these emotions constantly, but rarely any more. Why? Because I'm learning how to take these very negative emotions and turn them into a flashing light that illuminates lasting fulfillment. Let me give you an illustration of what I mean.

Using Negative Emotions as Positive Warning Lights in Life

Let's say Dr. Trent and I have just finished our seminar and we've asked Bob, the local chairman, if he'd take us to the airport. As always, we're cutting it close, but if he hurries we'll make the plane just in time.

As we drive to the airport, Bob is having a great time, asking us questions and commenting on how the conference went. He's moving down the highway at a steady clip when suddenly the red light on the dashboard comes on and starts blinking, indicating there's an oil problem with the engine.

I see the light and point it out to Bob right away. After all, this is the last flight out for the day, and we're really anxious to get home to our families.

"Don't worry," Bob assures me. "That thing comes on and off all the time."

Now, though, the light is shining even brighter and is staying on, not flashing. "Bob, are you sure there isn't a problem with your car?" I ask, beginning to wonder if something is actually wrong.

"Naw, nothing to worry about," he says. Just then his engine freezes up, stranding us in the middle of the freeway and causing us to miss our plane.

Actually, Bob had several options when that warning light came on. He could have pulled over and checked the oil, or flagged someone down who could help him fix the problem, or get us to the airport. He could even have done something like this:

When I asked him the second time about the red light on his dash, he could have said, "Gary, do me a favor. Reach into the glove box and hand me that little hammer that's inside there." When I handed him the hammer, he could have taken it and Wham! Wham! Wham!, smashed out the light. "There, now do you feel better? That light won't bother you any more!"

No intelligent person ignores a warning light. It's installed for a purpose. Rather than smash it, you should learn from it. It will alert you to a potential problem. Unfortunately, when it comes to experiencing negative emotions, many people try and "smash them" out of their lives instead of using them as positive warning lights.

Many people feel tremendously guilty when they experience anger, fear, worry, or hurt feelings. I've learned to use them in a positive way. These emotions are actually red lights flashing telling us our focus is in the wrong spot. We're expecting life from the wrong source!

You see, there's a fundamental problem with expecting fulfillment from people, places, and things. These are the *gifts* of life, not the *source* of life. Any time we expect the gifts of life to give us what only God can, we're asking for our cups to be drained of energy and life itself.

Now, when fearful thoughts come into my life, I don't degrade myself for feeling them. I simply say, "Thank You, Lord, for reminding me that you're the only One who can give life." Instead of resenting negative emotions, I can be thankful for their warning-light reminder that I'm looking for something other than the Lord to fill my cup. They can also be the prod that God uses to get us moving in the direction He has chosen for us. How can we learn to harness negative emotions to point us in the right direction?

People, places and things are the gifts *of life, not the* Source *of life....*

Seeking First the Source of Life

When the red lights of negative emotions fill my life, they are all ultimately tied into the same sensor. It's a spiritual sensor that is saying, "Smalley, you're expecting fulfillment from people, places, and things—not from the Lord." I'm focusing on the gifts of life and expecting them to be the Source of life.

Matthew 6:33 gives us a clear direction on what our Source of life should be. "But seek first his kingdom and his righteousness, and all these things will be given you as well." When I give God first place in my life, He promises to meet all my needs.

I try to love God with all my heart. In other words, He's the highest priority in my life. When I focus on Jesus Christ alone as the Source of my life, an amazing thing happens. Because He loves me and actually possesses the wisdom, love, peace, and joy I've always wanted—He alone can fill my cup to overflowing! That's exactly what He promises to do for His children. Ephesians

3:19–20 tells us that " . . . this love . . . surpasses knowledge—that you may be filled to the measure of all the fullness of God." Can you get any more filled than full? Absolutely not.

Do you understand now why very few people can hurt my feelings? Because I'm no longer expecting people to fill my cup, I'm not hurt when they don't respond in a particular way. Even if my wife or a close friend says something to hurt me, it is still a reflection that my focus was on what they could give or take away—not on what God gives.

Whenever those warning lights go off, I thank God for them. Then I pray and ask forgiveness for focusing on something that is less than Himself. Finally, I ask Him alone to fill my life. Psalm 62 says that we are to wait and hope in God alone. He's our rock, our salvation, our rear guard, our hiding place. He's everything we'll ever need!

Think of how many wives are manipulated by husbands from whom they "expect" life and vice-versa. The more we place our expectations on another person, the more control we give them over our emotional and spiritual state. The freer we are of expectations from others—and the more we depend upon God alone—the more pure and honest our love for others will become.

Tapping into a Limitless Source of Power

For twelve chapters we've looked at the various "skills" that can move a marriage from rock bottom right up at the top. We've also been careful to say that communication and intimacy skills alone aren't enough to build the kind of lasting love we all want. Why? Because if we really want a relationship "made in heaven," we must learn to appropriate the power of Heaven—and that power is available through prayer.

The key to powerful prayer is found in Luke 18. When I pray, I become a great deal like the little widow woman pictured in this parable of Jesus. He used her as an example to teach the disciples how to pray. Let me tell her story:

There was once a little old widow lady who went before a wicked judge seeking protection from people who were bothering her. The problem was, this judge had no respect for either God or man, and he repeatedly turned her away. Even with that kind of treatment, she never gave up.

Every day she got in line in front of that wicked judge. Finally, through sheer persistence day after day, she got the protection she was looking for. What was the point of this story? Jesus went on to tell His disciples that we have a God who loves us. "How much more will He hear and answer our prayers" when we line up every day with our requests.

That's how I pray. I line up every day before God and wait expectantly for His answer to my prayers. Of course, even before I pray, I make sure that I'm praying as I should. I always pray keeping 1 Timothy 6:3 in mind, checking to see that my petition is consistent with God's will and that it leads to godliness. If I'm careful that my request meets these standards, then I never get out of line—just like that widow woman. How does this apply to a marriage or having a strong family?

Remember John and Kay Hammer, the couple back in Chapters 1 and 3 who went through such terrible struggles? Kay learned all the "skills" I could teach her about how to have a strong marriage, but that wasn't all. She also learned how to tap into the one power source that could fill her cup to overflowing. That source was separate from anything John could ever do. Once her expectations for wisdom, love, peace, and joy were placed on her God and not her husband, she was finally free to love John. She also had the strength to keep persistently, expectantly praying for positive changes to happen in their relationship.

As she practiced the skills of growing a great relationship, she also prayed continually for a positive result in her home, in her own and her husband's lives. It was her attitude of prayer that gave her the power to keep going when all her feelings said, "Give up!"

Standing in line every day before God reminds me of the story of a man who died and went to heaven. The first place St. Peter took him was to a huge warehouse. It stretched for miles, and it was filled with millions and millions of presents.

"What in the world is this room?" the startled newcomer asked.

"This room is full of presents that were for God's children," Peter answered. "But they got out of line too soon."

I know many, many couples who began the work of forging a loving relationship—but they got out of line too soon. They weren't persistent enough. They ran out of strength to keep their relationship together, forgetting that "those who hope in the Lord will renew their strength" (Isaiah 40:31).

Whenever I wake up in the middle of the night and find my stomach knotted over some problem I'm facing, I've learned to do something that puts me right back to sleep. I've learned to thank God for my knotted stomach, because it's telling me that I'm focusing on one of the gifts of life for love, peace, and joy, rather than the Source of life. The level of my cup doesn't vary now from day to day, phone call to phone call, circumstance to circumstance, because His mercies are new every morning—a fresh full cup of life every day.

It's not Norma who fills my cup. It's not Kari, or Greg, or Michael. It's not my good friends or family members. They're "overflow," not my basic needs. John 17:3 says that to know God is life. Just knowing Christ is life. It's not knowing about Him, it's knowing Him. In 1 John 5:12 the apostle says, "He who has the Son has life; he who does not have the Son of God does not have life." It's as simple as that.

Is your life filled with negative emotions? Or all the fullness of Christ? As we close this chapter, let me share with you one example. I hope it will bring this concept closer to your heart. It did for me the first time I heard Linda's story.

A Single Place to Plug in our Lives

Linda was a young woman who had suffered terribly as a child. Her father adored her, but with his untimely death when she was only five, it seemed she was left without anyone to love her. Her mother resented her, and her brothers and sisters rejected her. All through her childhood, Linda could remember crying herself to sleep at night, wanting so much for things to be different, but they never were.

Linda's desires in life were the same as ours. She longed for others to highly value her. She wanted inner happiness, calm, and contentment. Yet growing up in a negative, non-Christian environment, she experienced only anger, bitterness, and defeat.

Up to this point, I've talked about the Lord filling our cup. Let me change the imagery to give us a different perspective. It was as if Linda's life were a lamp with a single cord.

She wanted desperately to see her life lit up with positive

feelings and a warm, inner calm. She wanted the joy of knowing she was accepted unconditionally by her mother and loved by her brothers and sisters. Yet every time she tried plugging into her family, she received a terrible shock.

Over the years, Linda had been shocked so many times by her family, she sometimes felt like giving up. The very people who should have given her love and acceptance had given her only pain and hurt. Thus she often considered taking her own life.

Linda was so tired of darkness and being shocked, so desirous of light in her life, that she went to another extreme. She spent years plugging into anything and anyone she thought might bring her power and warmth.

She tried lighting her life by plugging into friends, dating, school, jobs, houses, even "recreational" drugs and alcohol. Every time she plugged into one of these things, they, too, left her trapped in darkness and afraid she would never see the light she longed for.

Do you know someone like Linda? Has a difficult background or even some present relationship left you searching for the light of love and peace, and full of darkness and fear? Like Linda, there is only one place where any of us can plug in our lives and find the satisfaction we so desperately need.

Plugging into the Source of Life

When Linda finally discovered that she needed to plug into the Source of Life, Jesus Christ, she saw her life light up for the first time. In His love she found unconditional acceptance (Romans 8:38–39; John 10:1ff; Hebrews 13:5). In His power she found the strength to be joyful in spite of her circumstances (Philippians 4:11–14; 1 Peter 1:6–9). Guided by His hand, she found a spiritual family at a nearby church. They loved her unconditionally. Through His Word and Spirit she received the inner peace that had always eluded her (John 14:6, 1 John 5:1ff).

Perhaps you need to ask yourself what your life is plugged into. Many people try to carry around dozens of "extension" cords and plug them in to the Lord as well as many other people and things, but God has designed us with a single cord and only one place where we can plug it in to find lasting life and power—Himself.

One afternoon after a long conversation with a close friend, Linda made the most significant decision anyone can make. For the first time, she plugged her life into the Source of Life. For the next year and a half, she made a daily decision to look only to the Lord to light up her life.

Whenever she found herself angry with her husband or impatient with her children, she took time to realize that she was really plugging in to them, trying to use them for fulfillment or to meet an unmet need in her own life. Most importantly, whenever she thought about her terrible past and her light began to dim, she would immediately unplug from the hurtful memories and plug back into the positive words of Scripture to discover a special future her Heavenly Father had for her.

What happened when Linda found a single, unbroken source of life to plug into? Her life was never again the same.

Her marriage began to blossom as she finally stopped expecting her husband to make up for years of neglect she had experienced with her family. In her early fifties, she even called her estranged mother and began working to restore that relationship. Her mother was in her eighties!

Linda still met with the same painful, discouraging words, but somehow the shock had been turned off. She was finally free to love her mother because she wasn't expecting anything from her—and it made a major difference in their relationship. She never knew the joy of leading her mother to Christ, but at least Linda was free from the choking feelings of hatred and anger she had carried for years.

Are you expecting life from another person? Someone in the past, like your parents? Someone in the present, like your spouse? Are you struggling with forgiving them because they've "taken" something from you? Something only God could ever have given you in the first place?

For some of us, this single concept of plugging into Christ alone for wisdom, love, peace, and joy can be the most freeing experience in our lives. It certainly was for me.

For me, learning that the ministry, other people, and even my spouse would never fill my cup was the very thing that got me up out of bed when I was so depressed. Believing and practicing the fact that Jesus alone is the Source of life, wisdom, fulfillment, and purpose is what has kept me active and excited about life ever since. I've already accomplished more from a human perspective than I've ever dreamed possible—and in large part it's because I no longer look at life from a human perspective. I'm free to succeed or fail because Jesus Christ is the Source of my life, the fullness of my cup that can never be drained away.

There remains only one final area to discuss before we close this book. In many ways, it could be the most important. In addition to learning that Christ alone could free me from unrealistic expectations, I discovered something else during that difficult time. Even the very trials that led me to depression actually contained valuable gold for developing strong, lasting relationships.

14

The Source of Lasting Love

Some readers may be thinking, *All this talk about having strong relationships and even "plugging" into Christ as my only Source of life is great, it's inspiring. I can even believe it works for other people—but not for me. There's no hope for me.*

I can hear you saying, "You've never met my husband! You've never met my wife! She's been unfaithful! He's left me before! My kids have turned against me! She's turned away from God! I'm a pastor's wife, and I can't tell anyone our problems! I've already been divorced twice! I've had five jobs in the last year and none of them have worked out! . . ."

In almost twenty years of working with individuals, couples, and families, I've heard terrible stories of heartache and tragedy. Many of these certainly sound like "exception" clauses to God's power to turn a terrible situation into something positive. Let me tell you Diane's story:

Diane came to one of our seminars. In her early sixties today, as a young girl she had lived in a very beautiful home in the Northwest. Her father was a well respected attorney in the community, but he was a terror to live with at home. Verbally and sometimes physically abusive, he was always critical and unreachable.

When she was nine years old, her mother caught her father in the midst of an affair. In a fit of anger, she threatened to expose her husband and ruin his reputation in their small town, but like a wounded lion, he turned on her and successfully sued *her* for divorce first—thoroughly slandering her name in the process. Their "soap opera" courtroom theatrics became so bad, other parents forbade their children to play or even talk with Diane or her older brother at school. Then, one day, circumstances turned from bad to far worse than Diane could ever have imagined.

When Diane and her brother came home from school, the movers were in the house packing all their things and getting ready to cart them away. Their father had won the divorce decree and had even gotten a court order evicting his former wife from the house.

As the mother wept, Diane's older brother became furious. He stormed into the house and up to his father's room, grabbing up a gun he knew his father always hid in his bedside drawer. When he came out of the house, his grandmother was walking up the porch and saw him with the gun. In a burst of anger, he told her he was on his way to kill his father. She grabbed at him, trying to wrestle the gun away. But in the struggle the gun went off. In a terrible accident Diane's brother had killed his own grandmother.

Tragedy would follow tragedy that day. When the police came to the house, they tracked down the boy who was hiding in a neighbor's garage. A gun battle broke out, and an officer was critically wounded. Diane's brother was killed.

Can you imagine her feelings? Only nine years old, she had lived through the trauma of her parents' hostile divorce. She had lost her grandmother and brother in a single day. The community was blaming her because her brother had nearly killed a police officer. And now she was literally put out on the street after having lived in the lap of luxury.

There was nothing good about what happened to this woman or her family. The pain her father and brother caused will always be with her. And yet she told us, "It's taken many years, but I can actually say that God has used my terrible childhood to make me a much better person, especially with my own family. I've had to work through a lot, but I know God has made me a more loving wife and mother because of what I've been through."

Certainly, you say, her story is an exception. Exceptional perhaps, but an exception? Hardly. Here is another story that may be even worse. We share it to underline that whatever we're personally struggling with, if God can turn a situation like this into something worthwhile, He can bring about a similar result in our trials.

Two Roads to the Same Destination

During the Vietnam War, two very different men were part of a Navy SEAL Team, an ultra-elite group sent on dangerous search-and-destroy missions. One was Dave Roever.

Dave would sit on his bunk and strum his guitar, singing religious folk songs and telling his buddies how much God loved them. The other man occupied the bunk above him. His name was Mickey Block, and along with another soldier, he gave Dave a hard time, constantly telling him to shut up and to knock off his preaching. In fact, as in many combat units, they gave Dave a nickname. During his tour in Vietnam, his handle would be the "Preacher Man." Dave came up with his own nickname for them, calling them Pervert Number One and Pervert Number Two!

One night, while on an ambush raid in their heavily armed patrol boat, another American vessel mistook them for the enemy and started firing. Mickey was hit over a dozen times by shrapnel and large caliber machine-gun bullets. His right leg was shot to pieces, and the top of his left hand was torn to the bone by a grenade blast.

The next year and a half, Mickey spent in and out of the hospital in tremendous pain. The doctors tried valiantly to save his leg, but they couldn't. The rest of his body was held together with pins and tubes for months. He found his only relief in getting high, and he stayed that way until he had become addicted to painkillers.

Life moved on at the front, and Mickey heard little about those he had fought with in his SEAL unit, but he did hear about Dave—and he knew he had to be dead.

Not long after Mickey was wounded, Dave was out on a combat mission with a squad of men when they were pinned down by enemy machine-gun fire. Dave pulled a phosphorus grenade from his belt to light up the enemy's position and stood up to throw it, but as he pulled back his arm, a bullet hit the grenade, and it exploded next to his ear.

Lying on his side on the bank of a muddy river in Vietnam, he watched part of his face float by. The rest of his face and his shoulder alternately smoldered and caught fire as the embedded phosphorus came into contact with the night air.

Dave Roever knew that he was going to die, yet miraculously he didn't. He was pulled from the water by his fellow soldiers, flown directly to Saigon, and then taken to a waiting plane bound for Hawaii. But his problems were just beginning.

In the months that followed, he would have dozens of operations—but he almost didn't make it through the first one. The Navy surgical team had a major problem during that operation. As they cut away tissue that had been burned or torn by the grenade, the phosphorus embedded in his body would hit the oxygen in the operating room and begin to ignite again! Several times the doctors and nurses ran out of the room, leaving him alone because they were afraid the flammable oxygen used in surgery would explode! Roever survived that first operation and was taken to a ward that held the most severe burn and injury cases from the war.

The real struggle for both men came after the war. Roever would start each day putting his wig on his bald head, adjusting his false ear, un-taping his eye which has to be taped closed at night since he has no eyelid, and staring at a face that shows the horror of burned flesh. Mickey, at the same time, was surviving skin grafts, amputation, traction, and plastic surgery only to acquire a bone disease and recurring abscesses and infection.

The two had pain and trauma in common after they came home, but beyond that their lives were very different. Mickey would sit in his house at night with a loaded gun in his lap, hoping someone would try to break in so he could shoot the intruder down. His marriage was ruined, and his addictions were getting worse.

Dave, on the other hand, had fallen back on his faith. Soon he was speaking across the country about his experiences. One special night, I heard him speak on national television, and he said: "I am twice the person I was before I went to Vietnam. . . . I wouldn't trade anything I've gone through for the benefits my trials have brought to my life. . . ."

I know what some of you are thinking now. *These people are crazy! How can a trial like this benefit us?* But before you put down the book, read what happened next.

About the same time that Dave Roever was telling how his trials had given him a better spiritual and family life, Mickey Block decided to kill himself. He sat in a chair in his bedroom and stuck his gun in his mouth. Even though he was not a "religious" person to say the least, he recounted that he suddenly felt as if he had seen a vision.

In his mind's eye, he saw the scene a moment after he'd pull the trigger, his brains and blood splattered over the wall behind him. He saw his children come running into his room after school. He tried to get up out of the chair and tell them not to look, but he couldn't! He saw the horror and fear in their eyes as they found his lifeless body slumped in the chair. . . .

As he sat there, a second away from death, he blinked away

the terrible picture of what he had almost done and began crying for the first time since Vietnam. Then, also for the first time, he prayed. He thought back to all the "preaching" he'd heard from Dave Roever and other Christians he had known and finally surrendered what was left of his broken life to Jesus Christ.

What happened next, he would only explain as a peace settling over him. Nothing drastic changed that day. His marriage was still shattered, his leg was still gone. He still battled his addictions, but now there was hope in his life—and a deep inner knowledge that he was forgiven for a life turned against God. He was no longer alone with his problems. His wife viewed his conversion with skepticism but as the months passed, she knew he was a changed man.

Then the day came when a friend called who happened to be listening to a local radio program. "Hey, Mickey," he said. "There's a guy talking about God on the radio who was a member of the SEALs in Vietnam like you were. Do you think you know him?"

The Preacher Man? Mickey thought. It couldn't be. From the account he had heard from the men who put Dave's body on the helicopter in 'Nam, he knew he was dead.

He called the radio station, his hands trembling as he asked to speak to the Vietnam veteran who had just been on the show. After a few moments, a familiar voice came on the line and said, "This is Dave Roever. Can I help you?"

In a few moments of animated conversation, Mickey found out that the "Preacher Man" was in town to speak at a church that night. Dave warmly invited him to attend the meeting, and he agreed. Mickey hadn't been inside a church in years, but that night he went with his wife. By way of introduction he put a .308 caliber machine-gun bullet in the offering plate—the type of bullet they used on their patrol boats and that had torn off his leg.

When the bullet was given to Dave at the front, he stopped speaking and called for his combat buddy to come up with him. Mickey limped the length of the church to Dave's waiting arms, amidst the tears and cheers of the people in the church.

That night, two men stood at the front of that church. They had both lived through the same excruciating, horrible experience. Each had taken a different road to the same destination. One found a deeper faith through having his face nearly blown away. The other lost his leg and nearly his wife and family—but finally he gained everything worth living for. He had new life in Christ and new hope for his family.

Turning Wrong Around

Not one of us would want to experience the kinds of tragedies that Diane, Mickey, and Dave experienced. Yet in each case, these people became stronger in their personal and family lives as a direct result of their trials.

One of the greatest truths I know is that life is difficult and often unfair. What makes the difference between those people who experience difficulties and grow bitter—and those who find a better life produced by a similar or even more difficult trial?

I experience the joy of sharing all across the country that everyone who knows Jesus Christ as Lord and Savior can have the assurance that their trials will produce good in their lives. In fact, for the believer, I often say, every trial comes gift-wrapped with a treasure ready to be found inside.

When Trials Fall from the Sky

I once heard of a man who was walking along the sidewalk outside his high-rise apartment in New York City. It was very early on a bitterly cold winter morning, and he was hurrying to get out of the wind. Suddenly, from out of nowhere, he was hit on the shoulder by a heavy object and knocked to the ground.

For several moments he lay on the sidewalk, dazed, feeling to see if his shoulder was broken. Finally, he sat up and looked around. The street was deserted, so he ruled out a mugging. He looked up at the apartments above him, but he could see no lights on and no open windows. He glanced around the ground where he was lying and saw a shoe box next to him. It was heavily taped from end to end. He reached over to pick it up, but it was so heavy he had to use both hands.

He took the shoe box back to his apartment, got some scissors out, and cut through the tape. Inside were three fairly large cloth sacks. As he lifted out one of the sacks and opened it in the light he gasped. There were several small gold bars and dozens of gold coins! After a few more moments of gasping, he decided he'd better take this shoe box to the police station.

The police told him that more than likely the gold was stolen jewelry that had been melted down. Whether it had fallen from an apartment or from a plane overhead, they couldn't say. If he'd leave it with them for six months, they told him, it could be his if no one lawfully claimed it during that time.

The six months took forever to pass, but finally the day came. He hurried to the police station and there was the shoe box that had given him the sore shoulder. His shoulder didn't hurt anymore, and soon because of this treasure that fell from nowhere, his pocketbook didn't either.

> *. . . though apparent trouble may look as if it's destroying our home, it can actually turn into a benefit for us through God's power!*

Most of us would gladly suffer through a sore shoulder to end up with a box filled with gold. Yet we may not realize that we have the same chance of benefiting every time we are hit by problems. For every trial is like a box containing valuable treasures. It may knock us to the ground and bruise us, but once we learn how to open the box, we can find a golden opportunity inside.

"Gary, you're either crazy or oversimplifying the problem of pain," some may say. "It's hard to believe that every problem can have a silver lining." After all, what good can come from some serious trial? A trial like having your face nearly blown away? Or from losing your leg and being on drugs? Or from being put out on the street at age nine?

As Diane, Dave, Mickey, Joni Eareckson Tada, Corrie Ten Boom, and many others can testify, trials are often devastating at the time. Yet in spite of the pain, they can produce a gold of sorts in our lives. Like a refining fire, each trial can work to make us more pure and sound. The Bible says God will " . . . bestow . . . a crown of beauty instead of ashes . . ." (Isaiah 61:3).

Don't misunderstand me. I'm not implying that God causes all trials (James 1:13). Neither am I saying that we ought to cause trials for others so that they'll gain from the experience (Romans 6:1–2). But I certainly do believe that in His sovereignty and love, God *can and does* take anything that happens to us and use it for good (Romans 8:28; Isaiah 61:7).

It isn't wrong to avoid painful situations when possible, but it is wrong to deny problems, ignore them, or try to explain them away. As Christians, we are left with a much more positive option than denial or trying to delude ourselves into thinking tragedies didn't happen. Of all people we have a promise that whether we get blasted in the jungles of Vietnam, or in the front yard of our father's home, trials can produce the very things that can make us the most like Christ—His love, peace, and joy.

It's never easy to "welcome" trials as friends, but trials can train us to become more Christlike, if they're experienced in the right light. I've learned to "treasure-hunt" with every difficulty I face. This attitude has been one of the most important tools we can give our children to help prepare them for the large and small trials of life they'll inevitably face.

How God Turns Trials into Triumph

I'm writing this chapter because I know that trials can not only defeat individuals, they can ruin entire families—especially if that family doesn't know how to handle the trials effectively. So here's a summary of this entire book in three sentences.

In Chapters 1 through 12, there's a practical plan we can follow to strengthen our relationships and develop the specific skills necessary to practice that plan. In Chapter 13, we looked at the only consistent power source—the Lord Jesus Himself. Only He can give me the strength to love my spouse as I should over a lifetime. *Now in this final chapter, we have the assurance that although apparent trouble may look as if it's destroying our home, it can actually turn into a benefit for us through God's power!*

That means all trials, over all seasons of the life-cycle. Let me give you a personal example. I'll take you on a treasure-hunting journey through three of my own personal trials and show you the benefits that God ultimately gave me through each one. We'll begin with a trial I faced early in life. It has left a lasting mark upon me.

Being Held Back Moved Me Forward

Until I was in high school, I had moved at least once every year of my life. I'm not proud to admit it, but between bouncing in and out of so many different schools, I flunked the third grade. A number of children are held back before or after kindergarten at an age when it's socially acceptable, but how do you explain to your friends that you're being held back in the third grade because you can't read well enough?

While it may not make anyone's list of all-time trials, I can assure you that at the time, it was one of the greatest traumas I had ever faced. Now, as I look back years later, what did I get from the experience? Humility, to begin with.

Not being promoted with my friends kept me humble for many years. To this day I am self-conscious about my spelling. That's especially true if I have to write a note to one of my children's teachers, because my atrocious spelling was one of the reasons I was held back. Humility may not sound like such a great benefit, but a valuable gift of gold can be added to our character as a result of being humbled. It's found in a verse that says, "God opposes the proud but gives grace to the humble" (James 4:6). While I didn't realize it at the time, God was actually giving megadoses of His grace to me during the third grade!

Flunking third grade also made it difficult for me to read aloud in front of people. One of my most embarrassing moments was the time I was not able to finish reading a section of Scripture at my church. As president of a large college group, I was humbled even more by that experience. It gave me a deep concern for those struggling with dyslexia and other spelling and reading disorders such as mine.

Also, because I was so embarrassed, to this day I am extremely careful to try not to embarrass people who attend my seminars. My experience of embarrassment increased my sensitivity. This is also a fundamental requirement for being a loving person.

At the time I didn't feel there was anything good about flunking a grade, but there was. I received more of God's grace and added sensitivity to hurting people. Two major benefits from one trial, and that's just one trial.

When Our Ship Came In . . . and Ran Aground

During our first few years together, Norma and I lived on the edge of poverty most of the time. My poor accounting skills didn't help.

One year, we had absolutely no money—but we could see our ship coming in any day! Especially since we knew that a tax refund of $2,000 was on its way to us in the mail. When the letter came from the IRS, I hurriedly ripped it open, certain that I'd find a check inside that would be a tremendous help to us financially. Instead, I learned that I had made a major error on our tax form and that we actually *owed* the government $1,700—and they wanted it *now!*

At the time, I couldn't think of a single treasure I was getting out of this particular trial. In fact, I was dying trying to come up with every cent of earthly treasure we had, just to keep the Federal agents away from our door. As Norma and I look back on that experience, however, the real treasure didn't go to the government to play catch-up with the deficit. We learned several lessons more important than money, and they have stayed with us until this day.

The first benefit was the reminder that money is not the source of life. We had focused on our tax refund so much, it had shifted our focus away from Christ. That experience took away everything we had monetarily in life, but God showed us that neither money nor anything money could buy could take away what was more important—our relationship with Him. Because we had to struggle so much to pay the tax bill, the whole family learned the value of trusting God to meet our needs. (Including things like saying "thank you" for care-packages of food that were delivered mysteriously by some close friends.)

Finally, the trial forced me to get professional help with my taxes so that I wouldn't get any "surprises" in the mail again. It also forced me to take a more serious look at the management of our finances. Trial number two, and this time three major positive benefits by nearly going broke! Actually, I could count even more benefits, especially the love we gained through the experience

—remembering that we gain more of God's love in every trial (Hebrews 12:9ff).

A Matter of Life and Death

When it comes to my third example of treasure-hunting trials, to tell you the truth, I'm glad I'm still around to explain it. While it's not easy for me to talk about, for the last two years, my health has not been the best. Basically, at times I've felt I had one foot in heaven and the other on a banana peel here on earth.

You see, my brother died of a heart attack two years ago at the age of 51. My sister had a heart attack last year as well, and another brother had to have triple bypass surgery at age 51. For those who are believers in genetics, it seems that my father's background may have something to do with the hearts in our family giving out when they do. My father died of a heart attack at age 58.

With my family's health history in mind, something happened two years ago—when I was 46—that started me counting my days.

For years, I've jogged a short distance every day and carefully watched my diet, hoping that alone would keep me healthy and fit. Then one morning in Vail, Colorado, during a speaking visit, I walked out of my hotel for a morning jog. Before me were 50 to 60 people, all in running clothes, stretching out and pinning race numbers on their T-shirts.

Recognizing them as people from the convention I was addressing, I said, "Hey, what are you guys doing?"

"This is the annual three-mile race," several people said. "Why don't you come and join us? Everyone at the convention is invited to run."

"You're only going *three miles?*" I asked.

At the time I could do three miles without breaking a sweat in the near sea-level altitude of Phoenix. So I walked over to the sign-up table, got myself a number and joined in. However, I soon discovered that there was a slight problem. This wasn't the friendly three-mile jog I had envisioned. It was a flat-out sprint through two-mile-high Vail. I was a short-distance jogger, not a long-distance sprinter, but the male conqueror mentality inside me kicked in, and I decided I was not going to finish in last place if it killed me.

It almost did.

Before I reached the half-way point, there were small children and senior citizens passing me. It was as if all the breathable air had suddenly been sucked out of Colorado. As I struggled to reach the finish line, I could see that last place was either going to be me or to a woman wheezing alongside me who looked like she'd flunked out of Weight Watchers. So I gave it all I had at the end—and she beat me.

The moment the race was over, I knew something was terribly wrong. I was sick. I spoke that day, then got on the plane with chills and fever. Before I knew it, I was vomiting and bleeding internally. I spent two weeks in bed and even then my blood pressure and cholesterol levels didn't recover. My kidneys were secreting blood, and I was having massive headaches. They were so bad that one doctor wanted to do surgery on my sinuses to drill holes in them so they could drain. Something about the altitude, my health, and my sprint had turned my body inside out.

What good could come out of almost dying? Particularly when John and I had conferences to conduct and books lined up to write? All this required nonstop work.

In the last two years, I have been forced to learn how to balance my life—how to level out the "high-highs" and "low-lows." I have learned even more about healthy food, healthy eating habits, and healthy work habits. I learned what burn-out and stress can do to a body and how damaging out-of-control emotions can be on my system. I also learned how to seek the Lord in a way I'd never done before.

As I learned the concept I described in Chapter 13 (gaining my fulfillment from Christ). I also re-learned the "little widow lady" attitude of prayer. For months, I had to wait daily in that line for my own physical health and strength and to accept that I may not be able to walk through every door of "ministry" that's open to me. The treasure I've gained from that experience is a clearer understanding of how God does give His strength to the weak and of His faithfulness to those who seek Him alone.

These were three trials at different times in my life, some small and some large. Each resulted in similar gains in my store of God's love, peace, and joy. Herein lies the secret to successful treasure-hunting. We can gain a great deal through our trials or nothing at all—depending on our faith. It's not how *much* faith we have, but whether the faith we have takes God at His Word.

Great Faith or "Dinky" Faith

The secret to successful treasure-hunting is understanding two life-changing words: faith and love. The greater our faith in God's Word, the easier it is for us to treasure-hunt trials. The more we treasure-hunt, the more we'll be able to see the ways we're becoming more loving as a result of our circumstances. It all begins with faith, however. We have to take God at His Word. It's not more faith we need, but great faith. Here's what I mean.

Do you remember the story of the centurion who came to Jesus for the sake of his servant? It's one of the clearest descriptions in the Scriptures of exactly what "faith" entails. Read Luke 7 to see if I'm telling the story correctly.

The centurion was a powerful man who commanded an entire garrison of men. Yet one day he faced a problem he couldn't defeat on his own, and he pushed his way through a crowd until he stood in front of Jesus. Coming quickly to the point, he said, "Sir, my servant is lying paralyzed at home, suffering great pain." Even though the man made only a statement, not a request, Jesus answered, "I will come and heal him."

But do you remember the centurion's response?

"Lord," he said, "I am not worthy for You to come under my roof. I am a man used to giving and taking commands. Just say the word, and my servant will be healed." Amazed by the centurion's faith, Christ said to the people around him, "I have not found such *great faith* with anyone in all of Israel!"

Anyone? He was talking about a very religious country. This Roman soldier had greater faith than anyone Jesus knew? Even greater faith than the disciples who would one day die for Him?

"Have you ever wondered what the disciples must have thought about such a statement? Peter was probably saying under his breath, *Sure, Lord, embarrass us in front of our Jewish brethren!* There was no love lost between the Jews and Roman soldiers.

What had impressed Jesus so much about what the soldier had said?

The answer is like a picture-frame around the concept of faith. This soldier believed that Jesus had only to command it and his servant would be healed. "For I, too, am a man under authority," he said to Jesus, "with soldiers under me; and I say to this one, 'Go!' and he goes, and to another, 'Come!' and he comes, and to my slave, 'Do this!' and he does it" (Matthew 8:10). The centurion never doubted for a moment Christ's power and authority to heal his servant. Jesus had said it, and that settled it in his mind.

But why *didn't* he doubt? Problems in life are so quick to produce questions in most of our minds. Perhaps the centurion's faith came from facing the trials of spending many days, on many different battlefields. Perhaps it was a reflection of his own father's faith. We're never told how this man came about his great faith. In contrast, Christ's disciples showed theirs to be of "dinky" proportions almost immediately.

It had been a long day of speaking to the crowds and healing the sick, when Jesus told His disciples to "get into their boat and cross to the other side of the lake." Exhausted from the drain of the crowd, He lay down to take a nap.

When the disciples were halfway across the sea, a storm blew in. Waves crashed over the sides of the boat and the disciples panicked. In desperation, they woke Jesus and cried out, "We're perishing!" Jesus just sighed, stood up, and quieted the waves and the wind with a single command. Then, drawing on the living illustration of the centurion's faith, He said to His disciples: "Why are you so timid, you men of little faith?"

How did the disciples' faith differ from that of the centurion? Why did a Roman soldier have "great" faith and Christ's own disciples "dinky" faith? The difference was that in the midst of the storm, *the disciples forgot what Jesus had said to them.* They quit counting on His Word, and as a result they panicked and counted themselves in the "lost at sea" category.

Jesus specifically said to them before He went to sleep, "We're going to the other side," not, "You guys better hug everybody, because we're fish-food halfway across this lake." He had given them His word they would *all* cross to the other side. Yet they forgot His words when the water got choppy.

I'm not blaming the disciples—I'm too much like them. Many of us make the same mistake in our marriages and families, don't we? During difficult times. we forget that God promises we'll make it to the other side—He just never promises a smooth ride on the way there. *But as the waves crash around us, God promises He will produce maturity, righteousness, patience, endurance, and love in our lives.*

In James 1:2, the writer told us to "consider it pure joy . . . whenever you face trials" and in 2 Corinthians 5:7, Paul told us to "live by faith, not by sight." So questioning the waves and their effect on our trip through life is like saying, "God's promises don't apply to me. God doesn't understand my situation, so how can any good come out of all this suffering?" (Isaiah 40:27ff.).

We're Not the First to Be "Treasure-Hunters"

One look in the Bible shows story after story of gaining treasure from trials. How would you feel if you were hated by your brothers, sold for pennies into a foreign slave market, framed for adultery, thrown into jail without a trial, and then forgotten by the one person who could have saved you?

Joseph, in the Old Testament, knew what that felt like. Yet what did he say years later, when he, the Pharaoh's right hand man, brought his brothers to Egypt? Even as he forgave them he said, "You intended to harm me, but God intended it for good" (Genesis 50:20).

Adam, Noah, Abraham, Isaac, Jacob, Joseph, Moses, Elisha, Elijah, Jeremiah, David, Solomon, Esther, Ruth, Isaiah, John the Baptist, Peter, Paul, Mary Magdalene, James. . . . on and on the list goes. All these are people with whom we can identify. They all faced trials like we have. Even in cases of "failure" (remember, Elisha and Jonah ran away, Peter denied Christ, Paul persecuted Christ's followers, James deserted Him, etc.), God took tragedy and even "dinky" faith and turned it into eternal treasure.

Blocking Trials from Producing Love

I'll be the first to admit that there is a problem with experiencing trials. Namely, their worth to us often comes on a delayed basis. As the waves are bouncing us around, we are just like the disciples. All we can picture is surviving the immediate, not thanking God for how He's shaping us for eternity.

Remember how long it took the average family to turn disasters into "family glue" in Chapter 12? It often takes several weeks for the family to see those disasters in their true light and begin bonding as a result. The same is true with trials. It took time for Dave Roever to say he was a better man for having a hand grenade blow up in his face. Diane didn't stop crying herself to sleep for months after the tragedy she faced at nine years of age—but healing did come one fateful morning.

Experts say that it takes at least thirty days of consistent repetition before a habit becomes ingrained. In other words, don't give up on treasure-hunting when you're only a few feet from shore. When someone's experiencing a trial, it's natural to go through a stage in which anger or doubt takes over, but making a decision to remain angry or even to dwell on being a "victim" can block you from any positive effects the trial could have on your character.

If I wanted to, I could still be angry at my third grade teacher or my parents for not getting me the help I needed to pass the third grade the first time, but hanging on to resentment would simply act as a roadblock to any benefits God could bring me. I could blame Norma or the "Infernal" Revenue Service for a complicated tax system that nearly bankrupted our family—or I could admit my own mistake and look in faith to what God could teach me in what happened.

I could even hate my father's memory—and question God's wisdom—in giving me his genes that may put an early time limit on the years I have to serve Him. To do so, however, would be to kick and scream at a loving and sovereign—and—unfathomable God. (Remember from Chapter 5: Anger blocks God's working in our lives, so we're only cheating ourselves to hold on to feelings of being a victim.)

There's no earthly reason why Dave, Mickey, and Diane should be happy and fulfilled after what's happened to them—but there is a heavenly one. Solomon once said if we live long enough, we'll all see enough sorrow to knock the joy out of life if we let it (Ecclesiastes 12:1). Embracing the value of our trials and mining the constructive good God can bring from them is the only way I know to keep rejoicing for a lifetime.

Passing down the Faith to "Treasure-Hunt"

As I mentioned earlier in the chapter, there are important personal reasons for learning to treasure-hunt trials, but it doesn't stop there. For those of us who have children, it's vital that we begin teaching them lessons in centurionlike faith at an early age—especially if they seem destined to increase their sensitivity level by being slightly (or decidedly) accident-prone.

For whatever reason, my son Michael wins the "I've-experienced-the-most-natural-and man-made-accidents" award in our family. When he was two weeks old, he almost died from severe stomach problems that required major surgery. For the next several years, he suffered through a series of childhood illnesses and came close to death again.

Once when he was three, I was digging in the back yard and unearthed a yellow-jacket nest. Where was my "award-winning" son standing? Right where the nest fell. He was stung repeatedly before I could get to him. Then in the same year, Mike nearly drowned in a motel swimming pool.

He's suffered through a retainer to enlarge his mouth and then braces to pull his teeth in tighter. At age thirteen, he was in a major car accident. He broke an arm and was showered with so much broken glass, it took the doctors two hours to take out all the glass slivers from the side of his face and from his eyelid. Soon he'll undergo an operation in which he will have to get his jaw broken and reset.

What do you say to a child who has gone through so many trials? Why not let him do the talking? When the doctor told Michael that there would probably be some pain involved in his upcoming operation, Mike said, "Oh, don't worry about it. I've had so much pain in my life that this isn't going to faze me."

When people go through painful experiences, it often seems to enable them to go through future experiences with less trauma, as if they understand the process and the refining fire. Michael had already been through so many things that the automobile accident wasn't that traumatic for him. Even during the two hours they worked to take all the glass from his face, he was calm and joking. A week after the accident, Mike's attitude was still positive when he learned that he'd have to go through the entire summer in Phoenix with a cast on his arm and unable to swim. The same will be true when he has his jaw operation. At age sixteen, he's already an avid, well-seasoned treasure-hunter—and he's needed to be!

Teaching Them to Look for Love in an Unusual Place

When you teach your children what God's Word has to say about troubled times, you're providing a true "lamp unto their feet" for the rest of their trial-ridden life. As John and I explain in detail in our book, *The Gift of Honor,* it all begins with your first reaction during a trial. Calmly comforting them at the beginning of a trial lays the foundation for them to find value in their difficult experiences. It teaches them they can be calm, too.

And how do we remain calm at such a chaotic moment? Calmness comes from our own deep inner confidence in God's abiding care. As we discussed in Chapter 13, it's a deep conviction that will work for good in God's time (Romans 8:28).

Watching Mike's positive attitude through his pain gave us an opportunity to praise him for the way he was handling the situation. Yet we made a mental note to keep tabs, as the months went by, on how he was responding (a bit like watching for after-shocks of an earthquake). By doing so, we'd be able to spot early warning signs like depression or anxiety that could grow into major problems later on. That is a good idea for all parents as they smooth the path toward finding the treasure of their children's trials.

Biblical principles are like powerful beacons that can light up even the darkest trial your children may experience. Teaching your children that Romans 8:28 and Philippians 4:1ff speak of spiritual benefits they can claim in faith is a precious legacy you can leave your loved ones. If you take God at His Word yourself, you'll verbally and nonverbally convey this message to your children as they watch your responses to your own troubles.

Great faith is confidently knowing that what God promises will come true. Great faith is the confidence even during a trial that it will one day turn out to our benefit. "Dinky" faith is complaining or "murmuring" during a trial that there is no benefit on the other side, we're doomed. . . . finished . . . beyond help . . . unrepairable. . . .

I firmly believe that the mark of a person who grows through trials is the degree to which he or she is willing to take God at His Word. That is called great faith in the love of God, and only possible for those who . . .

Don't Bail out of the "Love Boat" When Trials Hit

As we've mentioned, the most precious treasure we discover as we unwrap any trial is gaining more of Christ's love. Troubled times have a way of funneling the love and care of God to us, and the love of God *through* us, to others. Only those who desire God's best, His love, truly benefit from trials. Trials are coming to all of us, and it's crucial that we learn to use them for good, rather than let them get us down.

In the weeks after Mike's accident, I sat down with him several times and discussed some of the benefits that were a part of his trial. Because we've done this with so many of his trials, he jumped in quickly, telling me he could see the ways in which he had already become more sensitive. No longer could he pass an accident site and not begin praying for the people instead of just "looking" at what happened.

There's no question in our home about who is the most sensitive family member. No one feels the hurt of people or even animals as deeply as Mike does, and I believe it has everything to do with how much he has suffered.

Recently, on the way to a doctor's appointment, I asked Mike what he wants to do in life. Do you know what he said? "I think I want to try to help protect people somehow. Maybe I'll be a policeman or in some kind of service organization. Maybe I can be a secret service agent or something. I want to do something to help protect people somehow."

How often in our own lives has someone ministered to us during a difficult time with caring eyes and loving ways—and later we learned that person had been through the same kind of problem? One of the clearest treasures a trial offers us is to make us loving and sensitive in its wake. That wonderful sensitivity is, I believe, a major factor in genuinely loving others. We develop more patience, tolerance, sensitivity and over all we become better lovers of people (Romans 5:3–5).

The apostle Paul understood this mystery when he wrote his famous explanation of love: "Love is patient, love is kind. It does not envy, it does not boast, it is not proud. It is not rude, it is not self-seeking, it is not easily angered, it keeps no record of wrongs. Love does not delight in evil but rejoices with the truth. It always protects, always trusts, always hopes, always perseveres" (1 Corinthians 13:4–7).

These qualities of mature love are given to us through trials better and faster than any other way I know. Trials put us in a "love boat" with Jesus. As the disciples we're able to ride out the storm. Just as with them, it's our choice whether we're going to take Jesus at His Word and believe He'll take us to the "other side" of the trial—and gain more love for Him and others in the process. Or whether we'll wake Him up continually with our cries of mistrust and "dinky" faith—and hear His gentle reproof, "Oh, ye of little faith . . . "

I know I can't keep trials from coming. The Bible promises me that trials will show up on my doorstep (James 1:2ff.). Over the years, though, I'm finally coming to the place where I've quit fighting something the Bible says can "Purify you and make you lacking in nothing" (James 1:4).

> *T*he qualities of mature love are given to us through trials better and faster than any other way I know . . .

Another way to look at trials is to treat them like long-term "interest-bearing" CDs. It may take time for them to mature and for God to produce a greater capacity to love through our trial, but there's a promise we can count on. We can take Him at His Word that we can cash in on that love one day. As the writer to the Hebrews says, no one enjoys trials, "No discipline seems pleasant at the time, but painful. Later on, however, it produces a harvest of righteousness and peace for those who have been trained by it" (Hebrews 11:11).

A Promise by Day and by Night

Faith is trusting that God's Word is reliable. If He promises, "We are going to the other side," then we are going to the other side. There are a number of promises in the Scripture that can keep us going, keep us searching for that buried treasure of love with a full and open heart. In fact, here's a quick list I offered in the book, *Joy That Lasts*[1] that contains just a few of the promises to remember as trials come to us day by day. I strongly urge you to memorize a list of scriptural promises like these, so that when the next trial hits—you'll stay in His "love boat" and be able to treasure-hunt more quickly when you reach the other side.

1. "And we know that in all things God works for the good of those who love him, who have been called according to his purpose" (Romans 8:28).

2. "Give thanks in all circumstances, for this is God's will for you in Christ Jesus" (1 Thessalonians 5:18).

3. "Consider it pure joy, my brothers, whenever you face trials of many kinds, because you know that the testing of your faith develops perseverance" (James 1:2–3).

4. "Our fathers disciplined us for a little while as they thought best; but God disciplines us for our good, that we may share in his holiness. No discipline seems pleasant at the time, but painful. Later on, however, it produces a harvest of righteousness and peace for those who have been trained by it" (Hebrews 12:10–11).

5. "Jesus replied: 'Love the Lord your God with all your heart and with all your soul and with all your mind.' This is the first and greatest commandment. And the second is like it: 'Love your neighbor as yourself.' All the Law and the Prophets hang on these two commandments" (Matthew 22:37–40).

6. "The goal of this command is love, which comes from a pure heart and a good conscience and a sincere faith" (1 Timothy 1:5).

7. "Dear friends, since God so loved us, we also ought to love one another. No one has ever seen God; but if we love each other, God lives in us and his love is made complete in us" (1 John 4:11–12).

8. Last, but certainly not least, is my favorite chapter in Scripture as I've gone through physical trials this year (Romans 5). To offer a paraphrase of these verses: "Therefore we have been made right with God through faith, peace with God through Christ, and enjoy the power of God in us through Christ. Not only do we have all we need in Him, but we can also be excited about our sufferings. Because trouble brings us endurance—the power to keep going—and endurance produces character (love), character brings hope, and we won't be disappointed (great faith)

because God will pour out His love in our hearts through His Spirit!"

So the truth remains: No one likes trials, yet no one can escape them. We can let them ruin our lives, allowing ourselves to become bitter, angry, resentful. Or we can look for the treasure that will let us love and serve our family and others better. Again, the choice is ours. *For loving God—like loving one's spouse and children—is first, last, and always a decision.*

Notes

Chapter 1

1. In the years ahead, our goal as a ministry is to produce small group follow-up materials that will provide families everywhere with biblically based resources to strengthen their most important relationships.
2. "Even youths grow tired and weary, and young men stumble and fall; but those who hope in the Lord will renew their strength . . ." Isaiah 40:30–31.

Chapter 2

1. Gary Smalley and John Trent, Ph.D., *Hardside/Softside* (Pomona, CA: Focus on the Family Publishers, to be released Spring, 1990).
2. From a training booklet by Jack Hilger, *Training Married Couples to Work with Premarital Couples,* Prepare/Enrich, Inc., 1987.
3. Joan Druckman, David Fournier, Beatrice Robinson, and David H. Olson, "Effectiveness of Five Types of Pre-marital Programs," *Education for Marriage* (Grand Rapids, MI, 1979). Gerald Cossitt, *Effects of Feedback on Idealism in Premarital Couples,* Doctoral dissertation, University of Alberta, Edmonton, Canada.
4. The biblical concept of "honoring" God and others is so important, Dr. John Trent and I wrote an entire book on the subject called *The Gift of Honor* (Nashville, TN: Thomas Nelson Publishers, 1987).
5. Reading books like Frank Peritti's *This Present Darkness* (Westchester, IL: Good News Books/Crossway Publishers, 1988) can help you believe that there may be a satanic cover-up of honor!
6. William F. Arndt and R. Wilbur Gingrich, eds., *A Greek-English Lexicon of the New Testament and Other Early Christian Literature* (Chicago: University of Chicago Press, 1957), 119.
7. Ibid., 120.
8. Men are motivated by the "awe" principle both negatively and positively. One major reason for the creation of affairs is that a woman outside the marriage will show a man "ah-h-h-h-h," and it draws him after her. See Proverbs 5, 6:20–35, and Chapter 7 for a picture of the adulteress who "flatters with her words" in working her destruction.

9. *The Gift of Honor,* Chapter 3.
10. For more on the tremendously damaging effects of negative word pictures, see Gary Smalley and John Trent, Ph.D., *The Language of Love* (Pomona, CA: Focus on the Family Publishing, 1988), Chapter 15, "The Dark Side of Emotional Word Pictures."

Chapter 3

1. For a long overdue look at the long-term negative effects of divorce on children, see the chilling book, Judith Wallenstein, *Second Chances* (New York: Ticknor and Fields Publishers, 1989); Diana Medved, *The Case Against Divorce* (New York: Donald I. Fine, Inc., 1989), and especially, Gary Richmond, *The Divorce Decision* (Waco, TX: Word Books, 1988).

Chapter 4

1. Allen P. Ross, *Creation and Blessing* (Grand Rapids, MI: Baker Book House, 1988), 126.
2. Robert Kohn, "Patterns of Hemispheric Specialization in Pre-Schoolers," *Neuropsychologia,* 12:505–12.
3. James J. Lynch, *The Language of the Heart* (New York: Basic Books, Inc., 1985).
4. For a definition of "word picture," see *The Language of Love,* 17.
5. Arthur Bragg, "What's Holding Them Back?" *Business Insurance* (March 1989).

Chapter 5

1. Leprosy was such a dreaded disease that one rabbi taught it was all right to throw stones at lepers to keep them "a safe distance away," cf. Alfred Edershiem, *The Life and Times of Jesus the Messiah* (Grand Rapids, MI: William B. Eerdmans Publishing, 1971), 1:495.
2. See *aphieimi*, which has the basic meaning of "let go, send away, cancel, remit, pardon, leave, let go, tolerate," Ardnt and Gingrich, *Lexicon,* 125–26.
3. In *The Blessing,* we discuss the physiological benefit of elevated hemoglobin levels in both people involved in the meaningful touch. When elevated, the hemoglobin levels serve to carry more oxygen to our bodies and actually energize us. For more information, see

Gary Smalley and John Trent, *The Blessing*, p. 40, and "Therapeutic Touch: The Imprimatur of Nursing," *American Journal of Nursing* (May 1975): 784.

Chapter 6

1. For a detailed description of the concept of "closing" or "reopening" a person's spirit, see Gary Smalley, *The Key to Your Child's Heart* (Waco, TX: Word Publishing, 1984).
2. For a detailed look at the negative physiology of anger, see Paul Meier and Frank Minirth, *Happiness Is a Choice* (Grand Rapids, MI: Baker Book House, 1978).
3. Ibid., 23–29.
4. Albert A. Kurtland, "Biochemical and Emotional Interaction in the Etiology of Cancer," *Psychiatric Research Review* 35 (1978): 25.
5. "They can sit through sermon after sermon about forgiveness in church, never once misunderstanding what the pastor says, but still refuse to put their son's or daughter's picture back on the mantle." From Gary Smalley and John Trent, Ph.D., *The Blessing* (Nashville, TN: Thomas Nelson Publishers, 1986), 137.
6. We're using "soul" here in a nontheological way and especially not in the way some new-age people would call a "floating soul" touching another.
7. For a more complete list, see Gary Smalley, *If Only He Knew* (Grand Rapids, MI: Zondervan Publishing House, 1979), Chapter 5, "Climbing Out of Marriage's Deepest Pit," 82–86.
8. For an excellent resource on dealing with strong-willed children, see James Dobson, Ph.D., *The Strong-Willed Child* (Wheaton, IL: Tyndale House, 1979).

Chapter 7

1. There are, unfortunately, exceptions. See Gary Smalley and John Trent, Ph.D., *The Language of Love*, "The Dark Side of Emotional Word Pictures" (Pomona, CA: Focus on the Family Publishing, 1988), 150–62; and M. Scott Peck, M.D., *People of the Lie* (New York: Simon and Schuster, 1983).
2. We'll talk about this more later, but physically, emotionally and spiritually a man benefits by developing relationship skills.
3. From the Greek verb, *epitrepho*. Ardnt and Gingrich, *Lexicon*, 343.

Chapter 8

1. For a very helpful resource on leaving your children a legacy of love, see Tim Kimmel, *Legacy of Love: A Plan for Parenting on Purpose* (Portland, OR: Multnomah Press, 1989).
2. For more information on this outstanding conference, contact the Campus Crusade Family Ministry in Little Rock, AR (501) 223–8663.
3. For an insightful, biblically based book dealing with sexual temptation, see Charles Mylander, *Running the Red Lights* (Ventura, CA: Regal Books, 1986).
4. Ibid.
5. For more information about our #1 favorite Christian sports camp for any youngster aged eight to eighteen, please contact Kamp Kanakuk, Route 4, Box 2124, Branson, MO 65616, (417) 334–2432 or 334–6427.

Chapter 9

1. In fact, one of our favorite marriage books is by our good friends, Chuck and Barb Snyder. It's called *Incompatibility: Grounds for a Great Marriage* (Sisters, OR: Questar Publishers, 1988).
2. This is such an important concept, Dr. Trent and I have written an entire book about it called *The Language of Love* (Pomona, CA: Focus on the Family Publishers, 1988).
3. James Ford Rhodes, *History of the United States.* Vol. 1: *Lectures on the American Civil War* (1913). On meeting her, Lincoln reportedly said, "So this is the little lady who wrote the book that made this big war!"
4. Even though you may not realize it, you probably have been using them all your life. Expressions like "I'm toasty warm," "His elevator doesn't go all the way to the top floor!" or "That went over like a lead balloon" are just three of the hundreds of word pictures that are a part of our everyday speech.

Chapter 10

1. H. Norman Wright, *Romancing Your Marriage* (Ventura, CA: Regal Books, 1987), 41.
2. Alice Chapin, *Four Hundred Ways to Say I Love You* (Wheaton, IL: Living Books, Tyndale House Publishers, Inc., 1981).
3. *Romancing Your Marriage.*

4. Dan Carlinsky, *Do You Know Your Wife?* (Los Angeles, CA: Price, Stern, and Sloan, 1984).

Chapter 11

1. Marc H. Hollender, "The Wish to Be Held," *Archives of General Psychiatry* 22 (1970):445.
2. This survey of several thousand women was conducted by Ann Landers and its findings are recorded in "Is Affection More Important Than Sex?" *Reader's Digest* (August 1985).

Chapter 12

1. See chapter 6 for more on "closing" a person's spirit.
2. If you're interested in contacting Bill to do a family enrichment event at your church or business, you can contact him at P.O. Box 2929, Grass Valley, CA 95945, (916) 447-7738.
3. John Piper, *Desiring God* (Portland, OR: Multnomah Press, 1986).

Chapter 13

1. See Proverbs 7:1ff for a chilling description of the high cost of immoral relationships.

Chapter 14

1. Gary Smalley, *Joy That Lasts* (Grand Rapids, MI: Zondervan Publishing House, 1987).